UPPER STRUCTURES, SYNONYMS & VOICINGS FOR JAZZ GUITAR

Chord & single line soloing concepts for jazz guitar

By Ged Brockie

Text and musical examples proof read by Douglas Urquhart

Copyright © 2021 GMI - Guitar & Music Institute

ISBN 978-1-9163024-9-5

www.guitarandmusicinstitute.com

https://gmiguitarshop.com

First published in Scotland in 2021 by GMI - Guitar & Music Institute

Cover - Ged Brockie. Ged's Eastman Pagelli PG2

THE INSTRUCTIONS FOR DOWNLOADING THE MATERIAL (mp3 files, PDF, video) THAT SUPPORT THIS BOOK ARE FOUND ON PAGE 118.

TABLE OF CONTENTS

Preamble from author.. 7

Legend... 8

INTRODUCTION: 9

How To Get The Most From This Publication 11

Understanding The Strengths & Weaknesses Of Chord Symbol Notation 13

Making Full Use Of Chords With Alternate Bass Notes 15

Why Upper Voicings, Slash Voicings & Synonyms Offer An Advantage In Some Areas 17

Melodic/Harmonic Flow Diagram 18

SECTION 1: 19

CHAPTER 1: MAJOR 21

Stacking Chords 25

Do You Really Know Your Triads? 27

It's In The Formula 31

Leave Out Another Note 32

Extrapolating New Material 34

How To Use This Material In Many Ways 36

    Harmonising a Major Scale 36

    Playing Over The II Chord 38

    Playing Over The V Chord 41

    Making Use Of The Flattened Fifth 42

    Playing The Triads Against A Dominant Seventh 43

    Combining All Lines Over A II-V-I Progression 46

Summary Of Material Covered In This Chapter 48

CHAPTER 2: MINOR 49

Minor Over Major And Dominant Chords 53

How To Choose A Chord, Voice Leading Is Key 53

What To Consider When Utilising Voice Leading 54

Four Ways Of Defining The Melody/Bass Relationship 55

    Contrary Motion - Ascending Melody Descending Bass 55

    Contrary Motion - Descending Melody Ascending Bass 56

    Parallel Motion Between Melody & Bass 57

    Similar Motion Between Melody & Bass 58

    Synonym Information 58

    Pedal Tone Between Melody & Bass 59

    Inverted Pedal Tone Between Melody & Bass 60

Do You Really Know Your Triads? 62

Hiding In Plain Site 65

Closer Minor Chord To The Dominant 69

Summary Of Material Covered In This Chapter 73

CHAPTER 3: DOMINANT SEVENTH 75

More Chords Within Chords 79

The Effect On Single Line Solo Ideas 82

CHAPTER 3: DOMINANT SEVENTH Continued…

Use These Principles To Create Voicings Across The Fretboard 84
Closely Linked Polychords & Slash Voicings 85
Further Use Of The Same Notes/Shapes 88
Using The Same Notes/Shapes…Again! 91
Summary Of Material Covered In This Chapter 93

CHAPTER 4: AUGMENTED & DIMINISHED 95

Symmetrically Speaking 99
    What Does All This Mean? 101
    Using Symmetrical Ideas In Your Improvisations 104
    Motif Shapes Played Symmetrically & In Position 105
Do You Really Know Your Triads? 106
Side Slipping Your Way Through The Cycle 109
Do You Really Know Your Triads? 112
Altered Voicings & Augmented/Diminished Chords 115
Summary Of Material Covered In This Chapter 117

HOW TO DOWNLOAD YOUR SUPPORT MATERIALS 118

SECTION 2: 119

A Lick Library Of Ideas 121
Lick Library Contents 121

CHAPTER 5: MAJOR LICKS 123

Major Nine Licks 125
Major Thirteen Licks 129
Major 6/9 Licks 133
Major Seven Flat Five Licks 137
Major Seven Sharp Five Licks 141
Major Nine Sharp Eleven Licks 145
Major Thirteen Sharp Eleven Licks 149
Major Seven Sharp Nine Sharp Eleven Licks 153

CHAPTER 6: MINOR LICKS 157

Minor Nine Licks 159
Minor Eleven Licks 163
Minor Thirteenth Licks 167
Minor Natural Seven Licks 171
Minor Nine Natural Seven Licks 175

CHAPTER 7: DOMINANT & ALTERED LICKS 179

Dominant Ninth Licks 181
Dominant Thirteenth Licks 185

CHAPTER 7: DOMINANT & ALTERED LICKS Continued…

Dominant Seven Sharp Five/Nine Sharp Eleven 189
Dominant Seven Flat Nine Licks 195
Dominant Seven Sharp Nine Licks 199
Dominant Seven Flat Five/Sharp Nine Licks 203
Dominant Seven Sharp Five/Flat Nine Licks 207
Dominant Seven Flat Five/Flat Nine Licks 211
Dominant Seven Sharp Five/Sharp Nine Licks 215
Dominant Thirteen Flat Nine 219
Dominant Thirteen Sharp Eleven 223

SECTION 3: 227

CHAPTER 8: I CAN'T HEAR A THING! 231

Comparative Analysis of the Harmony 233
Notated Solo 239
Melodic Analysis of the solo 243
Harmonic Analysis of the solo 251
The Chords Used In Large Format 257

CHAPTER 9: THE DAY WE RENAMED NIGHT 263

Comparative Analysis of the Harmony 265
Notated Solo 271
Melodic Analysis of the solo 275
Harmonic Analysis of the solo 283
The Chords Used In Large Format 289

CHAPTER 10: WHO'S DREAM IS THIS? 295

Comparative Analysis of the Harmony 297
Notated Solo 305
Melodic Analysis of the solo 313
Harmonic Analysis of the solo 323
The Chords Used In Large Format 329

APPENDICES 335

A   Upper Voicing Formula To Chord Symbol Visual Guide 336
B   List Of Polychords 338
C   "Short List Of Common Synonyms/Substitutions…" 340
D   "Synonym Selection Of Extended/Altered Dominant Guitar Chords" 342
E   "Graphical Dominant Seventh…" 343
F   mp3 Audio Reference 343
G   Upper Voice Memorisation Cut Out 351
H   Recordings & Other Books By Ged Brockie 353

Other GMI Publications 356

Online Resources 358

INDEX 359

PREAMBLE

I started playing guitar relatively late, at the age of fifteen, but I did have the benefit before embarking upon this course of action of a very musical childhood. For example, I was exposed to melody regularly as I sang in two church services every week. I also played piano from the age of five receiving lessons from an aunt. These lessons lasted two years or so until I discovered football.

Aged nine I got the chance to play the cornet at school. I passed the entrance exam which consisted of attempting to get a rasp out of the instrument's mouthpiece. I somehow managed it and I was in! For the next two years I was parping my cornet at home, in school and eventually as part of the Edinburgh Schools Orchestra.

Ged in a recent recording session

As a teenager my interest in music intensified as I tried to knock out pop tunes on my mum's old out of tune piano. At the age of fourteen my friends and I decided to do the done thing back then, start up a band. After a year of saving I bought my first guitar. On the 30th October 1980 I played the first notes on my own instrument and I haven't stopped playing the guitar since. I had, however, played a guitar before this. It was an old acoustic guitar a friend had which only had two strings and two holes; the sound hole and a hole in the back of the guitar. It didn't really make much of a noise worth hearing.

The learning process was exciting and I couldn't get enough of music, performance, theory, reading, you name it, I was into it. One thing that became apparent to me was that there were chords and there were really complex chords; long named (extended) chords and weird sounding (altered) chords. I wanted, of course, to be the best guitarist in the world like most teenagers set out to be. Learning these big, complex sounding chords seemed the way to go if I wanted to become a real player. I then figured that if I was becoming more competent and a better player I wouldn't need to play simple "triad" chords and in that one moment I missed a crucial point. The point being that the most complex harmonic structures are more often than not created by combinations of, or the re-purposing of the humble triad.

If this book does nothing more than open up your eyes to the incredible power of the triad then it will definitely have been worth the purchase. By playing triads and understanding how to use them together you will be able to create harmonic textures and melodic lines that would be beyond the musical reach of most who depend upon eureka moments to infer new knowledge.

Welcome to the world of "Upper Structures", often referred to as polychords when the entire structure is considered. We will by necessity, due to the close linked nature of certain topics and the limitation of a six string guitar, also study slash voicings and synonyms which are much used by jazz guitarists. I hope the concepts found in this book enlighten your musical world. I'm not saying that any of the ideas in this publication are original, but they are presented as I discovered them in my musical life. So in some way they feel authentic and original to me and I feel that's important when imparting knowledge to others.

Finally, you may find this text jumps about a bit but I have tried to maintain order by splitting the book into three sections. Hopefully this jumping around subjects will not put you off and you'll be able to work with the way my mind works. This book is, in places, as much musical research and discovery for myself as it, hopefully, will be for you.

My wish is that this book will open a door to new musical vistas which once may have seemed a distant far off dream. Best of luck with your guitar playing and musical progress.

Ged Brockie

LEGEND

Some points to consider:

1. The notes that are played "open", that is non-fretted, are filled in as the other notes, however, they have a further hollow circle within the black circle line to show that they are played open. Lighter shaded open string notes are considered root notes.

2. If additional symbols such as square blocks/pyramid shapes are present these are notes played after the main chord.

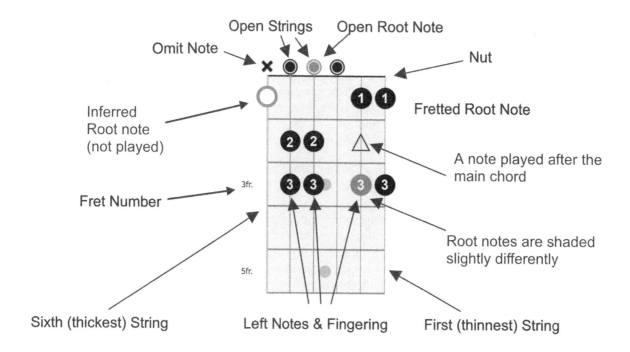

 Whenever you see this symbol there will be an associated mp3 file which will demonstrate the musical idea. Narration is provided by the author before the musical idea is played for all Section 2 lick ideas.

There is a code given beside each audio icon. Example: S1EX1 = Section 1 example 1, S2EX1 = Section 2 example 1 etc.

Please see appendix F to reference the audio code to the correct audio file. The audio files have the page that the respective file refers to as the first part of the mp3 name.

INTRODUCTION

HOW TO GET THE MOST FROM THIS PUBLICATION

This publication contains three sections with each section containing chapters. The chapters do not need to be studied in sequence in order to get the most from this book. You will find that some chapters within a section will often be used for reference whereas other chapters will be used more frequently as they offer practical and technical playing experience.

Section one is split into four chapters with each chapter headed by a chord type; major, minor etc. Each of these opening chapters in section one include ideas and concepts which relate sometimes closely and sometimes in a more loose way to the overall subject matter of upper voicings, synonyms and slash voicings. At other times, the author has strayed into musical territory that although distant from the original focus of the text, is still an important consideration when considering the subject of jazz guitar as a whole.

Section two is devoted to providing the player with a catalogue of guitar lick (line) ideas split up by chord type that demonstrate upper voicing use within common progressions found in jazz. These ideas can be applied and developed to reflect the player's own taste and musical style.

Within the second section, suggested arpeggio patterns for each chord type are provided as well as all the chord forms that were played in the demonstration tracks. With respect to the arpeggio patterns, the author does not expect the player to memorise all notated arpeggio patterns. The inclusion of these patterns, however, will prove a useful study aid in understanding how upper voicings from a single line perspective can be applied across the guitar fretboard.

Finally, section three provides the player with three recorded solos which demonstrate, within a playing context, the concepts outlined in this book. These solos are played over chord progressions that are directly attributable to popular jazz standards that most guitarists that wish to play jazz music will at some point learn as part of their repertoire. These three solos are analysed and commented on from both a melodic and harmonic point of view. A comparative analysis of each solo is also undertaken by the author to enable the player to see exactly how the various chords function within the context of a guitar solo.

GMI would urge you to download the free materials that have been created by Ged Brockie for you to use in conjunction with the following text. The materials include an introductory video, mp3 files for you to listen to and learn from, as well as backing tracks and a PDF to aid in memorisation of the upper voicings presented.

GMI - Guitar & Music Institute - creates books that are more akin to multimedia productions. The emphasis is on guitar players playing and learning through actual persistent practice while being provided with, hopefully, fun to play music examples. Almost all our publications include a download pack that is an integral part of the learning process.

We hope that you get a lot out of this publication. It has been carefully designed to help the advancing guitarist gain a lot of practical line improvisation, theoretical and chordal skills knowledge. From everyone at GMI we wish you all the best in your jazz guitar journey.

GMI - Guitar & Music Institute

UNDERSTANDING THE STRENGTHS & WEAKNESSES OF CHORD SYMBOL NOTATION

It's very easy to get attached to any system of understanding that has served you well. If you are comfortable reading and writing standard chord symbol notation, you may find it rather confusing to move to or to add another notation and reading system. More than this, you may feel resistant to other ways of understanding harmonic progression. If this is you, then here are some thoughts on the subject which I hope will make you pause for thought and reconsider.

Before becoming too misty-eyed about the current system of chord symbols, just remember what any system of notation sets out to do; enable understanding to the immediate viewer and to facilitate memorisation, replication and communication of ideas to others. Language is in a constant state of flux and so is musical notation. Look at the following example below which is often referred to as figured bass.

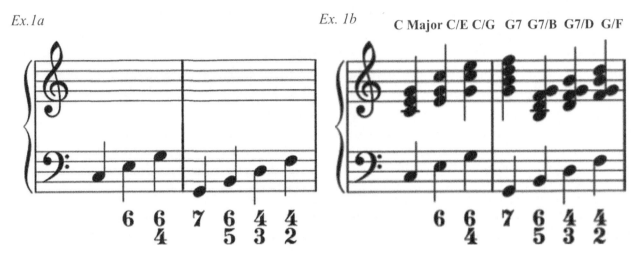

Most contemporary musicians will not use the above system of chord notation. As archaic as it may seem, if you only read chord symbols, figured bass has been around for hundreds of years and many people around the world still use it. The numbers underneath the bass line are a code of sorts which relates to interval distance from the note shown. This, in effect, denotes chords in root position and inversion.

In example 1b, the treble clef line displays the chords that a musician would play if faced with the first example bass line with an empty treble clef. I have added chord symbols for clarity of chord only.

If figured bass is of interest I'm afraid there is not enough room to go into it here but there are plenty of online and book resources available. What I am trying to impress upon you is that when a classically trained musician is reading a bass line and they see a bass note that has a six and a four underneath it, as in example 1a above, they will automatically play a second inversion with reference to the given note just as you would if shown a slash voicing chord symbol as displayed in example 1b. The process is fundamentally the same. The only thing that has changed is that the majority of contemporary musicians work with the "newer" system which is shown above example 1b's chords (these chord symbols would not be displayed in a real world situation).

When it comes to helping people know what chords you want them to play, for the most part these days, letters and numbers are in, numbers on their own, not so much.

So, hopefully, if you were unaware of the above you can now see that our chord symbol notation is nothing new and is but a re-imagining of an older system. One of the benefits of our current chord notation system is that it allowed expansion in terms of describing extended and altered chord structures, many of which may not have been musically acceptable hundreds of years ago.

I would now like to discuss a few areas that may just be taken for granted when it comes to the process of understanding and analysing chord symbols, specifically what they often do and don't tell you.

Study the chord progression below. Playing over this traditional chord symbol notation, which may come as second nature to many, actually needs a lot of knowledge and understanding before you can make an educated attempt using meaningful improvisational tools such as scales and arpeggios.

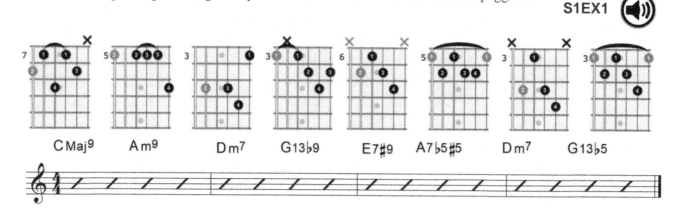

First of all, you would need to be able to analyse the chord progression and realise that it is in the key of C major. To do this you need to understand both scalar and harmonic theory to a high degree of competency.

- In the example above, if you know that all the notes found in the C major scale are all natural (no sharps or flats), you may then notice that all of the roots of the chords found in the progression are also all natural. This could be a big clue to the actual key of the chord progression.

- If you understand diatonic chord theory, you may realise that although many of the chords have quite complicated names, they are, for the most part extensions of the basic chord forms. By taking the respective scales into the next octave; for example, C Maj9 for C Major and A minor 9 for A minor. Note: Extending the scale into the next octave means the 9th is the same as the 2nd etc.

- Further to the last point, the understanding of how diatonic key centres work will enable you to pinpoint the position of each chord within the key and its probable function relative to the tonal centre (chord I). Understanding the malleable nature of certain chords concerning chord function within a diatonic key centre will also help with perception as to why there is such a prevalence of dominant seventh structures within the progression.

- Dissonance creates a sense of motion and instability within chord structures leading the ear to desire resolution of the chordal motion, as displayed in the complicated chords above. This dissonance would also include how 5th and 9th tones can be sharpened and flattened when employed using "voice leading", enabling heightened tension beyond what is already present. The prevailing tension is due to the tri-tone interval being present within dominant 7th chords.

- In general, when trying to locate the key centre of a piece of music or chord progression, work backwards. If you view the last chord and work backwards, you will realise that all of these chords are travelling around the cycle of 4ths/5ths and the probable final destination chord beyond the last chord shown will be C Major or possibly C minor. If the progression does lead to a C root chord, then the movement from G7 (alt.) to a C root chord as shown above would create a perfect V - I cadence.

- Finally, the chords do not tell you the notes needed to play an improvisational line that reflects both the guide tones (3rd and 7th) and other important extended and altered notes found within each chord structure. There is, however, every likelihood that regardless of the system used you would need to know something about the chords you were playing over and the notes found within them. I'm hopeful that you will agree with my point when I explain further.

So, let's carry on and see how else some of the chords shown in this example could be re-spelt or named.

I've displayed the previous chord progression again, but this time I have renamed some of the chords. I have deliberately not renamed the altered dominants as they are one of the main reasons this book was devised and will be covered in detail throughout this work.

So, you can see that the first three chords and the penultimate chord have been changed. I have renamed these chords by using slash voicings. It's vitally important to understand that these chord structures have the same sound regardless of the name they are given. *Note: a slash voicing is a chord symbol with a note other than the root in the bass. This bass note is shown under a diagonal line slanting forward at forty five degrees.*

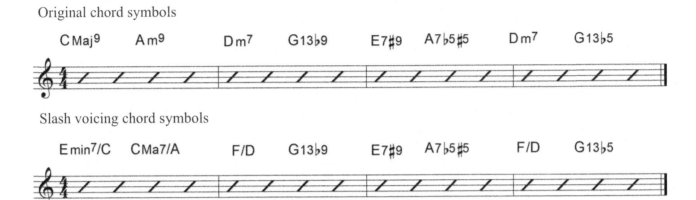

Slash voicings are an excellent way of understanding how many four note chords (and bigger chords) are constructed. When we leave the relative security of the triadic naming conventions, things start to get a little wobbly regarding defining a chord's true nature and harmonic intention. A chord can often only really be understood when considered within the context of the specific harmonic progression it currently inhabits.

1. CMaj9 can be viewed as Emin7 with a C in the bass.   2. Am9 can be viewed as Cmaj7 with an A in the bass.

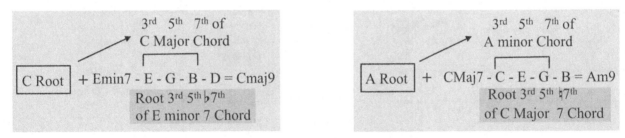

MAKING FULL USE OF CHORDS WITH ALTERNATE BASS NOTES

We can, by utilising this principle locate CMaj9 chord forms all over the guitar neck. Note: I have limited this to eight drop 2 voicing forms, but I could have included twelve. I've kept the number to eight because if you don't have a bass player or a seven string guitar, some of the lower voicings would begin to sound a little odd without that low C note laying down the harmonic foundation.

I've done the same for Am9 and the Dm7 chords. With reference to the Dm7, you'll see some duplication with the Em7 as these are shown first. The generic name for chords that can function in different ways with different names, depending on the musical context is a "synonym". There are many to consider, perhaps beyond the scope of this book but they will be referred to when necessary.*

Keep in mind that in each case an "inferred root" is shown. Just to clarify, on many occasions you will actually be physically able to play the inferred root should you wish, but not for every chord form shown.

Note: empty circles in the chord boxes are inferred roots; the root of the chord which does not need be played for the chord to sound and function as it is spelt.

* *If the voicings overleaf are of interest to you, you may be interested in another book I've written titled "Drop Two Voicings Uncovered : Volume 1" which deals with a wide range of ideas and concepts around drop two voicings. Synonyms are also dealt with in detail in this publication available from GMI.*

CMaj9 IN EIGHT POSITIONS (Emin7 with a C in the bass - Emin7/C)

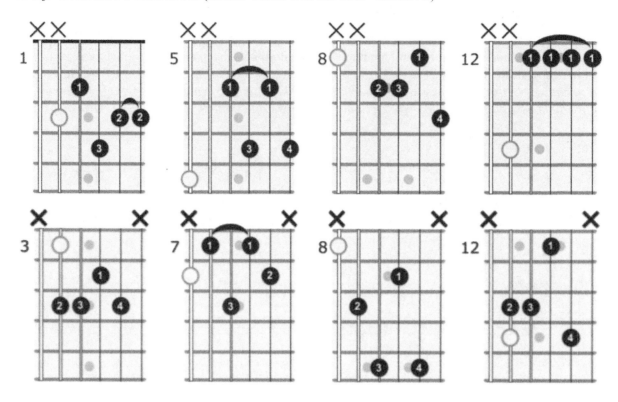

Amin9 IN EIGHT POSITIONS (CMaj7 with an A in the bass - Cmaj7/A)

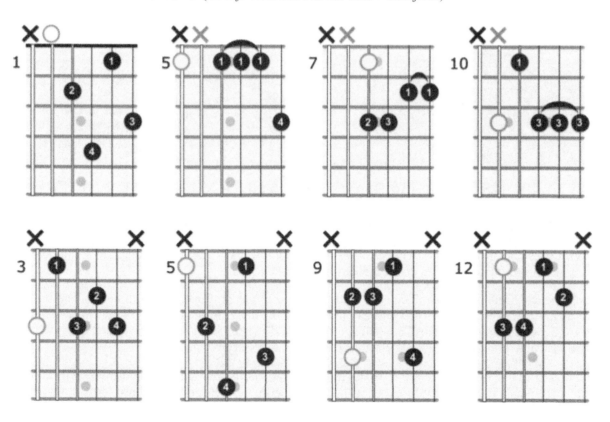

3. Dmin7 (can be viewed as F Major with a D in the bass - F/D).

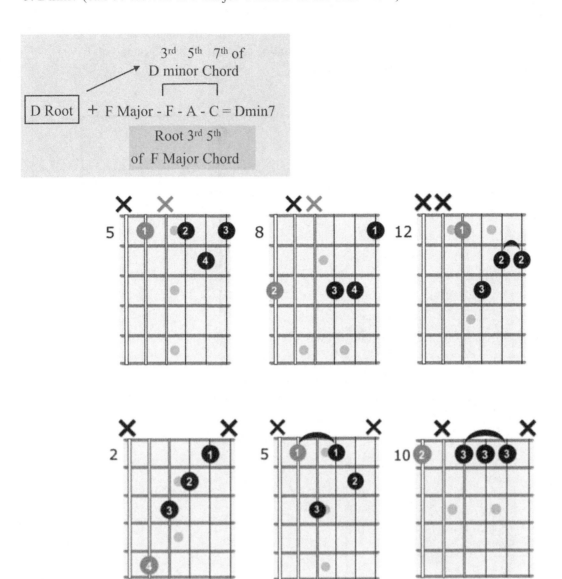

As I mentioned earlier, there are many other chord forms that I could have shown you but I'm not convinced that they would have been that useful or playable in many musical scenarios. I'll leave it up to you to take these ideas and work further on them if you feel compelled or interested enough to do so.

WHY UPPER VOICINGS, SLASH VOICINGS & SYNONYMS OFFER AN ADVANTAGE IN SOME AREAS

So, now that we've discussed chord voicings in general and slash voicings in particular and understood how much background knowledge you need to use them effectively, you're probably interested in finding out how upper voicings work with this material and what benefits they bring. You'll see a diagram on the next page that describes how this book works regarding polychords, slash voicings and synonyms.

I then go on to detail how chord voicings stacked one on another create rich and complex sounds. The first section has four chapters; major, minor, dominant seventh and augmented/diminished. Each section contains ideas that explore various concepts that come to the fore of my mind with the chord type under scrutiny. You will take these ideas and learn a library of licks in the second section of the book.

There's a lot to take in if you are new to these topics. I would urge you to read and reread certain passages to ensure you fully understand the full implication of what is being proposed at various points within the text.

MELODIC/HARMONIC FLOW DIAGRAM

Below is a diagram which outlines the connectivity of chord symbols, polychords, slash voicings and synonyms. This diagram will become clearer and will act as a point of reference for you once you have started to really work through the ideas presented in this book.

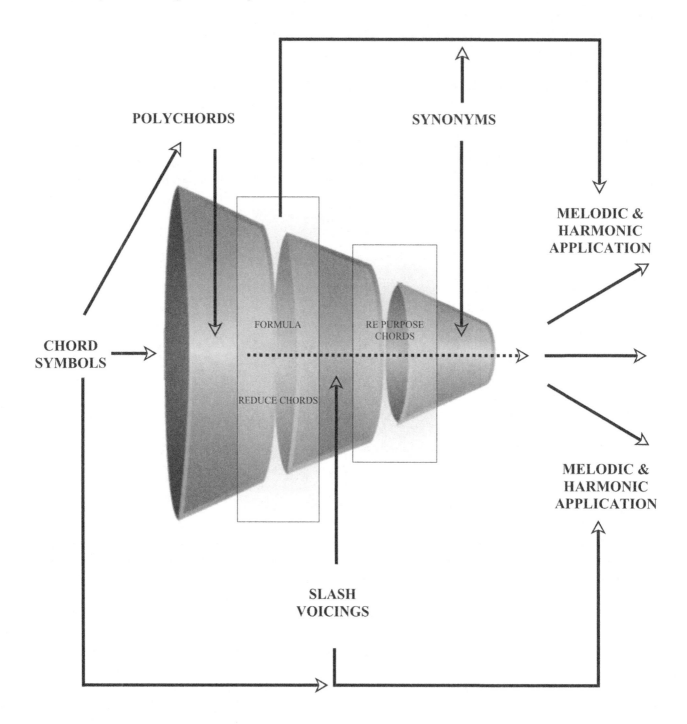

SECTION 1

MAJOR

CHAPTER 1

Chapter 1

What's discussed in this chapter...

stacking chords

chord extension & alteration

major triads as upper structures

chord formulae

making use of the cycle of 4th/5^{ths}

pseudo scales

inferring altered dominants

generating chords across the neck

chord & line superimposition

STACKING CHORDS

A good way to understand how upper voicings work, how to play them and what notes to use when improvising over them is to view a complex chord. The chord, shown on the next page, has been created from two simple major triads. First of all though, let's consider extended chord theory which is the usual way of thinking about such chords. Major triads consist of a root, 3rd and 5th as shown below. We can colour the basic triad by adding the 6th to make a Major 6 chord, and a 7th to create a Major 7 from within the first octave. By extending the same scale into the next octave, we can then add further notes (extensions) which are found in this upper register such as the 9th, 11th and 13th.

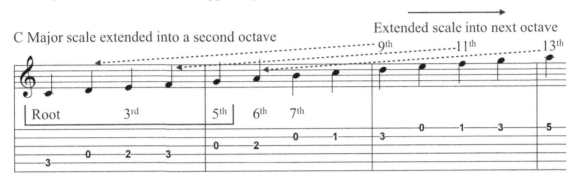

Therefore, a player could use triadic and four note chords and expand upon them by adding further notes for larger voicings such as Major 9th and Major 13th. For example, a Major 9th chord would consist of a major triad plus the 7th and the 9th. The Major 13th would consist of the major triad plus the 7th, 9th and 13th.

The 11th (which is also the 4th) creates an issue. A clash results between the 3rd and the semi-tone higher 4th. If both are present in a chord structure the result is a very dissonant sound. If, however, the 11th is sharpened a major chord with a ♯11 results in a sound that is lydian (mode) in nature and is one of the brighter sounding modes. Although now an altered sound colour, the chord still functions and is heard as a major chord tonality. As you can see below, by utilising upper triads things get considerably easier to understand regarding the nature and composition of large chord voicings

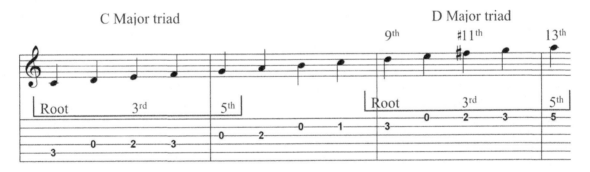

Looking once again at the C major scale with the sharpened 11th in the second octave, we can see that both C and D major triads can be identified within the notes. These two triads when combined result in the ever so complex sounding C Major13♯11 voicing; in essence just a C major triad with a D major triad on top.

Let's consider how this actually affects our understanding of a C Major13♯11 chord. If you don't know, or you are not sure about the composition of this chord and how it "functions" within the harmony, you might be a little confused about the scale to use when improvising. Armed, however, with the knowledge above, you have a complete six note scale, seven notes with the octave. These notes will work every time you play them over this chord as they are the only notes found within this complex chordal structure.

On the next page you will see in graphic form the chord and fingering that can be used and the notes that can be played with regards improvisation. As is often the case with these chord structures, there has been a note casualty when creating the C Maj13♯11 chord to enable it to be played with root on five and that was to omit the 7th from the chord.

25

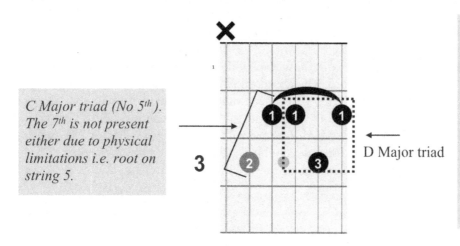

C Major triad (No 5th). The 7th is not present either due to physical limitations i.e. root on string 5.

D Major triad

This chord form is a good example of the approach that a guitarist needs to take to create "sounds". The "A" note in the chord could be thought to be in the position of the 6th but we refer to it as the 13th. There is no 5th and no 7th present due to the root being placed on the 5th string.

3

Slash voicings have the chord and the bass note separated by a diagonal slash. Polychords, are shown one above the other and are separated by a horizontal line.

EXAMPLE OF SLASH VOICING

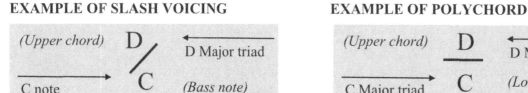

(Upper chord) D / C D Major triad (Bass note) C note

EXAMPLE OF POLYCHORD

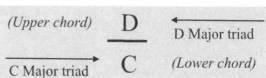

(Upper chord) D / C D Major triad (Lower chord) C Major triad

As mentioned earlier, because we only have six or fewer strings to work with, on many occasions we need to omit one, two or more notes to physically play the chords we are trying to build. In the form above it's the 5th of C Major, the "G" note that has been left out as well as the 7th. We can relate to and use the theoretical concepts of polychords, but in most cases, as guitarists, we can only express them through slash voicings.

You can see that we have the root and 3rd of C Major and the D Major triad above it. Now, let's observe how this chord looks on the manuscript both as a structure and with all notes in arpeggio and scalar form.

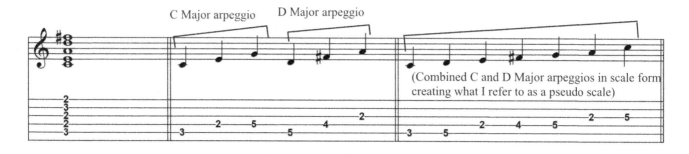

C Major arpeggio   D Major arpeggio

(Combined C and D Major arpeggios in scale form creating what I refer to as a pseudo scale)

The chord C Maj13#11 as written in music notation is shown on the left. Then we can see the two triads played one after the other in II position on the guitar neck (2nd finger over fret 3) and finally the notes of the two triads laid out in ascending order as a pseudo scale. Almost a complete C lydian scale but no 7th.

As I have pointed out, if you do not know how the chord shown at the top of this page functions and you don't know a scale that will work, upper voicings actually give you plenty of musical ammunition to play at least within the chord sound.

Are there other notes that could be played over this chord in addition to the six different ones shown above? Absolutely; as pointed out in a prior paragraph. What this does show you, however, is that by deconstructing then reassembling a chord into easy to understand chunks of information, you then have a simple starting point for both soloing and chordal development. Later in this section we are going to see how we can build a wide range of chord forms all over the neck that would not be that apparent if it was not for the understanding that upper structures brings.

DO YOU REALLY KNOW YOUR TRIADS?

One recurring problem in being able to use and visualise potential polychords effectively is not the theory but the technical building blocks that may have been overlooked in the early stages of playing. Knowing your triadic shapes in all possible inversions over all string sets is a must. Many players will think that knowing all of these probable shapes is just too massive a job; it's just not true. The following twenty five shapes will serve most potential scenarios. All major arpeggio forms you need to know for most music are shown below.

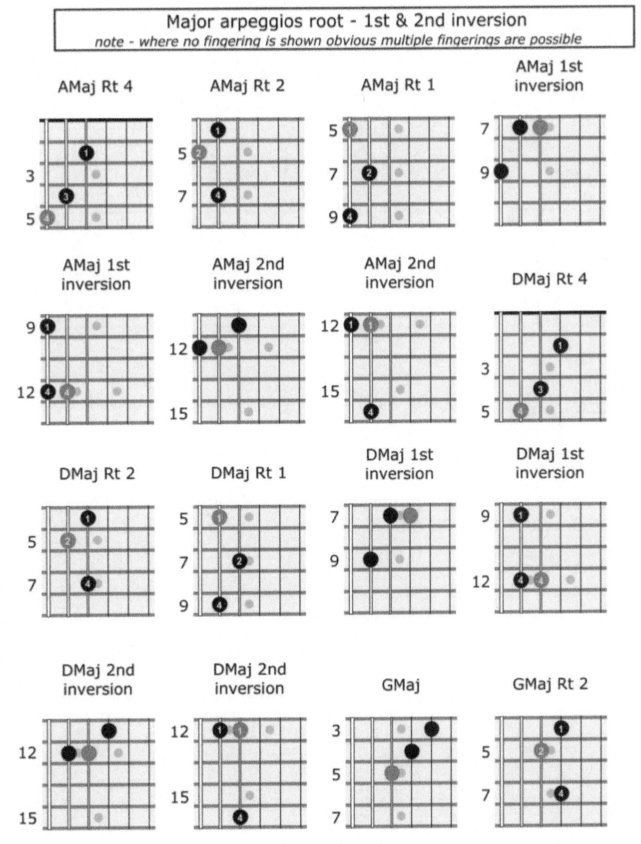

Major arpeggios root - 1st & 2nd inversion
note - where no fingering is shown obvious multiple fingerings are possible

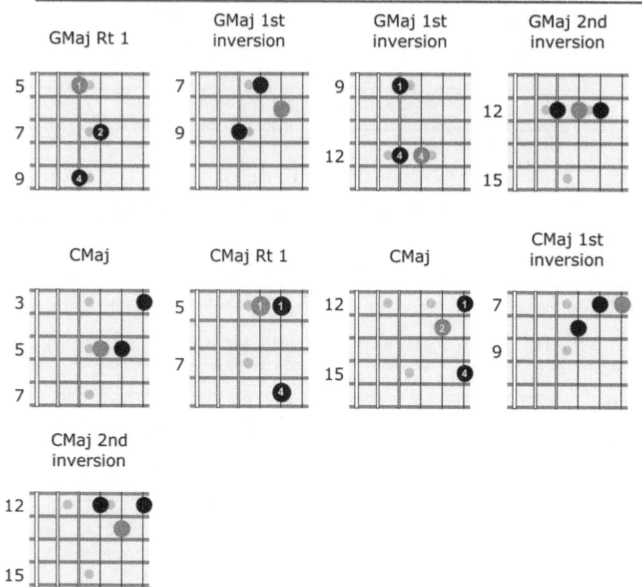

GMaj Rt 1

GMaj 1st inversion

GMaj 1st inversion

GMaj 2nd inversion

CMaj

CMaj Rt 1

CMaj

CMaj 1st inversion

CMaj 2nd inversion

Major chord (triads) in root, 1st & 2nd inversion

note - fingering are shown however in most cases multiple fingerings are possible

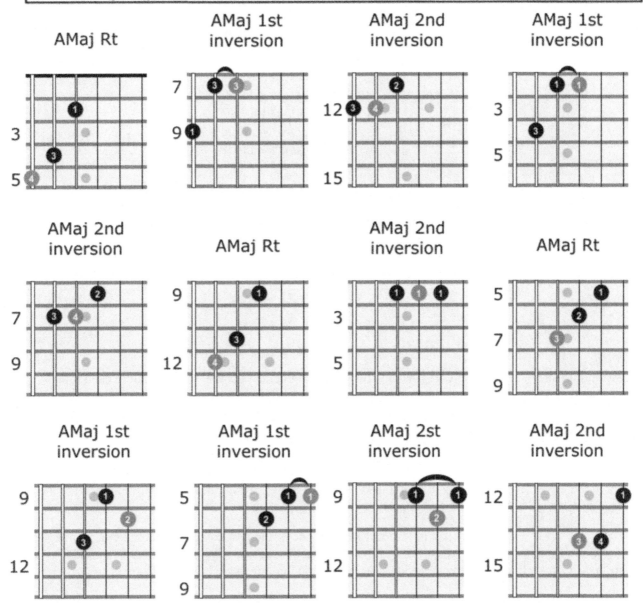

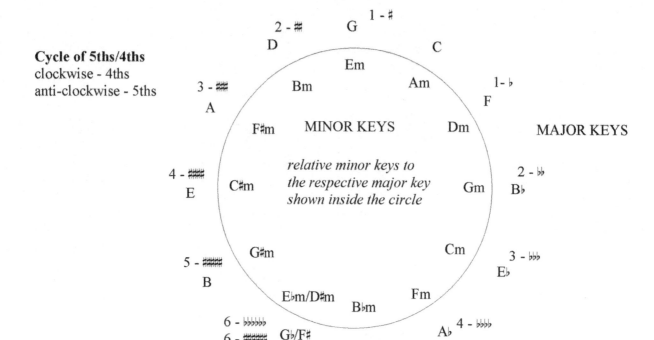

Cycle of 5ths/4ths
clockwise - 4ths
anti-clockwise - 5ths

MINOR KEYS

relative minor keys to the respective major key shown inside the circle

MAJOR KEYS

Understanding and using the cycle of 4ths/5ths for your practice and general understanding cannot be overstated enough. So much of the musical language created over hundreds of years uses the musical wheel you see above. Think of it like a clock with the twelve numbers being replaced by twelve key sounds. A couple of things to keep in mind.

1. Memorise the cycle if you do not already know it, you will never regret this.

2. There are obviously other ways to spell the keys shown above, we are dealing with sound. Name the keys any way you wish or that feel appropriate.

3. The cycle has many uses, not just in terms of knowing keys and practising chords, scales and arpeggios. It also is a great help in understanding many theoretical concepts from the notes in scales to how progressions work to more advanced ideas such as the "alternate cycle".

IT'S IN THE FORMULA…

One thing that you will need to be aware of to get the most from upper structures is the need to memorise. If we consider our current example, which is C Maj13♯11, what we have found is that this chord name and sound equals a major triad played at the same time as the root note major triad but played one tone higher.

Extrapolated to other chords you'll find that if you play a G major triad over an F major triad you will get the sound of F Major13♯11. If you play a C major triad over a B♭ major triad you will be playing a B♭ Major 13♯11 and so on. The formula for a given chord symbol's polychord alternative is given in Roman numerals wherever possible and can include accidentals such as flats and sharps. Understanding and memorising these simple formulae and what they create in terms of traditional chord symbol notation is highly desirable, if not a necessity.

$$\frac{\text{II Major}}{\text{I Major}} = \text{Maj}13\sharp11$$

Just to recap, the above formula is founded on the structure of a major scale and works from that interval basis. Here is an example of how a major scale is created from a chromatic scale although I did make the assumption that most people purchasing this book would know this information already, but just in case…

The underlined notes shown above are the notes that are used from the chromatic scale in creating the C major scale. The resulting major scale both ascending and descending is shown below. When creating your own major scales you should always end up with seven different notes, the eighth being one octave higher than the first note of the scale. The interval between the seventh and eighth tone will always be a semi-tone. The tone, semi-tone structure both ascending and descending is also shown below. Remember, all major scales follow this tone/semi-tone pattern in exactly the same way.

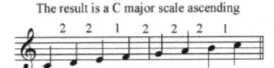

The result is a C major scale ascending

Descending C major scale

So, in the case above you can see that the 2nd or II degree is D which is a tone above C. This way of relating one chord to another and the relationship this represents in Roman numerals will be used for the rest of this publication's text unless stipulated otherwise.

When I started out I would have been thrilled to know two chord shapes for the same "complex" chord but we can use what we've learned in a very dynamic way to find many shapes. We will now look at how we can use this simple formula to build chord forms for Maj13 ♯11 chords all over the guitar neck. The important thing to remember is that, armed with the principle outlined above, you can use it to create extended and altered chords of all types all over the guitar fretboard.

LEAVE OUT ANOTHER NOTE?!

To create a form that can be used to generate many possible chord forms I'm suggesting that you actually leave one more note out of our original example, in addition to the fifth and the seventh. From a music history point of view, as the twentieth century has moved into the twenty first century, many musicians have taken to paring down the notes played within chord voicings to create what is thought of as a more "modern" and "open" sound. You will no doubt have heard the phrase "less is more" when it comes to playing, well this is exactly one of those scenarios.

In a nutshell, many players are looking for the essence of a chordal sound. This does not have to mean that the guitarist needs to play a full bodied six note six string voicing every time. I'll demonstrate this by revealing the note that can also be left out whilst preserving to a large degree the original sound in a moment.

The final point I'd like to make is that by leaving out a further note we will in fact go full circle and end up with a triadic slash voicing and another case for making use of synonyms. The reason that both of these subjects should be looked at within the context of this publication, which highlights the subject of polychords, is that the resulting forms are incredibly malleable and can be applied in numerous musical circumstances.

Further, due to the limitations of six strings, root placement and tuning, slash voicings are never far away from consideration and will through necessity be used often when referring to a polytonal sound. This musical consideration is, however, very much down to the individual's musical taste.

The 3rd of C will be left out which gives us a D/C chord. Basically a D Major chord with a C in the bass which could be heard as a D7 3rd inversion; D major with the ♭7th in the bass.

This is where a chord's function within a harmonic progression becomes paramount. The key centre, the chords that surround the voicing and of course the melodic line all work together to establish how we "hear" a chord and it's relationship to the progression in general.

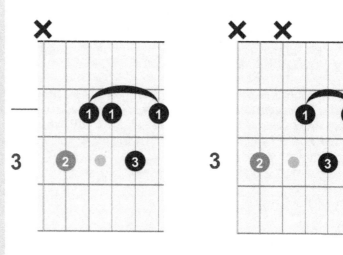

So here we are now looking at a chord that could be described as one of the following depending on musical context (with all the provisos as given in this chapter taken into account):

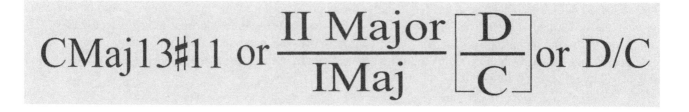

$$\text{CMaj13#11} \quad or \quad \frac{\text{II Major}}{\text{IMaj}} \quad \boxed{\frac{\text{D}}{\text{C}}} \quad or \quad \text{D/C}$$

CMaj13♯11 alternative voicing ideas (D/C)

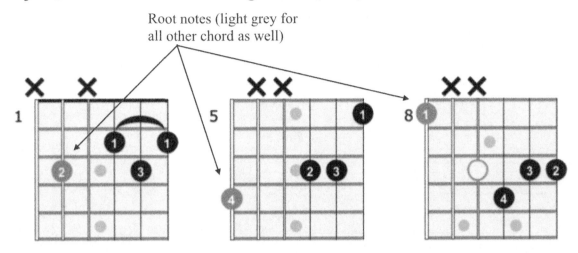

Hopefully, you are looking at some shapes you have never viewed before. If this is the case, then just remember this; it's important to see the major shape with the root note being added on. This is how the actual function and sound of the chord changes by the addition of that one note which is considered the root.

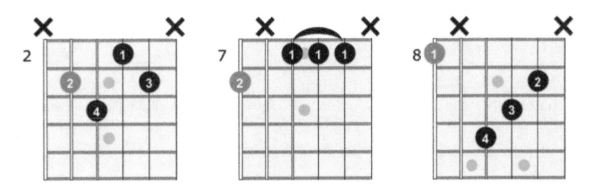

Potential ideas but perhaps fringe voicings…

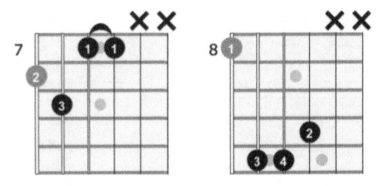

Remember, all of the above voicings could also be thought of as D7. That is, a D major chord with the flattened 7th in the bass, a 3rd inversion.

EXTRAPOLATING NEW MATERIAL

We're now going to explore how we can take our C major chord with a D major chord above it and create new ideas for improvisation by utilising various melodic techniques.

By isolating each individual triad and thinking of it as a building block or motif, we can create a lot of new material by simply changing the direction that each subsequent inversion of these triads take. This idea of shape and melody is often expressed or referred to as "melodic contours".

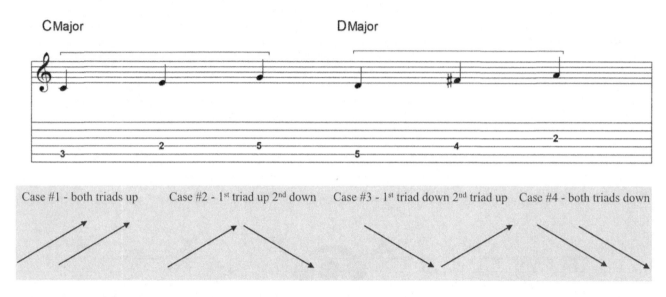

What follows is C and D major triads combined and utilising one of the four cases shown above. In each case I have created the line in two positions on the neck for variety, however, up to another five positions are possible. This book would be too big if all were listed. Work out these ideas in other scalar patterns.

All triads are played first in root, then 1st inversion (3rd in bass), then 2nd inversion (5th in bass) and so on up the fretboard.

Case #1 - both triads up

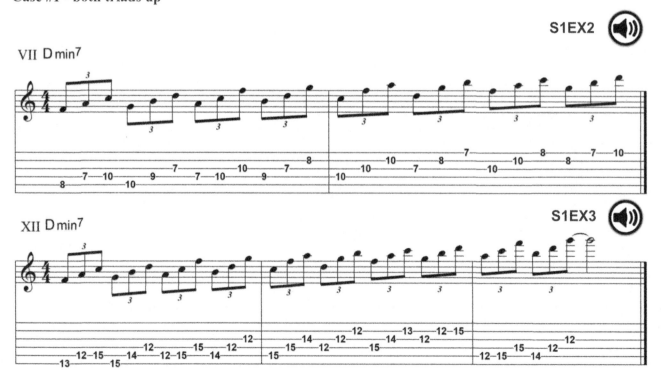

Case #2 - 1st triad up 2nd down

II CMaj13#11

 CMaj13#11

VII

Case #3 - 1st triad down 2nd up

II CMaj13#11

VII CMaj13#11

Case #4 - 1ˢᵗ triad down 2ⁿᵈ down

HOW TO USE THIS MATERIAL IN MANY WAYS

One way to really pull listeners in to an improvisation is to have a thematic idea that runs through the music and works over various chords and progressions. I'd like to show you how to do this with the material we have just viewed which will bleed into other areas that will be discussed later in this publication. I'm also going to touch briefly on theoretical concepts presented later in the minor and dominant seventh chapters within this section of the book.

We will look to create a line that is consistent and thematic and works over a II - V - I chord progression. First of all, here is a short recap on how to harmonise a major scale in both three and four note systems.

HARMONISING a MAJOR SCALE

This theory may be a little basic for some, but it will give a grounding as to where we get II - V - I. progressions from and will help those who have never looked into this aspect of key centres before.

By harmonising a scale we can find out the chords/scale relationship relevant to the key of the scale in question. This is often referred to as diatonic harmonisation.

Three note harmonisation of major scale (all chords build from major/minor 3rds)

1. Write out a major scale:

Re-write out the C major scale starting on both the 3rd and 5th degrees. This is known as writing the scale out modally or in modes.

C major from the 3rd   C major from the 5th

Now stack the scales you generated from the 3rd and the 5th on top of the original scale. You should end up with the following:

This completes the three note diatonic harmonisation of the C major scale with all chords in root position.

Each of these eight vertical structures is a chord. Below, the same chords are shown but with a higher rhythmic value for ease of note identification. The last chord is the same as the first and not used.

| Cmajor | Dminor | Eminor | Fmajor | Gmajor | Aminor | Bdiminshed | Cmajor |

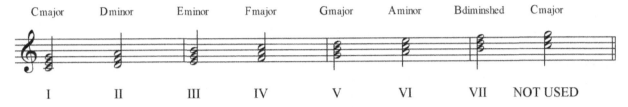

| I | II | III | IV | V | VI | VII | NOT USED |

Each chord is assigned a Roman numeral which points to its position within the key. In the C major example above, E minor is chord three and G major chord five etc. The results above are the same for all major scales and always follows the following pattern:

(x)major - (x)minor - (x)minor - (x)major - (x)major - (x)minor - (x)diminished

"X" is a variable. That is to say you can place any major scale that you know into this pattern and you will automatically generate the chords that are diatonic to that key. Further examples are as follows:

Gmajor
Gmajor - Aminor - Bminor - Cmajor - Dmajor - Eminor - F#diminished

Dmajor
Dmajor - Eminor - F#minor - Gmajor - Amajor - Bminor - C#diminished

Four note diatonic harmonisation of major scale

To create a four note harmonisation of a major scale take the three note harmonisation as shown earlier and add a fourth line of notes on top which begins from the seventh degree of the major scale.

\ seventh degree

This scale will now be added to the previous three note structure which is shown below. Again, the note values have been changed for ease of reading.

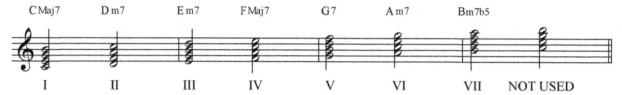

As in the previous three note harmonisation each chord is assigned a Roman numeral. In the C major example above the new chord structures are: major seventh at position I and IV, minor seventh at positions II, III and VI, dominant seventh at position V and minor seven flat five at position VII.

(x)major7 - (x)minor7 - (x)minor7 - (x)major7 - (x)dominant seventh - (x)minor7 - (x)minor7♭5

As in the last example "X" is a variable. Any major scale inserted into the above formula will give the key chords for four note structures. Here is a further example:

B♭ major
B♭Maj7 - Cm7 - Dm7 - E♭Maj7 - F7 - Gm7 - Am7♭5
I   II   III   IV   V   VI   VII

Therefore, in the key of C major a II - V - I chord progression would mean we played the following chords:

Dm7 - G7 - CMaj7

II   V   I

There are several chord progressions that are very commonplace in jazz music but this progression is found in a huge number of jazz guitar standards and is very much a cornerstone chord progression within a given timeframe for the art form. Knowing how to play lines and chords over a II - V - I is of paramount importance for any guitarist interested in playing jazz guitar. We will now look at how we can utilise the material presented earlier (C major and D major triads) over an entire II - V - I progression.

PLAYING OVER THE II CHORD

The relative minor of a major chord can be located on the major chord scale's VIth degree (up a major 6th). So you can see that at the top of the page, the Amin7 is the relative minor of C major.

The same is true the other way if we ask the question "what is the relative major of a minor chord?" We are interested in Dmin7 as that is the first chord in our II - V - I chord progression. The relative major of D minor is F major (up a minor 3rd).

F major is the first of our two triads that will be played over the minor seventh chord. Overleaf you can view a D natural minor scale which can also be thought of as a "D" Dorian mode. All the notes found within the scale are the same as C major. I have indicated the extension notes in a similar way to the major scale.

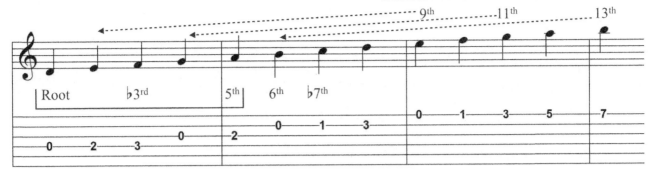

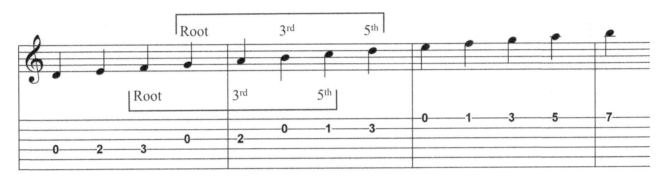

To keep things simple, you should know that the two major chords a tone apart idea which we utilised over the altered major chord will be used over the minor seventh chord. For the minor seventh, we will use F and G major triads.

By playing the F major triad we include the b3rd the 5th and the b7th of Dmin7. Then, by playing the G major triad we are including the extended notes of G (the 11th) and B (the 13th) as well as reinforcing the root note of the minor seventh chord. So in it's entirety we are inferring the sound of Dm11 and/or Dm13 arpeggios by playing these two major triads which is pretty powerful stuff in terms of melodic potency.

You can now view in music notation the result of what we have just covered theoretically. Now, before you start tearing out your hair regarding all these new lines remember this salient fact...you're playing exactly the same ideas as you did in the C major examples, just in a different position on the guitar neck!

Case #1 - both triads up

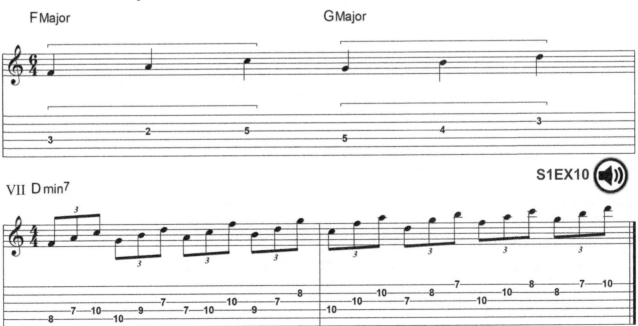

XII Dmin⁷

S1EX11

Case #2 - 1st triad up 2nd down

S1EX12

VII Dmin⁷

XII Dmin⁷

S1EX13

Case #3 - 1st triad down 2nd up

S1EX14

VII Dmin⁷

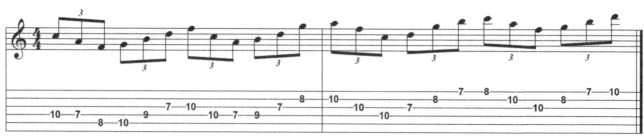

XII Dmin⁷

S1EX15

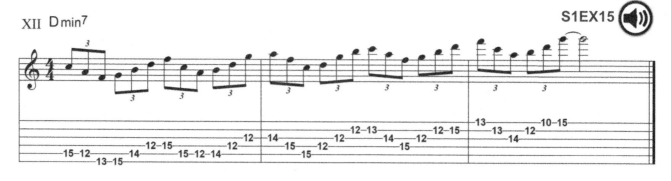

40

VII Dmin⁷

S1EX16

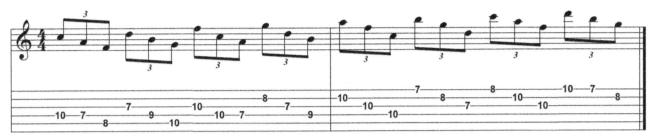

XII Dmin⁷

S1EX17

PLAYING OVER THE V CHORD

The final piece of the jigsaw is how we utilise our two major triads to enable us to play over a dominant seventh chord. To do this we are going to make use of a flat five substitution to create an altered sound over the G dominant seventh.

When dominants are moving up a fourth (see the cycle below) from, for example, G7 to C major, we can increase the level of dissonance heard in the V chord (G7 in this case). To do this we can alter (alt (sharpen or flatten)) the 5ᵗʰ and/or 9ᵗʰ tones in any combination. The amount of altered chords at our disposal are vast.

POTENTIAL ALTERED DOMINANT CHOICES

C7♭5, C7♯5, C7♭9, C7♯9, C7♭5♭9, C7♯5♯9, C7♭5♯9, C7♯5♭9

C9♭5, C9♯5

C13♯11, C13♭9, C13♯9

With so many choices you may be forgiven for thinking that there is too much choice.

Ultimately, the altered dominant you pick should be decided by your voice leading choices when moving between V7 (alt) to I.

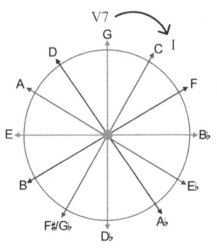

Example: D7 would be the secondary dominant of G7 as viewed on the left.

Here you can see how the cycle can help you identify both perfect cadence and *secondary dominant movement to chord V7 to chord I. From any note on the circle, by moving anti-clockwise from any chosen root note you are given the Vᵗʰ of that chord.

As outlined above, V7 chords can have their dissonance greatly enhanced by altering the 5ᵗʰ and 9ᵗʰ tones as shown in the list above. Whether you should do this or not is very much down to the style of music being played and musical taste. * Any chord can be approached by it's V as per this cycle i.e. a 7ᵗʰ chord's secondary dominant.

MAKING USE OF THE FLATTENED FIFTH

I go into some detail regarding dominant seventh chord construction, tri-tone and flat five substitution in the dominant seventh part of this section.

Simply put, the cycle of 4^{ths}/5^{ths} can be used to inform us about the flat five substitute of any given chord by looking at a chosen chord's diametrically opposite value. As we are interested in G7, the opposite note from G, by studying the cycle diagram below is D♭. This is the major triad that we will choose as our first triad. Therefore, using the same concept as before, the other major triad we will play against G7 will be E♭, a tone higher than D♭.

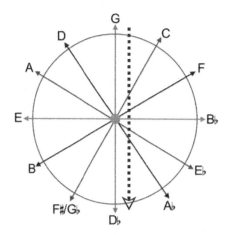

Diagram showing that the flat five substitute can be found at the opposite end of the axis from the chosen chord; in this case D flat is the flat five substitute for G.

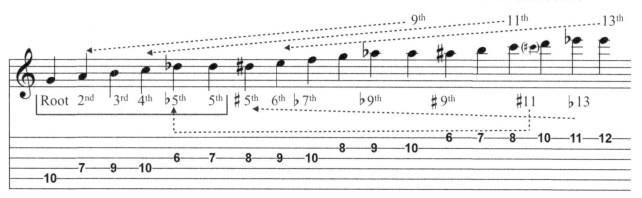

The diagram above is very busy so let's go through it bit by bit.

- The root, 3rd, 5th and ♭7th are shown as usual above the bracket.

- The extensions are mapped out in the second octave (the 9th, 11th, 13th). The extension, as before, point to their duplicate note one octave lower.

- Finally, the alteration notes are shown. These are the flat five (sharp eleven), flat nine and the sharp five (flat thirteen), sharp nine. One final point is that the flat thirteenth has been added as it's commonly used. I don't tend to use this nomenclature opting for the sharp five instead. I've added the dotted line pointing to the sharp five one octave below for clarity.

On the next page you will see how the notes of D flat major and E flat major triads create quite extreme altered chord forms from the list on the last page.

PLAYING THE TRIADS AGAINST A DOMINANT SEVENTH

First of all you can see the two triads played in third position. In the second example, once played, you will hear the inferred tonalities sounding against the G7 chord due to the tension of the major triad notes.

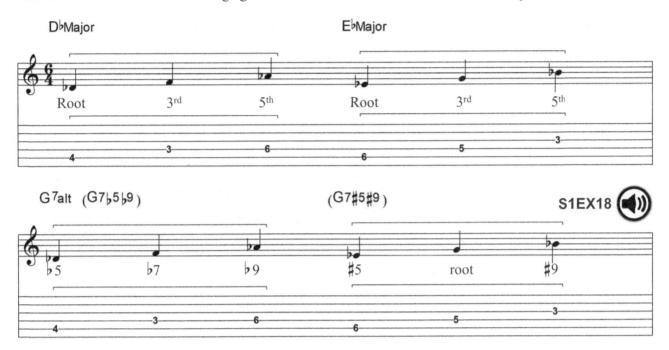

So, how can we sum up or quantify what we have just heard and played so we know what is happening and why it's happening so we can repeat this on demand? This is where we have to use our formulae approach again.

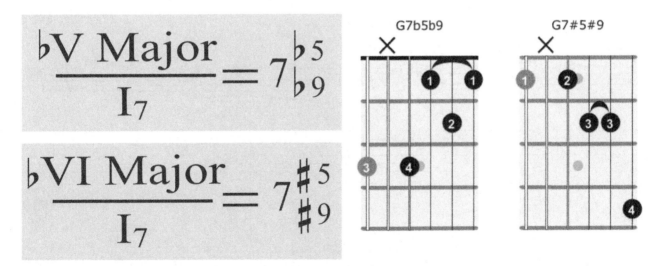

These are two examples of how we can take a simple triad, play it above another chord and come up with a new complex sound. The flat five flat nine and the sharp five sharp nine chords are often heard in series together. Not so much a cliche as a tasteful way of creating a whole host of musical devices from intros to endings and a lot in between, with both line ideas and chords.

We will use this chord/line relationship going forward to complete our II - V - I line based on the single concept of two major triads a tone apart. What follows is the complete musical example and then we'll finish this chapter off by considering the line from a guitarist's technical point of view.

Remember, what you are about to play is exactly the same material re-purposed harmonically as played over the minor seventh and altered major voicings shown earlier.

Case #1 - both triads up

S1EX19

S1EX20

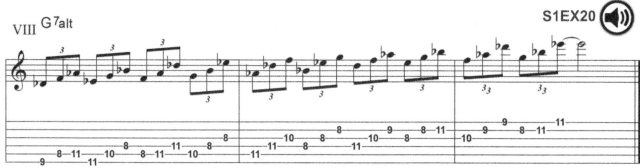

Case #2 - 1st triad up 2nd down

S1EX21

S1EX22

Case #3 - 1st triad down 2nd up

Case #4 - 1st triad down 2nd down

Hopefully you are enjoying hearing a musical line you now know inside out and which sounded "light" but is now starting to sound darker simply by what is being played underneath it. In many ways, this "shading" or colouring behind a melodic line is how composers and specifically film music composers manage to play with our emotions so much within the artistic fabric of motion pictures. A talented film composer will take a melodic line and manipulate motifs as needed, using, amongst many tools, the harmonic background to suggest a specific emotional subtext to underscore the onscreen action.

Back to the guitar. Now we'll put this line into a completed II - V - I progression for you to practise.

COMBINING ALL LINES OVER A II - V - I PROGRESSION

Now that the line idea has been demonstrated over individual chords, let's now look at playing a complete idea over all three chords found in a II - V - I chord progression.

Below you can see the chords that will be in the progression and the superimposition of the triads used over them as outlined earlier. From this, an actual line idea is shown below.

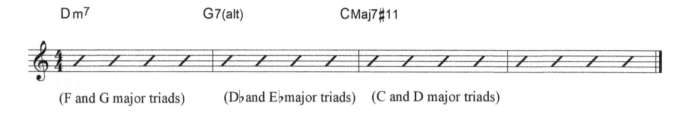

(F and G major triads)   (D♭ and E♭ major triads)   (C and D major triads)

Some points to consider:

1. The minor chord is shown as a minor seventh chord, however, if the chord was a minor ninth, sixth or thirteenth you can still use the triads as shown underneath the chord.

2. The same is true of the dominant chord. It simply stipulates "alt", short for altered. You can use any combination of notes you wish here and the aforementioned triads will be used.

3. The major chord is not a major 13 with a sharpened eleventh but again this does not matter. The improviser can make a decision on how much he/she wishes to colour a given chord symbol.

4. We will use the same melodic contour throughout this first idea, that is all motifs moving upwards. The idea will be shown in two distinct positions on the neck for variety and exploitation potential.

Here is the same idea in another position on the guitar neck.

Listen to the audio file of the previous example and, hopefully, you will agree it is a rich and complex line idea over the chord progression. From a technical perspective, it is a little difficult because the player has to move all over the guitar neck to actually facilitate the line. What would be better is if the idea was played in more or less one position and that is what the example below demonstrates.

The notes are exactly the same, however, the positions used on the guitar neck have changed to create a much easier way to execute the line. This does mean that the player should be confident playing triads across all string sets.

Finally, here is the same idea again further up the guitar neck but as close to one position on the fretboard as possible.

SUMMARY OF MATERIAL COVERED IN THIS CHAPTER

- How stacking chords (triads) one on another can lead to complex chords and/or inferred sounds.

- Knowing your major triad shapes is vital both from a chordal and melodic point of view.

- By relating chord symbols to simple formulae we can better understand how polychordal structures work.

- The leaving out of notes is often used and a necessary part of creating chord structures on the guitar.

- We can generate new voicings by reducing chords to inferred sounds and slash voicings (see point above).

- How to create melodic lines from harmonic material by combining the notes found in two triads and creating a "pseudo scale".

- It is possible to create a wide range of sounds by using melodic contours for practice and development. With simple devices such as considering a triad as a motif in its own right and altering its direction of play, many new contours are possible.

- Extrapolating the ideas around melodic contours to other chord forms such as minor and altered dominant can mean the creation of lines that have a unifying melodic "story" or sound.

- Learning how dissonance over dominant chords can be enhanced by employing altered 5th and 9th tones. These altered tones are organically produced by superimposing simple triads over dominant seventh chords, targeting strategic notes within the structure.

- Introduction of secondary dominants.

- Introduction of of flat five substitution.

MINOR

bIIIm
I7

Chapter 2

What's discussed in this chapter…

parallel harmony

voice leading

vagrant harmony

minor triads used as upper structures

contrary motion

pedal tones

similar & oblique motion

inferring altered dominants

MINOR OVER MAJOR & DOMINANT CHORDS

Minor triads layered upon major triads or dominant chords offer the guitar player access to a host of extended and altered voicings. The ideas presented in the previous section are all still pertinent. Knowing the formulae in regards to the relationship of the stacked triad over the lower triad is very important. Learning to hear the sound that these formulae represent, is of paramount importance.

We utilised major over major triads with a chosen formula in the last section creating sharp five/sharp nine and flat five/flat nine chords. Utilising minor over dominant chords using specific relationships offers the ability to access several chords that are often hard to use in an effective manner. Knowing when to use a specific chord type is the area we will be mainly addressing in this chapter. The two chords that we will be considering are shown in the box below.

POTENTIAL ALTERED DOMINANT CHOICES

C7♭5, C7♯5, C7♭9, C7♯9, C7♭5♭9, C7♯5♯9, ⟨C7♭5♯9, C7♯5♭9⟩

C9♭5, C9♯5

C13♯11, C13♭9, C13♯9

HOW TO CHOOSE A CHORD - VOICE LEADING IS KEY

I'm sure I was not alone in scratching my head when viewing chord diagrams of the two chords outlined in the box above when I first learned them all those years ago. At the time they sounded like another bunch of odd sounding voicings which I'd throw into the mix whenever I could and it never made much sense.

The key to making effective use of these chords is to employ good voice leading between chord changes. Voice leading (V.L.) is when you consider each note in a chord as a voice in its own right. In simple terms, as a chord of four notes transitions to another chord of four notes, voice leading assumes that there are four "voices" (one for each note in each of the structures). You would then take the closest interval route to a note which can be found in the next chord on the same voice level (1,2,3,4). In this way you create smooth interval transitions between the voices and therefore the chords.

Below is an example in this context of good and bad chord combinations. The first example represents poor voice leading and the second represents good voice leading. You will hear how, in the second example, the chords flow effortlessly into each other in a natural way.

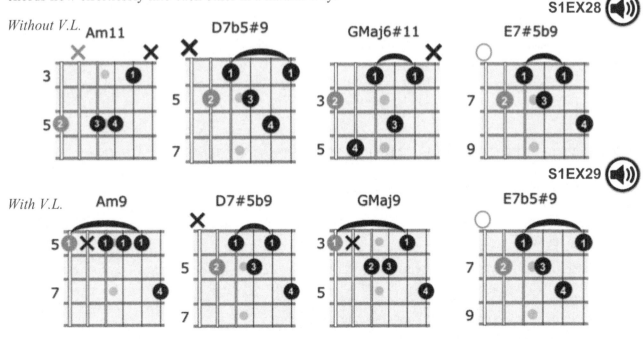

53

A cursory glance at each of the voices in these chords will enable you to see that in the second example the notes in each chord move to the adjacent note in the next chord much more smoothly. Note that the doubled root notes which are shown in brackets in the examples below are not necessary for the chord to function.

Example without V.L. in notation

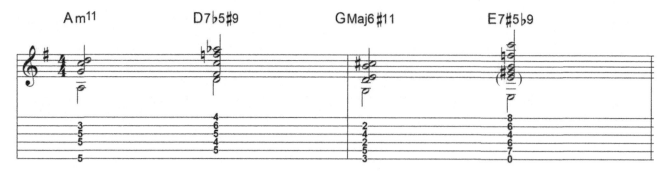

Here is a zoomed up version of the first bar in the second example above, which clearly shows the close movement of each voice from chord to chord apart from the strong root movement which moves up a perfect 4th from "A" to "D". This is how "awkward" chords such as the altered D7 below can be used effectively within progressions

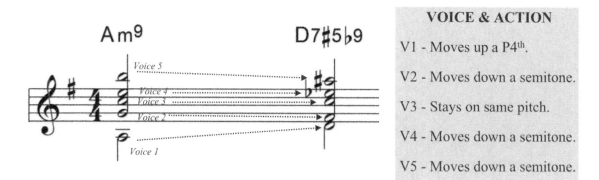

VOICE & ACTION
V1 - Moves up a P4th.
V2 - Moves down a semitone.
V3 - Stays on same pitch.
V4 - Moves down a semitone.
V5 - Moves down a semitone.

WHAT TO CONSIDER WHEN UTILISING VOICE LEADING

You can see that the overarching aim of voice leading is the smooth resolution from one chord to the next, ensuring that the voices found within adjacent chords are as close as possible to the perspective of the intervals used. Within this concept we can utilise specific aims for example, the movement of the bass in relation to the melody.

These concepts are central to how I perceive and hear the harmonic progressions I play. I try to create interest and as a by product (due to the guitar being a transposing instrument (-12 semitones)) create counter melodies to the main theme or improvisation taking place. In this vein, what follows are four areas of interest and study to help you advance your chordal playing.

FOUR WAYS OF DEFINING THE MELODY/BASS RELATIONSHIP

The most important relationship for me in chordal harmony within a progression is the one between the melody and the bass. Thinking about how you wish to "sculpt" this crucial relationship and move through the chords will have a big impact on the final sound(s) you create.

So, here are four melody/bass relationships to consider:

1. Contrary motion. This is where the melody rises or falls and the bass line will do the exact opposite. This is the most powerful of movements between melody and bass and can be used to create great emotional impact from solo guitar through to orchestral arrangement.

2. Parallel motion. Parallel motion describes how the melody and bass keep exactly the same interval distance throughout, whether they rise or fall.

3. Similar motion. Both melody and bass move in the same direction but not necessarily keeping the same interval distance as asserted in point two above.

4. Pedal Tone *(sometimes referred to as oblique motion)*. This technique involves either the bass or the melody playing a constant note with the other voice(s) playing notes against it. Pedal tone comes from the use of an organ blasting out a low note that the singers or instrumental players would use as a point of reference to help keep them in tune. When the pedal tone is the highest note played then this is often referred to as an inverted pedal tone.

   Generally speaking, bass notes have historically been employed more than melody for pedal (or inverted pedal) tones. Also, again as a general rule, the dominant (5th) or tonic (1st) are primarily used as pedal tones but any note can be considered for use. In the end it's up to you, the player, to decide what does and does not make musical sense and is in good musical taste.

The four cases above will now be demonstrated to let you hear and play an example(s) of each idea. I will be using the flat five/sharp nine and sharp five/flat nine chords mentioned earlier as much as I can within these examples. A "I - VI - II - V - I" chord progression will be used although at times heavily substituted.

CONTRARY MOTION - ASCENDING MELODY DESCENDING BASS

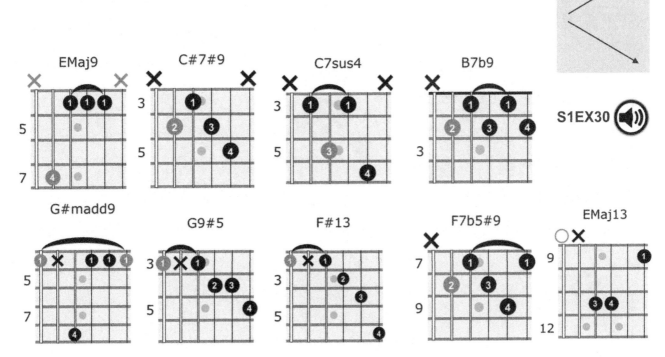

55

For the most part the melody is rising and bass is descending. This changes as we arrive at the penultimate and last bar where the F7 altered chord has its bass note "F" taken up an octave due to stretch considerations and a low "E" is used in the last bar as explained below.

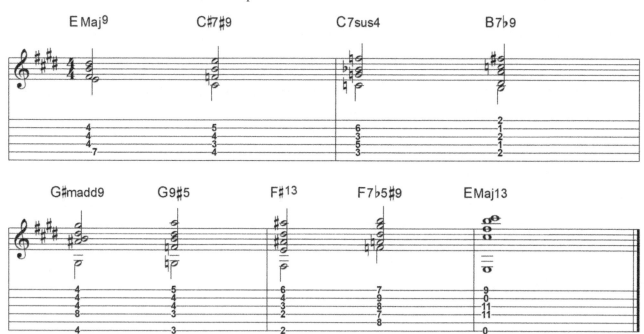

The C7 suspended chord in the second bar is a flat five substitute for the expected II chord, F sharp minor. In the next bar the G sharp minor add nine chord is a direct substitute (chord III) for chord I which is a common substitution technique. The F sharp dominant chord (with thirteenth extension) is preferred to F sharp minor to continue the motion inherent within the progression. The aforementioned F7 flat five sharp nine chord is itself a flat five substitute for an expected V chord, B7, which continues the chromatic movement in the bass. This leads to an E chord with the root "E" being played an octave lower to create depth to the sound through the wide interval spacing between melody and bass.

(NOTE: the subject of flat five substitution is covered in the next chapter in greater detail.)

CONTRARY MOTION - DESCENDING MELODY ASCENDING BASS

S1EX31

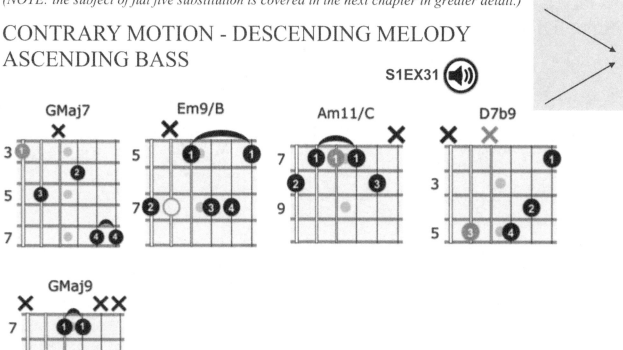

For the descending melody and ascending bass example it can be a challenge with the descending range available between the top and bottom notes. This is where knowing chord inversions and many shapes that can be altered to fit really can come in useful. Two examples right in the middle are the 2nd inversion E minor nine chord and the 1st inversion A minor eleven. Without making use of inversions it would not have been possible to create the final chordal ideas.

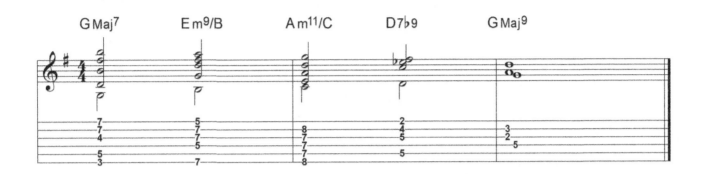

PARALLEL MOTION BETWEEN MELODY & BASS

S1EX32 🔊

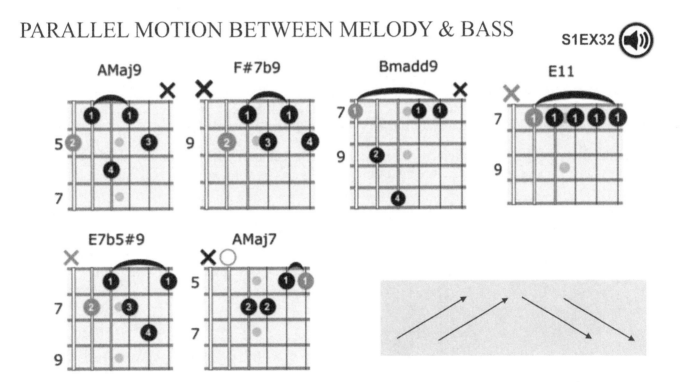

The thing to keep in mind is that the interval between the bass and melody is consistent throughout thus parallel, apart from the penultimate chord where I squeeze in a flat five/sharp nine for melodic interest.

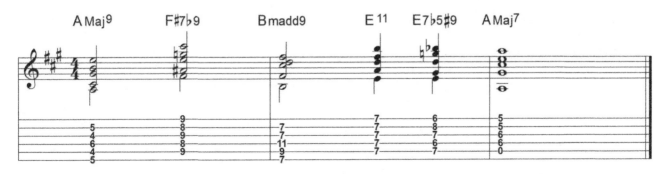

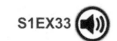
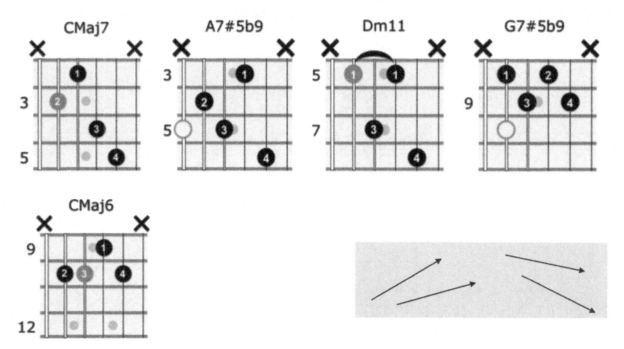

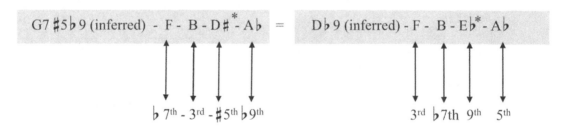

This example includes two voicings that do not contain a root note within the notes played. The A7 and G7 chord diagrams display an inferred root as shown above. Sharp five/flat nine chords are used in both examples but utilise different fret board shapes. Note that in both of these examples the sharp five/flat nine chord can also function as a dominant ninth chord within a different harmonic scenario; see below.

The similar motion of bass and melody in the example above is defined as the interval distance between elements not being consistent throughout. For example: first interval - 10th, third interval - perfect 11th etc.

SYNONYM INFORMATION

* = Enharmonic equivalent

$$G7\sharp5\flat9 \text{ (inferred)} - F - B - D\sharp^* - A\flat \quad = \quad D\flat9 \text{ (inferred)} - F - B - E\flat^* - A\flat$$

$\flat7^{th} - 3^{rd} - \sharp5^{th} \flat9^{th}$ $3^{rd} \quad \flat7^{th} \quad 9^{th} \quad 5^{th}$

One way of recalling this synonym is to know your flat five substitutes. The flat five of G is D flat and from that point you need to remember the type of chords that these note groupings within the synonym create. Flat five substitution was covered briefly in the last chapter but will be covered in greater depth within the next chapter which looks at dominant seventh chord structures. The chord progression, shown again below could have been notated as C major seven, E flat nine, D minor eleven, D flat nine then C major six.

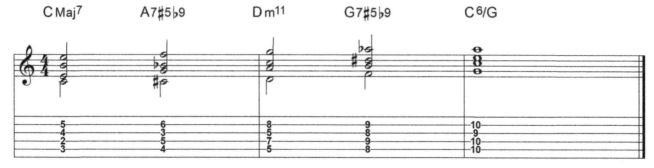

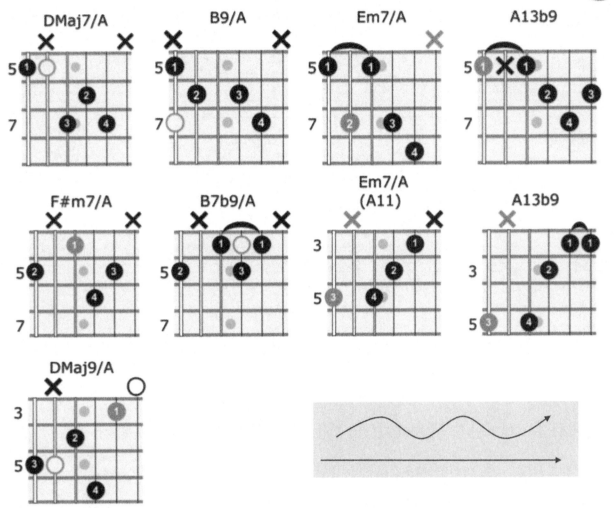

For the most part, there are four pedal tones used in traditional music.

1. Tonic - root of chord I in the bass.

2. Dominant - root of chord V in the bass.

3. Inverted tonic - chords move underneath a recurring root note which is the highest note.

4. Inverted dominant - chords move under a recurring V note which is the highest note.

The example above is case two: dominant (root of chord V) in bass. This example is a I - VI - II - V - III - VI - II - V - I example in D major so an A note is the dominant root and therefore the pedal tone.

As you can see and hear, the pedal tone has in each case a strong relationship to the chord it is underpinning. This does not always need to be the case which will be shown in a later example.

The B9/A is in reality a B7 3rd inversion. If you stack a major triad a sixth higher than a given root note a 13 flat nine chord will be created. In this example, (A thirteen flat nine) the flattened seventh note "G" is also further supporting the dominant seventh sound.

The F sharp minor seven is often visualised and heard as an A major six (which through synonyms it is). The B7 flat nine shape utilises symmetrical harmony; basically a diminished seventh chord.

The A11 is often thought of as a major chord with a root a tone higher in the bass (G/A).

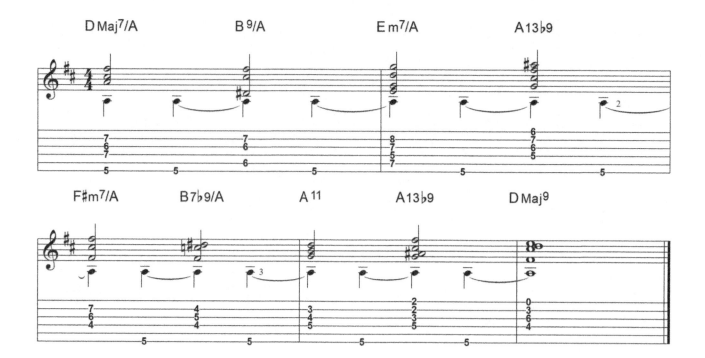

Most of the chord examples have been kept rhythmically simple, using half notes for the most part so scrutiny can fall on the chords and voice leading used. Here I've added a syncopated bass note to the pedal tone to create some additional interest within the example.

INVERTED PEDAL TONE BETWEEN MELODY & BASS

S1EX35

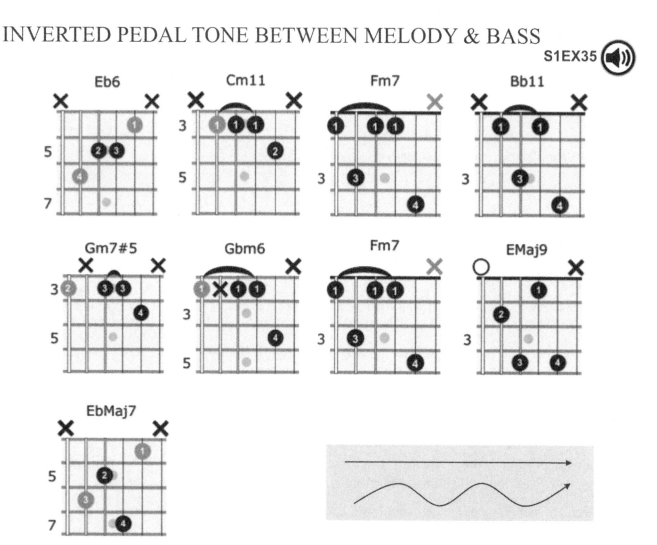

Here you can see the third type of pedal tone from the list given, which is a tonic pedal above chordal movement. Its full name would be an "inverted tonic pedal" and in this case an E flat note is played throughout.

In terms of harmonic analysis, chord III is again substituted for chord I in bar three, as mentioned earlier, a common substitution to help create longevity to what is ultimately the same recurring pattern. The fact that the chord is a minor seventh with a sharpened fifth is very much down to the organic outworking of having to keep the E flat note as the uppermost note in all chords.

The penultimate chord is again a utilisation of flat five substitution in order to continue the chromatic movement downwards towards chord I from G to E flat. On this occasion an E major seventh is used as the substitute for chord V, giving a fresh ending to the progression.

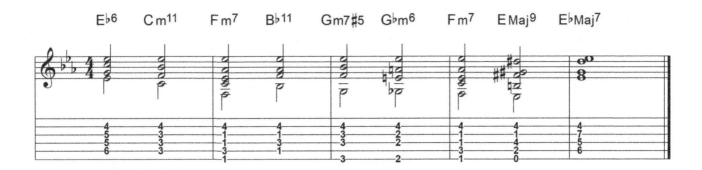

In this final example you can hear how parallel voicings can be employed to great effect over a recurring pedal tone. The tonic pedal underpins a vagrant harmonic idea which consists wholly of major chords in first inversion played at various positions on the guitar neck. The chords used in the second bar are (all major): B, C, D, E flat, D, C, B, C, B, B flat and A flat. I have not displayed chord boxes to keep things simple.

What binds these disparate major chords together? The melody. A sense of wandering and freedom, where the music is not tied down to any specific key centre is obvious. The harmony is both skipped over and bound at the same time by the melodic idea presented. The tension inherent within the idea is only resolved with the activation of the final chord.

S1EX36

I hope that you can see now how the chords discussed at the beginning of this chapter, sharp five/flat nine and flat nine/sharp five can be found to integrate meaningfully within a chord progression if used in conjunction with a sound understanding of voice leading. When talking about such chords my mind is inexorably taken to the subject just looked at; how bass and melody can work together. I now want to look at the composition of these chords from an upper voicing point of view and how to improvise over them.

Just before we do that, however, we'll look at our minor triads as we did major triads in the last chapter to ensure that everything that needs to be under the fingers is under the fingers for both arpeggios and triads.

DO YOU REALLY KNOW YOUR TRIADS?

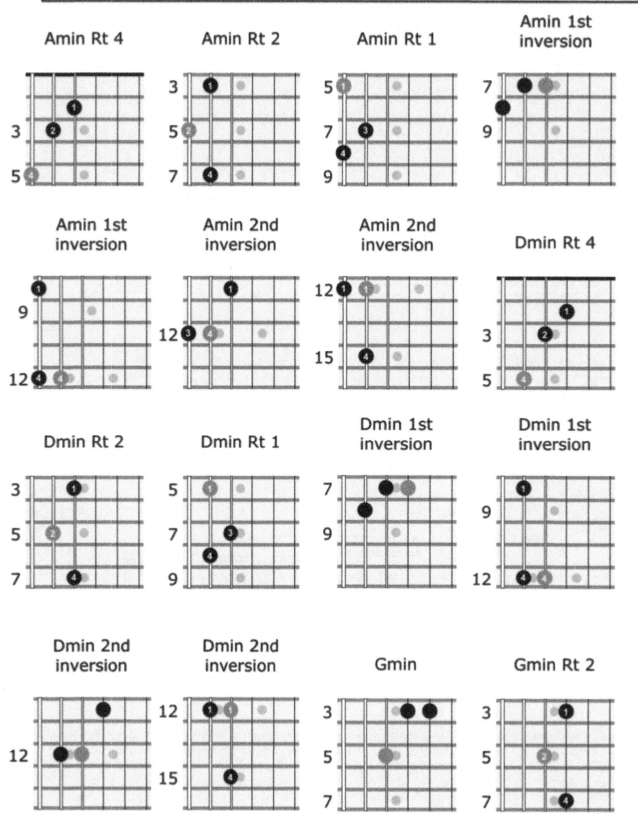

Minor arpeggios root - 1st & 2nd inversion Page 2
note - where no fingering is shown multiple fingerings are possible

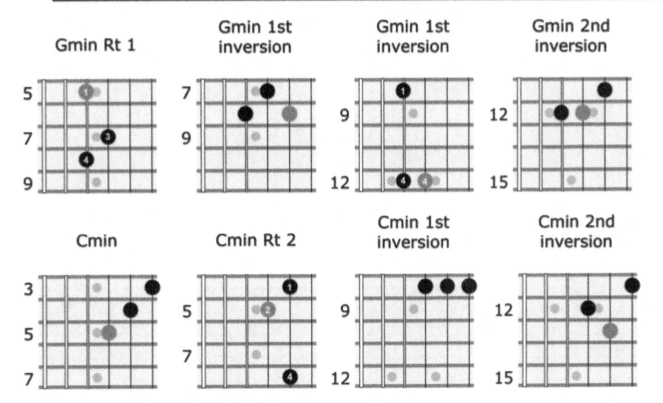

Gmin Rt 1

Gmin 1st inversion

Gmin 1st inversion

Gmin 2nd inversion

Cmin

Cmin Rt 2

Cmin 1st inversion

Cmin 2nd inversion

minor chord (triads) in root, 1st & 2nd inversion
note - fingering are shown however in most cases multiple fingerings are possible

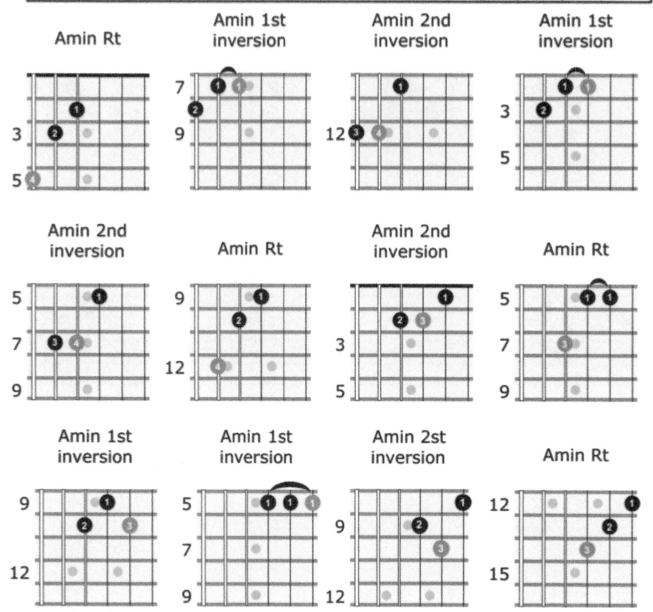

HIDING IN PLAIN SIGHT

Just as with flat five/flat nine and sharp five/sharp nine chords, the chords of "sharp five/flat nine" and "flat five/sharp nine" can be viewed as chords that include upper structures (triads) within them. If you've struggled to play arpeggios that represent these chord sounds when improvising, this knowledge will really help make things much clearer for you.

One thing I would like to point out is that when I state dominant seventh below, I am only referring (at most) to the root of the dominant seventh, it's 3rd and flattened 7th tones. In many cases, the root note will be omitted, as well as the 5th, so often we only consider the tri-tone interval with another triad sitting on that (the upper structure). If you are not sure what a tri-tone is, it's explained in the next chapter.

The make up of our first chord is as follows - chord symbol, formula, chord stack:

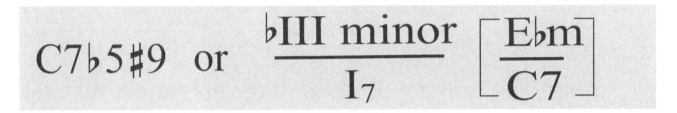

Here is a chord diagram of a couple of dominant seven flat five/sharp nine chords.

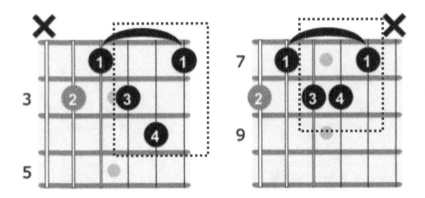

Common triadic minor chord shapes can be clearly seen within the dotted boxes. The visualisation of chord forms within complex chord structures can be key to understanding their make up and composition. What you will now view is an arpeggio created from the above.

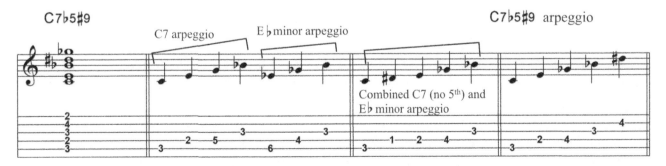

Although this final arpeggio is not that easy to play, my hope is that you will see (if you've studied the minor arpeggios and triads provided earlier) a C note, an E note and an E flat minor arpeggio played in 1st inversion as shown in the final example of the arpeggio pattern.

So, now that we have done all the background work, let's hear an arpeggio based around this chord played within a musical idea that you can practise and use when improvising.

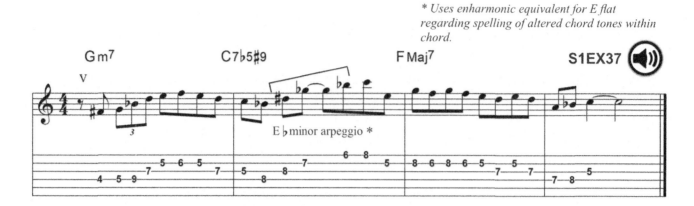

* Uses enharmonic equivalent for E flat regarding spelling of altered chord tones within chord.

Many more musical lines which outline a wide range of upper voicings are available in the second section of this book.

It would be good at this point to consider again how the essence or inference of a sound is created from the full harmonic structure. By stripping the flat five/sharp nine chord down to as few notes as possible we increase the possibilities of what can be achieved.

For this to happen we will take away the 3rd and leave the chord as a slash voicing. This will not be the same chord as we had before, but as mentioned, it does "infer" the sound of a flat five/sharp nine. By doing this (as we will see with other chords) it offers flexibility in finding new shapes and places to play the original voicing.

Leave out the 3rd

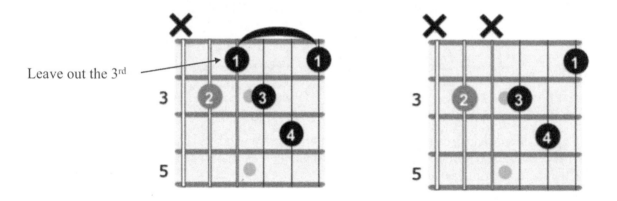

The eagle-eyed amongst you will now have realised that the chord that we now have is the same as a half diminished chord. The minor seven flat five chord is without doubt one of the most harmonically "pliable" chord structures available to the jazz musician. As you will see in the next chapter, the chord can represent a 9th, minor seven flat five, minor sixth and, added to that list, it infers a flat five/sharp nine chord.

Overleaf you are given six usable shapes that outline the sound of a flat five/sharp nine chord. II - V - I progressions with this chord concept integrated and in context, are then displayed. Full use of voice leading is also demonstrated.

C7♭5♯9 CHORD FORMS & SAMPLE PROGRESSIONS

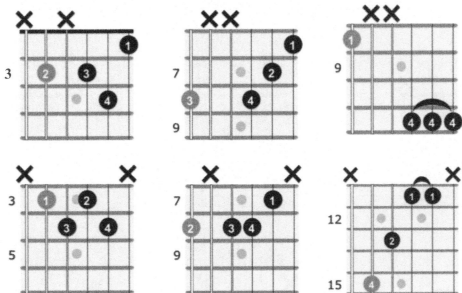

Ebmin/C (inferring C7b5#9) In a II - V - I Progression

S1EX38

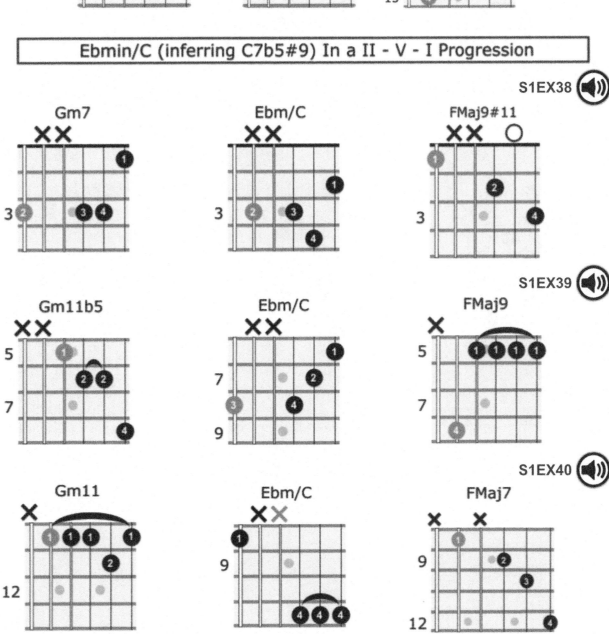

Gm7   Ebm/C   FMaj9#11

S1EX39

Gm11b5   Ebm/C   FMaj9

S1EX40

Gm11   Ebm/C   FMaj7

Ebmin/C (inferring C7b5#9) In a II - V - I Progression

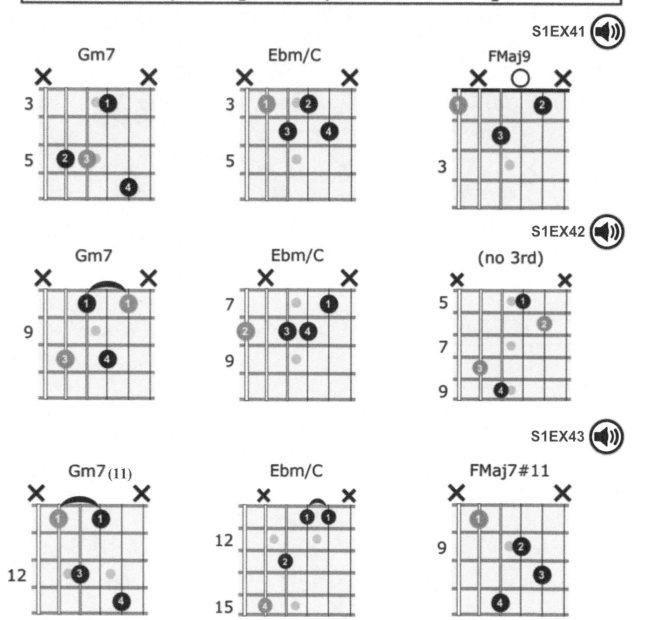

There were other forms that could have potentially worked but I have not included them. For the most part it would have been the E flat minor voicings found on string set 3 - 5. If you are curious to hear what they sound like then why not do some investigation. You will, however, be limited to a root note "C" which can only be found on the 6th string due to the E flat minor string set in this particular case.

Also, when creating chord voicings, the lower limits in regards to low intervals such as 3rds start to sound "muddy" and this needs to be considered. That's the main reason I have not added these other potential voicings.

CLOSER MINOR CHORD TO THE DOMINANT

Just as a flat five/sharp nine chord consists of two chords, a minor triad and a dominant seventh played together that are a minor third away, so this cousin makes use of an upper structure minor triad which is even closer. Seven sharp five/flat nine chords consist of a minor triad a minor second interval (semitone) from the root of the dominant chord in question.

Remembering the formulae to create or improvise over the chord being played is not difficult, but, remembering which formula equals which of the two chords is a little trickier.

For example, does a minor chord played over a dominant seventh chord a semitone lower create a flat five/sharp nine or a sharp five/flat nine? If you had to look below, then that makes my point. Try and link a flat II triad with the sharp five (flat nine) and a flat III minor triad with the flat five (sharp nine). Remembering the 5th and how it relates to the complete altered chord will, hopefully, help you.

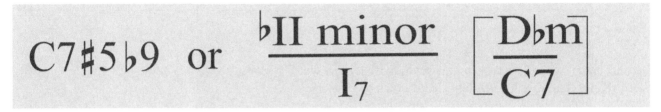

Two chord diagrams of the most commonly used dominant seven sharp five/flat nine chord shapes.

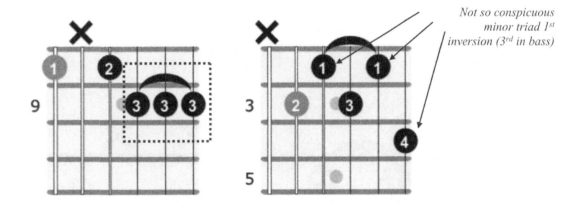

Not so conspicuous minor triad 1st inversion (3rd in bass)

The first chord shows an obvious minor triad in it's construction I have outlined where it occurs in the second diagram because it's not that easy to spot right away.

Below is the chord, the two arpeggios, arpeggios combined into a pseudo scale and this chord's arpeggio.

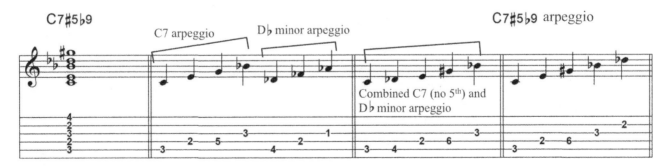

The last arpeggio for the flat five/sharp nine chord was not that easy to play and this one is, if anything, just as challenging! One thing that does muddy the waters slightly is that the final arpeggio is an amalgam of both arpeggios. The 3rd of C7 is also the 3rd of D flat minor with the flattened seventh of C7 appearing before the flat nine tone at the end.

Here is an example of the sharp five/flat nine arpeggio integrated into a musical line idea with the upper voicing arpeggio being clearly emphasised for clarity over two separate altered chords.

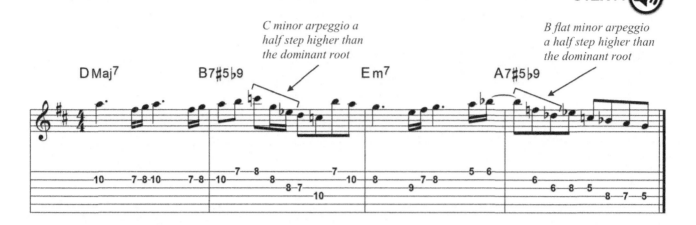

C minor arpeggio a half step higher than the dominant root

B flat minor arpeggio a half step higher than the dominant root

So, once again we are going to tamper with our chord to see if by doing so we can come up with a range of chord shapes that infer the original sound/voicing.

I accept that it's difficult to know what's going on in the boxes below, but fundamentally one note is being left out and two other notes are being rearranged.

The left hand chord shows a traditional C7 with a sharp five/flat nine. What you see on the right is the hollow circles being moved to their new positions represented as a triangle in each case. The black square in the second diagram is actually denoting that this note is being removed.

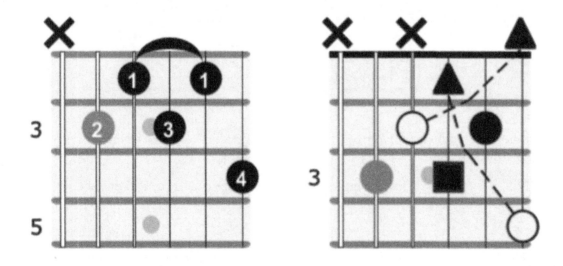

Basically, what you will end up with is the first chord shape that you see on the next page. This chord is titled D flat minor with a C in the bass. It infers the sound of C7 with a sharp five/flat nine. These new chords do not contain a tri-tone as the B flat note has been removed. Keep this in mind if your chart/song explicitly needs a dominant sound, which of course relies on the underpinning of the tri-tone.

Dbmin/C (inferring C7#5b9) In a II - V - I Progression

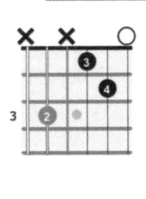
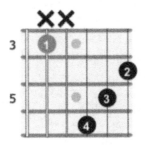
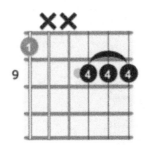

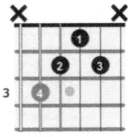
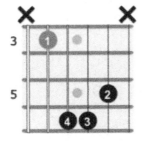
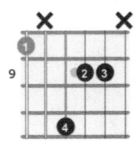

Dbmin/C (inferring C7#5b9) In a II - V - I Progression

S1EX45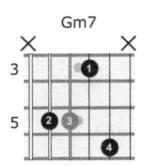

Gm7

Dbm/C

FMaj7

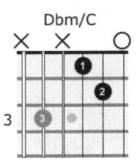

S1EX46

Gm9

Dbm/C

FMaj9

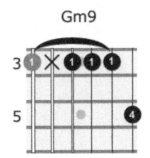
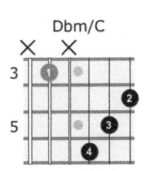
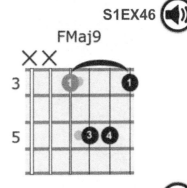

S1EX47

Gm9

Dbm/C

F6/9

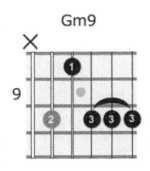
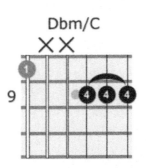
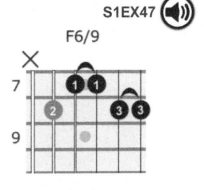

71

Dbmin/C (inferring C7#5b9) In a II - V - I Progression

S1EX48

Gm7/Bb
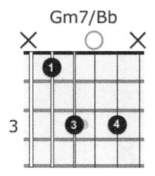

Dbm/C
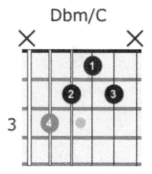

FMajadd9/A
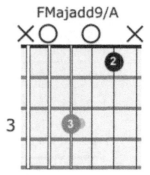

S1EX49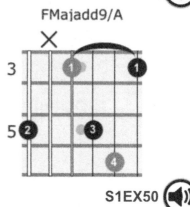

Gm9
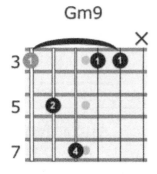

Dbm/C
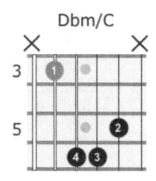

FMajadd9/A

S1EX50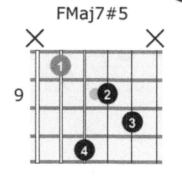

Gm7b5
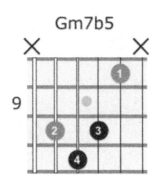

Dbm/C
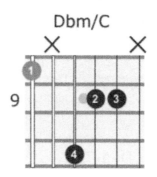

FMaj7#5

72

SUMMARY OF MATERIAL COVERED IN THIS CHAPTER

- A list of common altered chord voicings available to the guitarist.

- Explanation and demonstration in regards to voice leading and why it helps bring clarity and focus to the consideration of dissonant voicings and the many options available.

- Examples of four different voice leading techniques using contrary motions and pedal tones.

- An example of how to bind parallel voicings and vagrant harmony within a pedal tone idea.

- Further understanding of the construction of specific altered dominant chords that make use of minor triads.

- How minor triad superimposition within single lines soloing gives a wide range of altered dominant seventh sounds.

- Explanation of and method on how to re-purpose chords for use in different harmonic situations.

Dominant Seventh

$$\frac{VI_{Maj}}{I_7}$$

Chapter 3

What's discussed in this chapter…

single line solo ideas

tri-tones & what they create

flat five chordal relationships

chromatic movement

flat five substitution

Re-purposing chords across different chord progressions

deconstructing complex altered dominants

synonyms

MORE CHORDS WITHIN CHORDS

Guitars, the majority of which have only six strings, obviously offer no more than six potential notes to play at anyone time. If we could stack one triad upon another then that would be the end of our harmonic options because the six notes (assuming no tones were doubled) and therefore strings, would be used up. By the way, I'm making the assumption that the player is playing a guitar in a conventional manner of pick and fingers and not ten finger tapping…

We will yet again need to omit certain notes to facilitate the "stacking" of triadic voicings one on another as we have seen in earlier chapters. This is desirable, if only from a practical physical necessity: the hand would quickly become tired if no allowances were made for the rather difficult shapes that can and at times must be created. From a musical point of view, lightening the sound of a harmonic structure and creating a less dense timbre, especially multiple lower string intervals, is for the most part, in my view, desirable. Remember, the guitar is a transposing instrument so we already sound one octave lower than notated on the music page with regards to concert pitch. This is worth remembering when creating voicings that consist of multiple intervals in the lower string and fret extremities of the instrument.

Despite the fact that we do need to omit notes (in many cases the root and/or fifth can be left out with no impact on the integrity of the chord) to enable such stacking, we can still see in many chordal forms a triad being added on top of an interval foundation consisting of the remaining 3rd and 7th tones. This visualisation is key. For years I learned hundreds of chord forms but never visually recognised triads within shapes. What follows is an example of what I am talking about. First of all, if you've never played the following chord before, then try it out now. It's challenging, that's for sure and sounds, well, we'll get into that later.

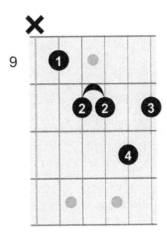

Okay, the following text is going to get a little technical and may sound like gibberish at first but hang in there. A "♯5 ♯9" chord can be viewed as a dominant seventh with a major triad based on the sharpened 5th (or enharmonic equivalent named ♭6th) of the original dominant seventh's chord tone placed on top.

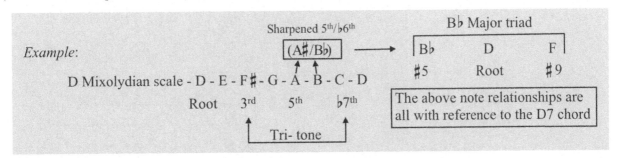

As mentioned above, this chord will sound rather "fringe" at first until you know how best to incorporate it into chord progressions, especially if you make use of "voice leading". That said, if you actually look at the shape above, it clearly displays a triad sitting on top of a tri-tone. Just so you know, I never noticed this for years when I was starting out as a guitar player trying to play jazz guitar.

So here is the chord shape again with its component parts labelled.

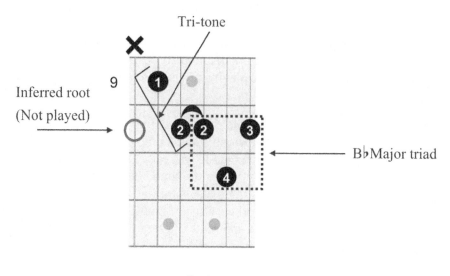

D7♯5♯9

What we have here in note order from the lowest note to the highest is the 3rd then flattened 7th of D7. This creates the tri-tone which generates the dissonance heard in dominant sevenths. Sitting on top of this is a B flat major triad second inversion. The note order being F, B flat and finally D. Note that F is the 5th of B flat major and played as shown is a 2nd inversion chord voicing of B flat. Also, the 3rd of B flat is a D which is also the root note of the original dominant seventh chord below the B flat triad. Finally, if we consider the "F" as part of the D7 chord we see as stated earlier, that the F is the ♯9th of D7.

> Major triad
>
> NOTE ORDER: F♯ - C - F - B♭ - D
>
> Tri-tone

With this one example I hope that you can see the power of the upper structure concept from a guitarist's point of view and from which all other examples and concepts can flow. It defines the structure of a chord in a visual way using what is, hopefully, already known from past study (the learning of triadic voicings) and overlays it, in this case over a tri-tone pairing.

At this point I'd like to introduce you to another consideration regarding the above chordal structure. Due to the fact that there are only six tri-tone pairs (see cycle of 4ths/5ths below which confirms this fact) the chord D7♯5♯9 actually has a counterpart that is created from exactly the same tri-tone. The cycle below not only tells you the tri-tone pairings, but the chord they belong to (go counter clockwise two steps from the flattened seventh of the respective dominant seventh) and the other chord the tri-tone relates to (the flat five substitute which sits directly opposite the D note at 5 o'clock).

Cycle of 4ths/5ths

Note: (pairings given in no particular order re numbering system)

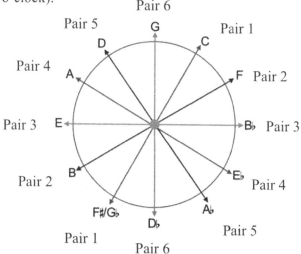

If you look again at the cycle of 4ths/5ths you will see that the D7 chord contains the tri-tone of the notes F♯ and C. That is, as already noted, where F♯ is acting as the 3rd of D7 and C is acting as the ♭7th. Due to the fact that each tri-tone addresses two dominant seventh chords, the C can be seen as the 3rd and the F♯ (in this case re-spelt as G♭) as the flattened seventh of A♭13♭5. Notes within a tri-tone always switch around like this when the harmonic polarity of the chord is flipped over.

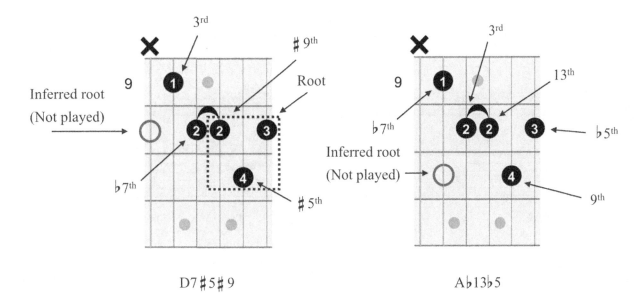

D7♯5♯9   A♭13♭5

To recap. As there are only six tri-tone pairs and twelve dominant seventh sounds, each tri-tone must address two dominant seventh chords and in each case, the mirror image dominant seventh's notes switch from being a 3rd to a ♭7th and vice versa as shown above.

One interesting fact to note when we are dealing with the cycle of 4ths/5ths is that many songs contain harmonic progressions that make use of and travel around this cycle. If a song has consecutive dominant seventh chords that go around the cycle, the tri-tones descend in chromatic movement with the thirds and sevenths switching "harmonic polarity" so to speak, as seen in the example below.

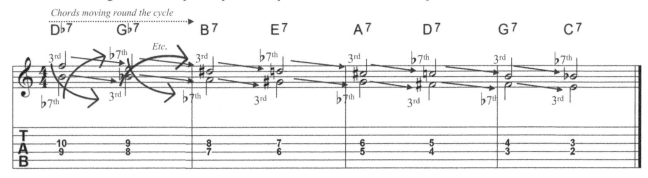

This example contains exactly the same tri-tones as the one above but addresses the "other" dominant seventh chord. This is often referred to as a flat five substitute, in this case with respect to the above chords. Again, the 3rd and ♭7th flip as shown (rather messily) in the first bar above and left out for tidiness below.

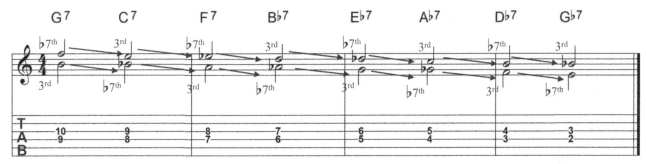

In this example we can see that the reason for flat five substitution is to create chromatic movement and to free ourselves harmonically from the constrictions of the cycle of 4ths/5ths. I often see flat five substitution discussed as if it were an end unto itself with no clear explanation or reference to its true purpose. Again, all the notes are the same, as in the last examples, but in the first example below, the 3rd stays on the top line throughout and in the second the b7th stays on top throughout, in relation to the notated chord at that point. To reinforce this point, the constant note (either 3rd or b7th) on top is due to the now chromatic movement of the root notes as observed in the chord symbols in both examples.

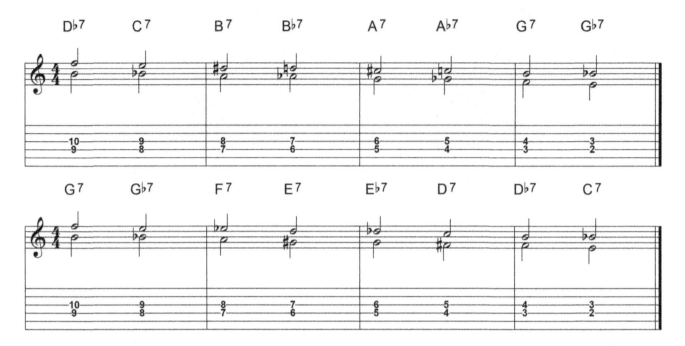

Regardless of whether this chord structure acts as a sharp five/sharp nine or a thirteenth flat five, the fact remains that as far as the guitar player is concerned, a tri-tone with a major triad as an upper voicing based on the #5 of a D7 or the 2nd of an Ab7 chord will create this dissonant and dense sonority.

THE EFFECT ON SINGLE LINE SOLO IDEAS

How does this affect our knowledge in the way we solo over chords? As we now know, a major triad whose relationship to a root note is either a b6th or the 2nd and is superimposed upon a tri-tone will result in one of two chord types; either a #5#9 or a 13b5 depending on how we perceive the tri-tones relationship to one of two potential root notes. We can utilise this concept in our approach towards soloing and the patterns that we create and use.

What you can see above is one of two potential chord/melody outcomes we've been discussing, written out in arpeggio form. In the second bar both arpeggios have been combined to form a usable arpeggio/line pattern. Take special note of the new combined arpeggio notes. Due to the fact that the #5 is not present in the original D7 chord, we have dropped the "A" natural note in the final #5#9 arpeggio pattern.

This is an improvisor's choice in the purest musical sense, as in, if you're playing a $\sharp 5\sharp 9$, you will probably not wish the natural 5th to be present. Also, it would weaken the dissonance that you're trying to create by superimposing triads on the original structure in the first place. On the other hand, on another day, the improvisor may decide to keep the natural 5th in. That's the beauty of being a musician who improvises.

From a guitarist's point of view, again, the B♭ triad is clearly distinguishable within the arpeggio pattern as a "major triad" shape. This is one of the great strengths of utilising upper voicings. You can actually see what is happening on a physical level, once you know how chords stack up and what the result is.

Of course, this is not the only way to view this collection of notes. We could see them not from a D7 perspective but from the A♭7 perspective due to the aforementioned tri-tone substitution.

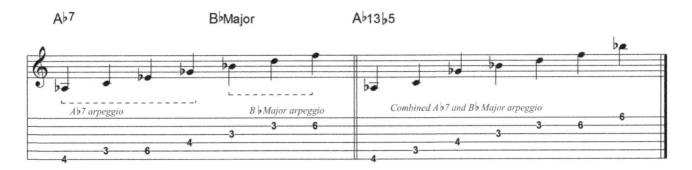

As before, by adding these two basic arpeggios together we then create the sound of an A♭13♭5. Sonically, I tend to leave the root note out when mixing chords and arpeggios together as this opens the sound of the chord up and de-clutters the lower end of the structure. By leaving out the root, we can then base the lower voicing in both these examples on the dissonance of the tri-tone, which, as shown in specific harmonic progressions will underpin the prevailing sound of the altered dominant.

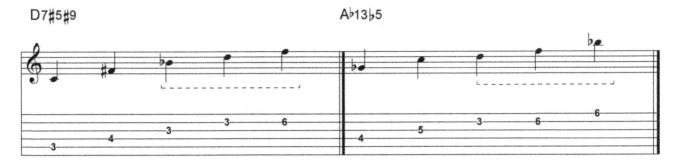

Something to keep in mind if you do want to leave the root of the flat five substitute in situ is that you may unintentionally change the chord voicing. Overleaf you will see exactly the effect that this seemingly innocuous idea can have.

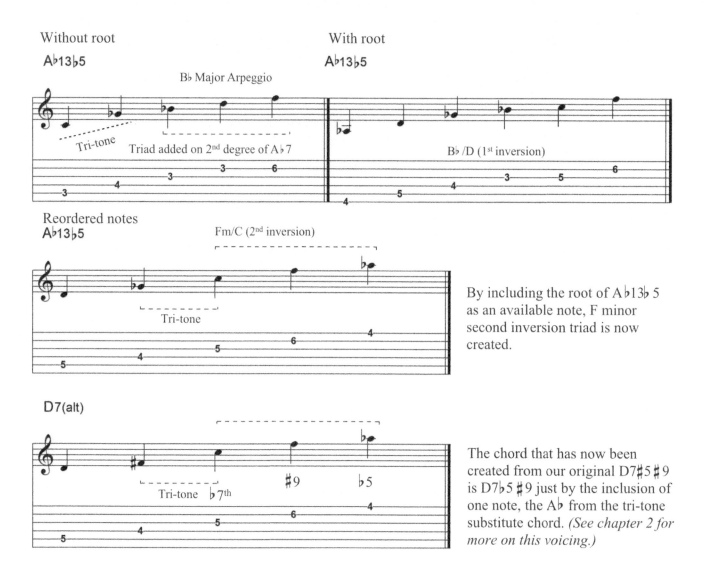

Without root

A♭13♭5

B♭ Major Arpeggio

Tri-tone   Triad added on 2nd degree of A♭7

With root

A♭13♭5

B♭ /D (1st inversion)

Reordered notes

A♭13♭5

Fm/C (2nd inversion)

Tri-tone

By including the root of A♭13♭5 as an available note, F minor second inversion triad is now created.

D7(alt)

Tri-tone ♭7th   ♯9   ♭5

The chord that has now been created from our original D7♯5♯9 is D7♭5♯9 just by the inclusion of one note, the A♭ from the tri-tone substitute chord. *(See chapter 2 for more on this voicing.)*

USE THESE PRINCIPLES TO CREATE VOICINGS ACROSS THE FRETBOARD

I'd like to use part of what we have worked on to show that the information given can be used as a force multiplier for learning, in this case, new chord forms. Playing a chord like D7♯5♯9 can be daunting to begin with and if you know even one such chord you've got every right to feel pleased with yourself.

The thing is, it would benefit you greatly if you could create this chord in many different places across the guitar neck. Indeed, not just this one chord, but other chords that have bearing and context on the music you play. To do this, we will take the chord we examined at the beginning of this chapter, the D7 sharp five/sharp nine.

To create a more usable form I'm suggesting that you actually leave one more note out of our original example, in addition to the root and the fifth. Now, this is very much down to the individual's musical taste and the sounds they wish to generate and hear. By leaving a further note out, you will see how pliable the remaining chord forms can be.

CLOSELY LINKED POLYCHORDS & SLASH VOICINGS

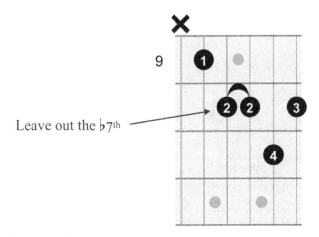

Leave out the ♭7th

By omitting the note shown above which makes up the tri-tone, we are left with the 3rd of D7 in the bass and a major triad in second inversion analysed as the flat six or sharpened fifth of D7. If we therefore find, in this case, F sharp notes and put B flat triads above them (a slash voicing), we will have created the musical essence of a sharp five/sharp nine chord. Here are examples:

D7♯5♯9 represented by B♭Major/F♯

Alternate F sharp bass note

These empty circular notes are alternate inferred roots although the dominant seventh root can be found within the chord itself and is shown as a light grey (not black) circle.

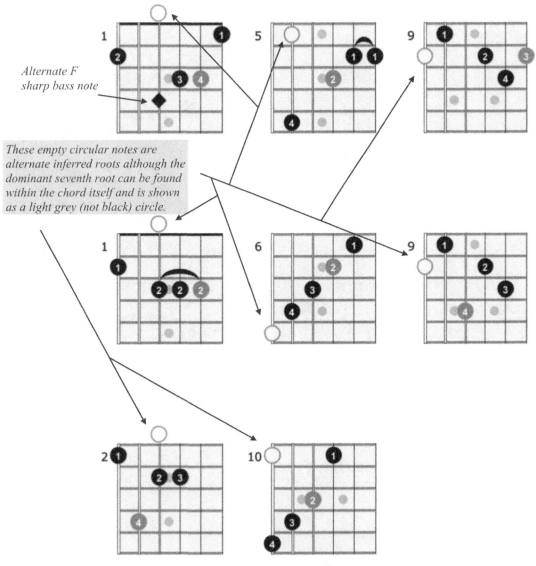

BbMaj/F# (inferring D7#5#9) In a II - V - I Progression

Examples of Major II - V - I progressions

S1EX51

Am/G
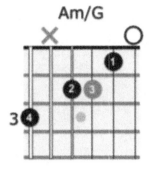

Bb/F#
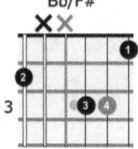

GMaj7
Note: Tilt barre
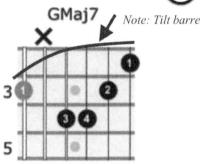

S1EX52

Am11
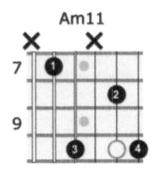

Bb/F#
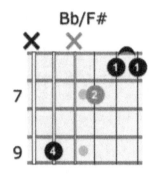

GMaj7
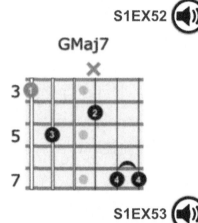

S1EX53

Am7
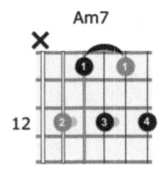

Bb/F#
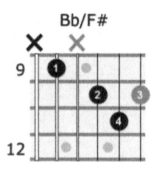

GMaj7#11
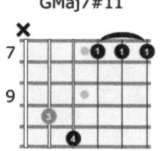

S1EX54

Am7/E
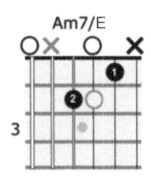

Bb/F#
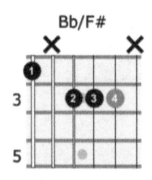

GMajadd9
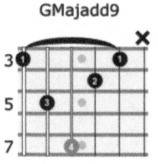

86

S1EX55

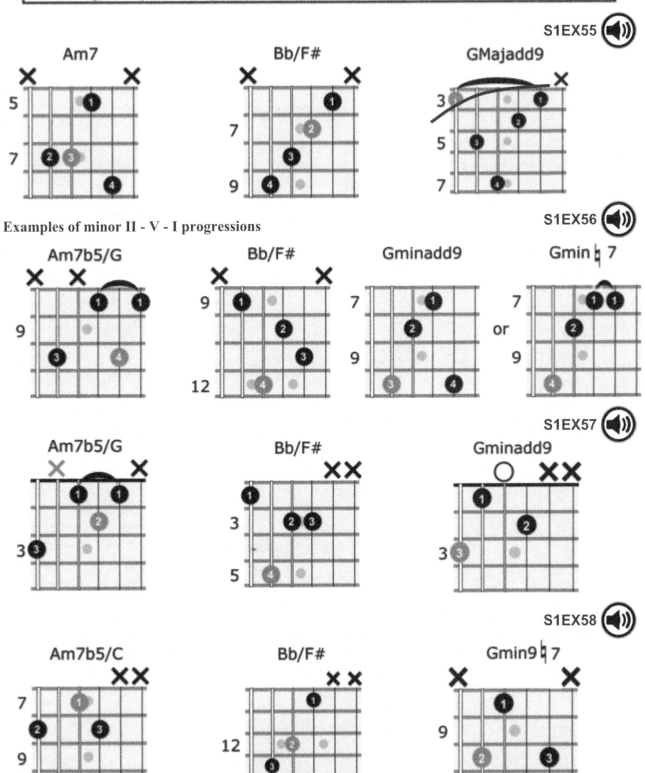

Examples of minor II - V - I progressions

S1EX56

S1EX57

S1EX58

To recap, the notes that we are now playing in this chord structure that infer the sound of a D7♯5♯9 chord are as follows:

D7 ♯5 ♯9 (inferred) - F♯ - F - B♭ - D

FURTHER USE OF THE SAME NOTES/SHAPES

Now do you remember I mentioned synonyms a while back? A chord which can have more than one name depending on harmonic context can be labelled, or is referred to, as a synonym. This is an excellent example of a chord that we can consider using as a synonym. The notes found in this chord structure are the same as D♯m9♮7. Here is the analysis of the chord structure:

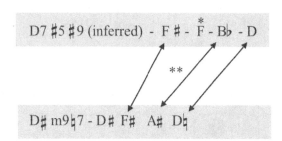

D7 ♯5 ♯9 (inferred) - F♯ - *F - B♭ - D

D♯ m9♮7 - D♯ F♯ A♯ D♮

*= Note the "F" note functions as the sharpened 9th in D7 and the 9th in the minor chord equivalent below i.e. E sharp.

** = Enharmonic equivalents

To emphasis just how powerful understanding and utilising synonyms can be, consider the following chord progression. The first line displays chords that could be used and the second line displays the same chord shape considered in three different ways that carries out exactly the same harmonic role. The key used in this example is E minor.

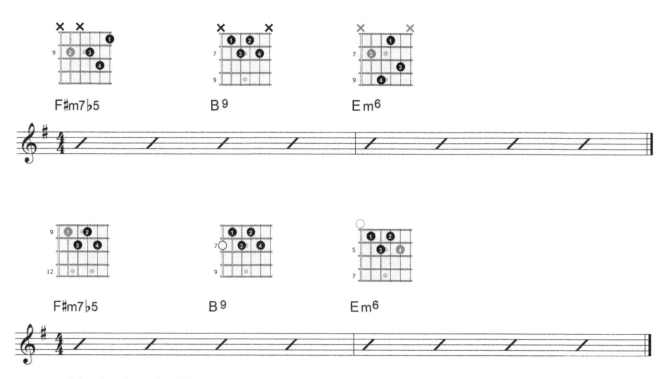

F♯m7♭5   B9   Em6

F♯m7♭5   B9   Em6

now consider the sharp five/sharp nine chord as a minor nine with a natural seventh chord in a progression.

The minor ninth natural seventh chord form used will be in the same order as the inferred seven sharp five/ sharp nine order as given three pages ago. We will continue to use E minor as our focus key rather than D sharp minor, to help reduce the harmonic complexity of what we are currently considering.

The dominant shapes (now functioning as I minor throughout) will be one semi-tone higher due to this new key and in some cases have been moved to adjacent string sets to create an easier to play chord form.

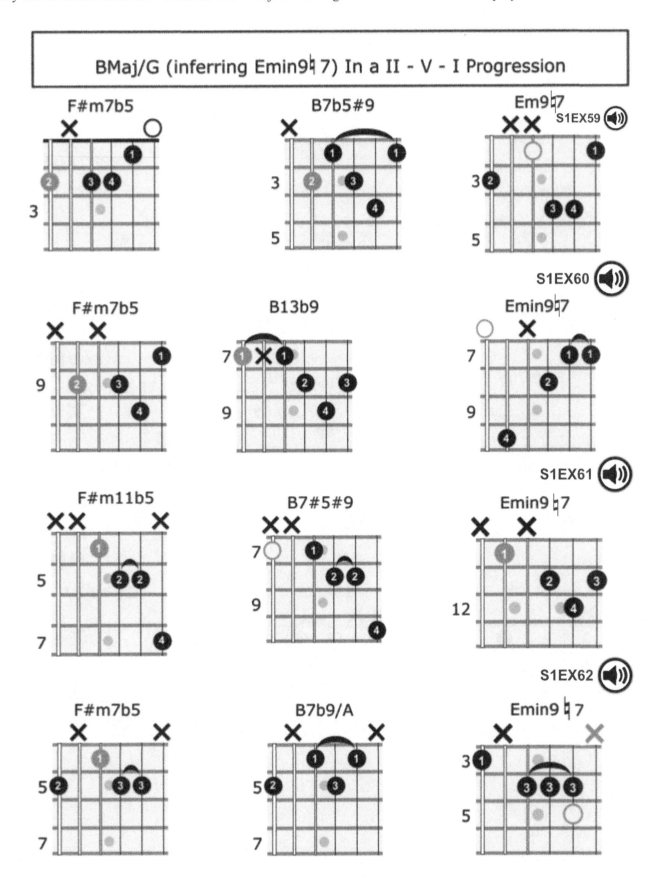

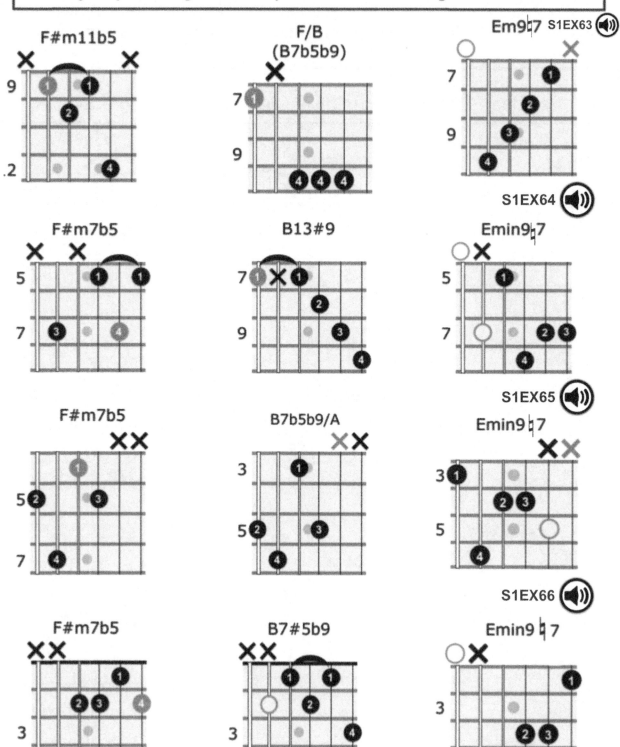

USING THE THE SAME NOTES/SHAPES…AGAIN!

Yes, we can yet again re-purpose the same shape, this time thinking of it as an altered major seventh form. This should come as no surprise due to relative major/minor relationships and the closeness this has on sound and meaning.

Once again we will be using a II - V - I to demonstrate how the chord works within a harmonic centre. In many cases voice leading using contrary motion, pedal tones, parallel and similar motion has been employed.

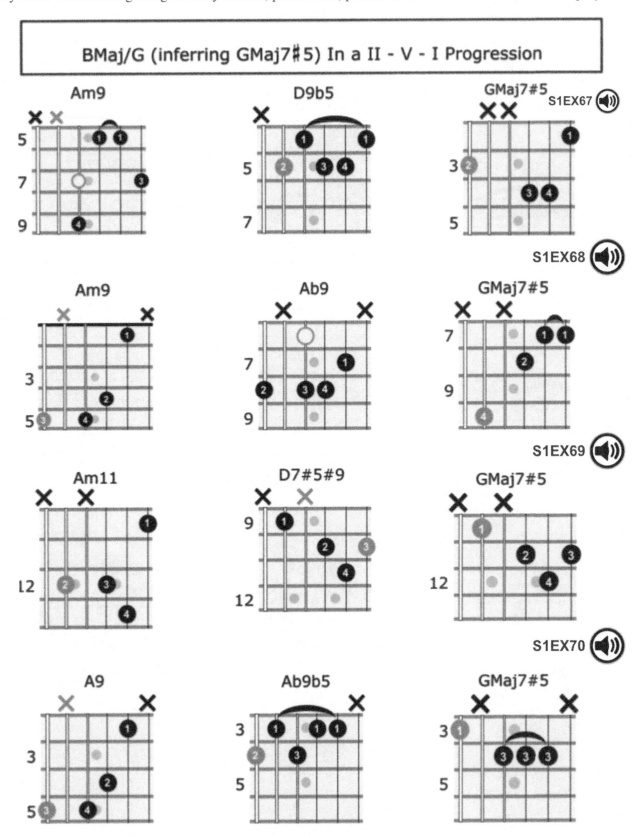

91

S1EX71

Am6
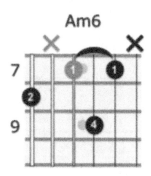

D7b9
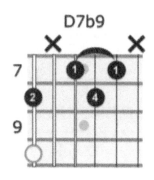

GMaj7#5
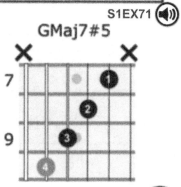

S1EX72

Am11
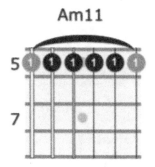

D7#5b9
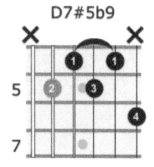

GMaj7#5
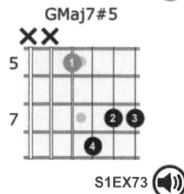

S1EX73

Am7
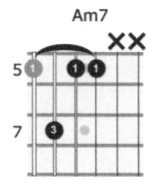

Ab7
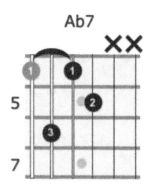

GMaj7#5
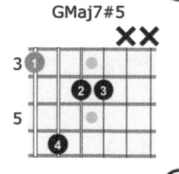

S1EX74

Am9
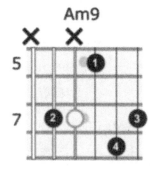

D7b5b9
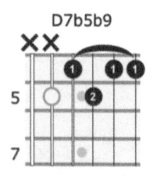

GMaj7#5
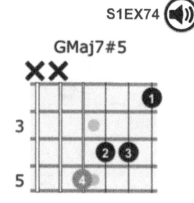

SUMMARY OF MATERIAL COVERED IN THIS CHAPTER

- The most complex of chords are often amalgams of simpler harmonic structures.

- Tri-tones address two chords at the same time, which is why we can make use of flat five substitution.

- Flat five substitution is not an end in itself but a way of creating chromatic movement that enables the player to escape from the cycle of $4^{th}/5^{ths}$.

- Due to the limitations of the guitar, in only having six strings available at any one time, understanding that roots and fifths are dispensable in order to create usable chord forms is desirable.

- Make use of what you already know (or should know) both physically and visually of basic triadic voicings and arpeggios, both major and minor across the neck.

- A voicing or line that is created with dissonance for a dominant seventh chord may well have relevance in regards to the flat five substitute alternative chord.

- Synonyms are powerful and when understood and applied can have far reaching effects, both in a harmonic and melodic sense.

Augmented & Diminished

Chapter 4

What's discussed in this chapter…

symmetrical harmony

diminished chords

cascading chords

movable solo lines

whole tone scales

motif development

inferring altered dominants

sidestep line movement through progressions

how augmented chords relate to scales

SYMMETRICALLY SPEAKING

Jazz guitarists want to learn how to improvise with freedom. The other big desire of most players is to have the freedom of chordal expression. Being able to play chord patterns seamlessly up and down the fretboard sometimes over just an individual chord symbol was certainly something that I always aspired to.

If you cannot do this yet and wondered how players make this happen then here is a common progression that players regularly face which will be used to explain a common harmonic technique.

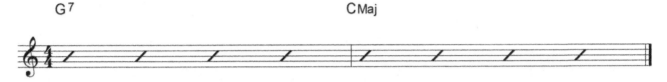

Now, let's assume that this is the first two or last two bars of a ballad. From this simple chord chart, some players would play the following…

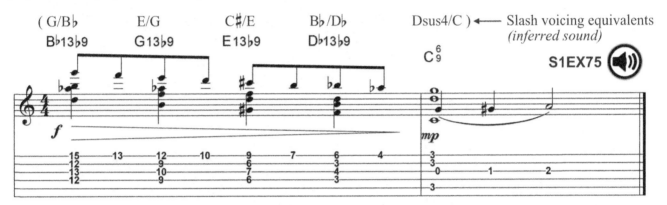

If you don't know why the chords used in bar one have been played, or perhaps you know this chordal idea but don't know why this works, then this chapter will help you understand and enable you to take your playing, both melodic and harmonic, to a new level.

Below is some text and overleaf a diagram I've copied directly from my book "Scales You Can Use!" (published by GMI - Guitar & Music Institute) which details how symmetrical harmony works and diminished chords in particular. Although the text is talking about scales, this information is equally true when dealing with harmonic structures.

A diagram is viewable on the next page which details in graphic form the information shown below. There are only three diminished scales due to the fact that the scale is symmetrical and repeats every minor third. If you learn one diminished scale, you've actually learned four. From a playing perspective, the scale patterns and any musical ideas created from them repeat every three frets. The whole step half step form is primarily used to play over diminished chords and the half step whole step form is utilised over altered dominant seventh chords.

Scale 1 = built from the root notes G - B flat - D flat and E.

Scale 2 = built from the root notes C - E flat - G flat/F sharp and A.

Scale 3 = build from the root notes F - A flat - B and D.

The roots of the three diminished scales in graphical form.[*]

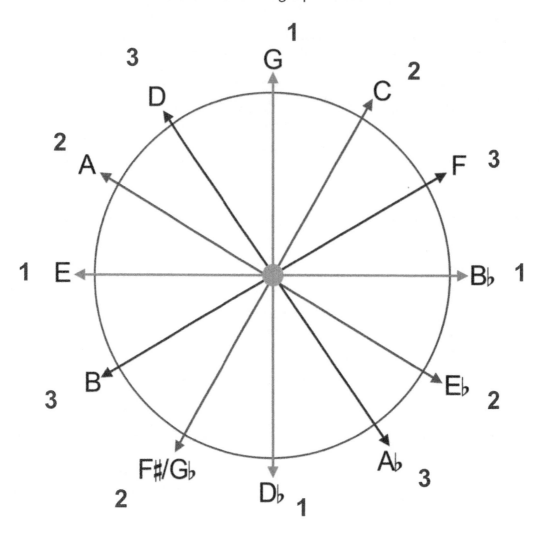

From this graphic you can see that the following scales all equal each other:

1. G diminished = B flat diminished = D flat diminished = E diminished

2. C diminished = E flat diminished = G flat diminished = A diminished

3. F diminished = A flat diminished = B diminished = D diminished

The Half Step Whole Step Form

The diminished scale can also be played starting with a half step as noted earlier. This form of the scale is used to play over altered dominant seventh chords. The reason for this can be seen below.

G diminished chord = G - B flat - D flat - E

G flat seven flat nine = G flat - B flat - D flat - E - G

NOTE: The original diagram and all other diagrams in "Scales You Can Use!" are printed in full colour.

WHAT DOES ALL THIS MEAN?

The practical working out of all this musical theory is that each diminished chord and its respective dominant seven flat nine chords (whose root is a half step lower than the diminished chord root) can repeat every three frets. What's more, you can start the chord from any one point from the four points shown in this cycle. Let's look at that musical idea again.

The progression is V - I in the key of C major as shown above. When working harmony out, work backwards, it's usually much clearer. We have a major chord that is preceded by a chord that is found in position five in its diatonic key centre. Taking the symmetrical harmony as used and applied by diminished chords, I have re-set the circle of 5th/4th as displayed below.

NOTE: the dominant seventh chord roots are shown on the circle on the right, but as mentioned above and outlined at the bottom of the last page, each of these dominant seventh flat nine chords map to a diminished seventh chord one half step higher. So G seven flat nine maps to G sharp diminished seventh etc.

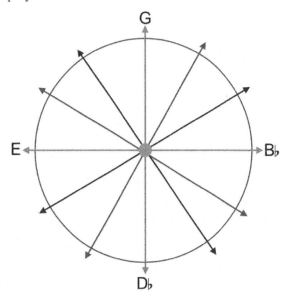

The G note which is the root, in this case of our V chord can be seen at twelve o'clock. Its flat five can be seen directly opposite; D flat. Due to the recurring and symmetrical nature of the diminished scale and harmony, we also have access to the B flat and E flat notes. All of these notes taken together would equal the case one diminished chord as shown on the previous page. I've blanked out all notes apart from the four we are interested in, which lie at opposite ends of each axis for you to clearly see the options available.

If you now study the chords below, you will see that the *roots* of these chords directly relate to the notes shown in the wheel above. Any one of the chords can then work and generate with any of the other three root note options. In the example below, we cascade the chords down the neck but the chords could have ascended. This is up to the musician. I've detailed more examples with different chords on the next page.

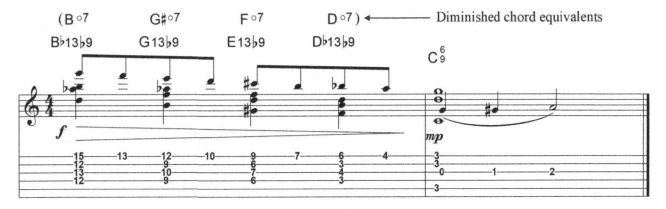

Here is another example using exactly the same chords but over a V - I in F major. The chords are ascending and the idea starts on an altered C7 chord, but it didn't have to, it could have started on any of the four chords played.

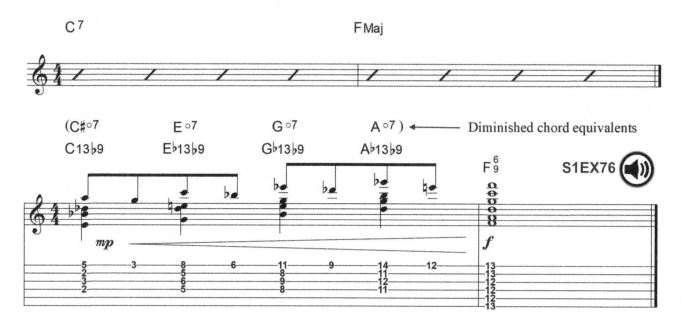

In this next example I've moved the idea to the inner four strings using the same shape. With the regular tuning of a guitar being what it is, the fundamental chord type played has changed from a thirteen flat nine to a plain ninth with no alterations. This makes no difference to the concept of symmetrical harmony and chord forms such as these can be used just as effectively as shown below. An example is shown below.

I've added, not exactly to be honest, an appoggiatura in the shape of a 13th tone of the chord in each chord instance to create some further interest.

The other thing to recognise is that I did not play a cycle of symmetrical movement but went back to a previously played form in the line. Again, this makes no difference to the musical integrity and resolving motion of the idea.

Note the dynamic layer added as well as the major seven sharp five in the last bar, which is in effect an E flat note with a G major triad on top. There is an endless amount of ideas you can create with this technique. The main thing is to have a go and not to be scared of experimentation.

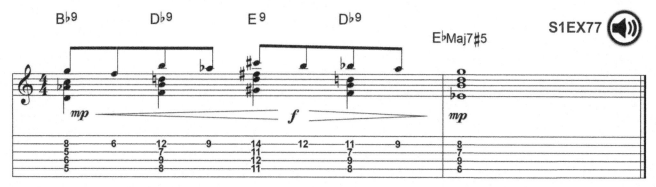

The final chordal example on this subject in regards to harmony combines several concepts that have been explained over several chapters within this book.

1. This idea could work either as an introduction or an ending. This of course would depend on the harmony of the song and how you reconfigured the idea to work in other keys.

2. The chord shape that is being moved around symmetrically up and down the neck is a dominant seventh with a flattened fifth and a sharpened ninth. This altered chord nomenclature is quite loose, as the melodic idea (or motif) that is repeated over all chords organically throws up different potential chord voicings.

3. As noted earlier, the seven flat five/sharp nine chord rendered as a polychord structure would consist of a dominant seventh (root (optional), 3rd, flattened 7th) with a minor triad up a minor third from the root of the dominant seventh chord. For example, E seven flat five/sharp nine is an E dominant seventh tri-tone with a G minor chord simultaneously played on top.

4. The chords do not move up systematically by minor third intervals in one direction but move between potential chord positions that can be played on the musical axis as detailed two pages earlier.

5. The piece is in A major and a dominant pedal tone has been combined with the chordal idea to create a foundation to the movement of the chords and the recurring melodic motif.

6. A rallentando is shown, which means that the fourth bar should slow down exponentially in relation to the original tempo.

7. Although not shown, due to the rather busy nature of the music notation, a decrescendo could also accompany the rallentando over the last two bars.

8. The squiggly line in the last bar before the final chord tells the player to slowly arpeggiate with pick or thumb. Gently strike the strings upwards through the notes in the direction of the arrowhead.

9. Notice how the root notes of the four chords create a diminished seventh chord.

10. The last note at the end of the third bar is not in keeping with the motif played throughout but it created a smoother transition to the final chord.

S1EX78

103

USING SYMMETRICAL IDEAS IN YOUR IMPROVISATIONS

It hopefully comes as no surprise that the ideas presented of chordal forms being moved about symmetrically can also be applied to single line soloing as well. Below is a diagram representing the sonic tension and release experience that is prevalent in common chord progressions.

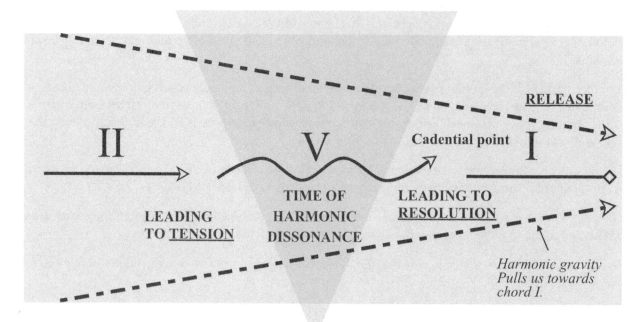

From the diagram above, which to some will no doubt look rather strange (which is fair), the dissonant quadrilateral area is where we can make the most obtuse melodic ideas and they will still make musical sense if resolved. That last point should also have "if you want to" attached to it. Keep in mind that you can play outside *all the time* if you really want, it's just that you may end up ploughing a lonely musical furrow if you do. *Outside as in melodically distant from the key being played over.*

So, take a solo line idea of three or four notes and then repeat it every three frets. This is in effect a rather crass way to explain motif development. What should be remembered is that you can get away with playing a lot of unconnected material in regards to the home key as long as you resolve the idea at the end of the line.

S1EX79 🔊

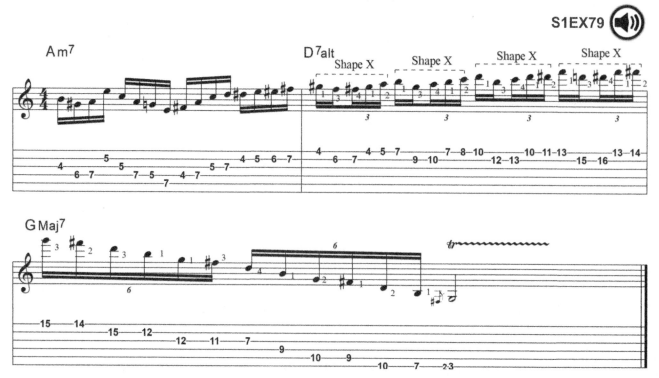

MOTIF SHAPES PLAYED SYMMETRICALLY & IN POSITION

Here we see a musical motif which can be "viewed" as a physical fingering sequence. It is knocking on the door of a full diminished scale lick idea, but not quite.

The idea is found in beat one of the second bar. This concept is then taken down in minor third intervals, as an opposite melodic direction to what we did in the last example. The other big difference with this line, however, is that the line is played in one position as much as possible. I would strongly advise that you learn to play such lines not only moving up or down the fretboard, but also in position as well.

This idea is over a minor II - V - I progression. One point that is worth making when you start creating your own lines is that if you consider the notes used in the initial motif idea in bar two beat one, they are all strong notes within an altered dominant sound. There is no 3rd present (which could have been added) but there is a flattened 7th. Also, the flat five and flat nine are present in this first beat idea. This is, in effect, a line that infers the sound of G dominant seven flat five/flat nine. From a polychord perspective it is D flat major over G dominant seven.

This sound is set in the listener's ear, if very briefly, and the exact same interval structure superimposed upon the diminished/symmetrical concept does the rest in leading the listener to the resolution at chord I. The following movement of the idea works because the initial motif element was harmonically and melodically strong in its own right.

Another element that helps bind the relationship of, at times, disparate note choices played within a recurring motif idea is the rhythm used as can be seen below. The rhythmic content of the notes played over each beat throughout the second bar is exactly the same throughout the repetition.

This constant is how familiarity and a homogenous melodic idea is built up over the length of a symmetrical musical concept.

DO YOU REALLY KNOW YOUR TRIADS?

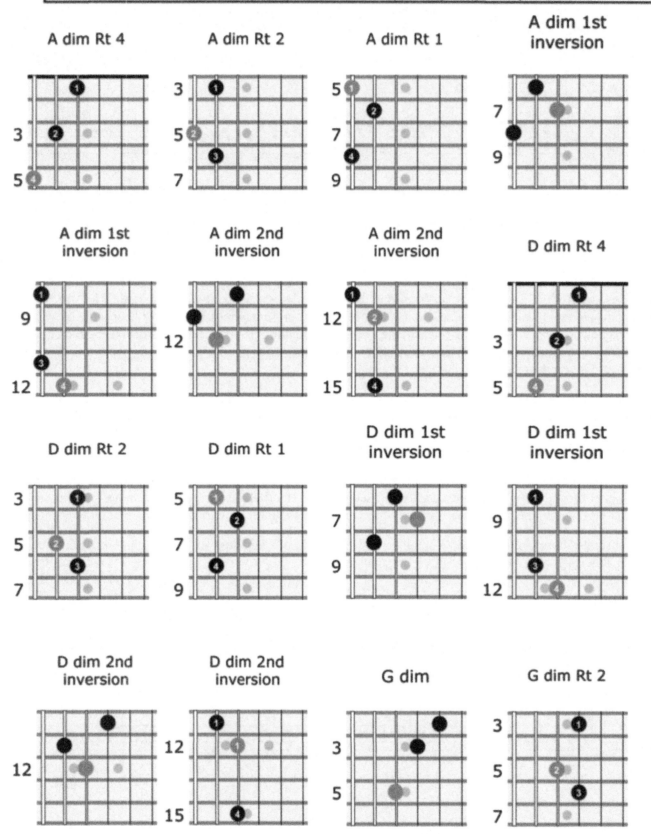

Diminished arpeggios root - 1st & 2nd inversion
note - where no fingering is shown multiple fingerings are possible

A dim Rt 4

A dim Rt 2

A dim Rt 1

A dim 1st inversion

A dim 1st inversion

A dim 2nd inversion

A dim 2nd inversion

D dim Rt 4

D dim Rt 2

D dim Rt 1

D dim 1st inversion

D dim 1st inversion

D dim 2nd inversion

D dim 2nd inversion

G dim

G dim Rt 2

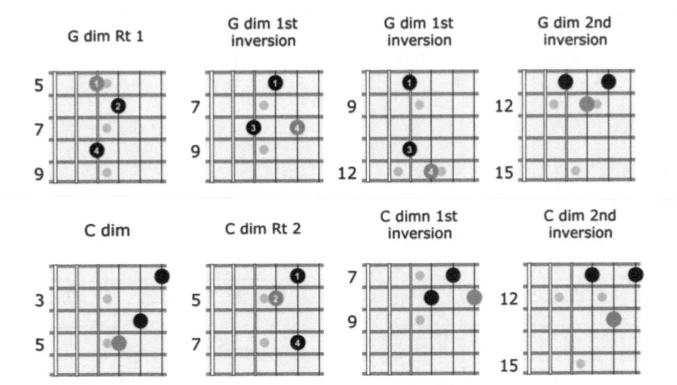

G dim Rt 1

G dim 1st inversion

G dim 1st inversion

G dim 2nd inversion

C dim

C dim Rt 2

C dimn 1st inversion

C dim 2nd inversion

Diminished chord (triads) in root, 1st & 2nd inversion

note - fingering are shown however in most cases multiple fingerings are possible

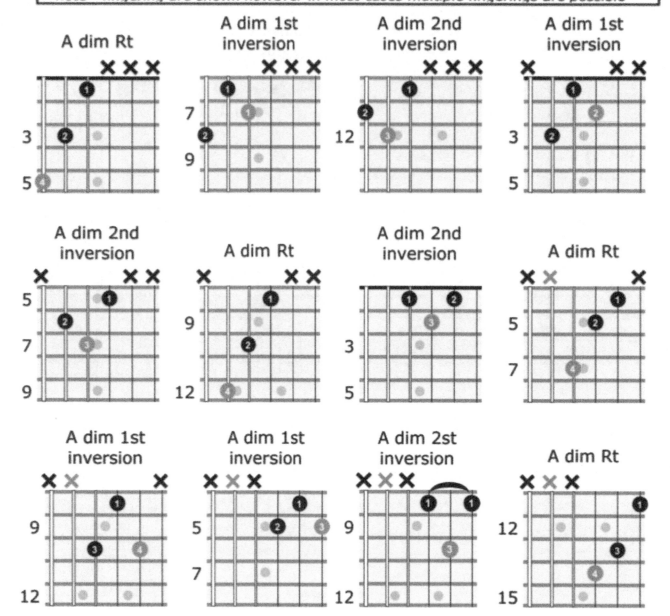

SIDE SLIPPING YOUR WAY THROUGH THE CYCLE

Back in chapter three I wrote the following text and provided a progression which was made up entirely of dominant seventh chords moving round the cycle. To recap, here is what I said and what the progression looked like:

"One interesting fact to note as an aside as we consider the cycle of 4ths/5ths is that many songs contain harmonic progressions that make use of and travel around this cycle. If a song has consecutive dominant seventh chords that go around the cycle, the tri-tones descend in chromatic movement with the thirds and sevenths switching "harmonic polarity" so to speak as seen in the example below."

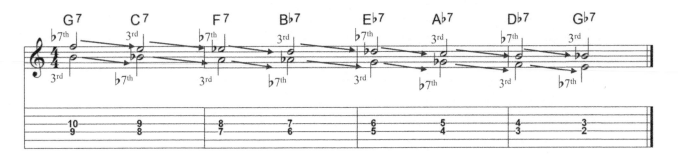

This switching harmonic polarity is an interesting aspect of moving around the cycle as we have seen. However, it can be also be thought of as a binary state as well, as we shall see.

The whole tone scale is often a poor relation for guitarists in terms of knowing the scale and using it effectively in a playing scenario. It can have what may be described as an odd, or a slightly disturbing sound. The scale's composition is different from the modal forms such as the major and minor scales. Here again is some material from my book "Scales You Can Use!" which detailed how this scale is constructed.

> The whole tone scale is perhaps peculiar in that it only contains six notes (excluding the resolving octave note). As the scale only has six notes, this means that in effect there are only two whole tone scales.
>
> The composition of a whole tone scale as applied to a chromatic scale can be seen as:
>
> W - W - W - W - W - W
>
> Circle 1 = G - A - B - D flat - E flat - F (Outer circle)
>
> Circle 2 = C - D - E - F sharp - A flat - B flat (Inner circle)

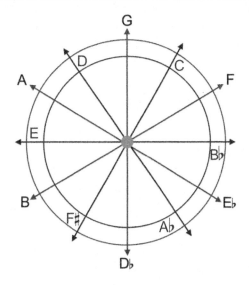

The type of chords that a whole tone scale can effectively be used to solo over are dominant seven flat five and sharp five structures. The whole tone scale can also be used over a host of related chords found within each scale. The resulting note relationship values of scale to chord are always the same as seen below.

WHOLE TONE SCALE 1

Notes for G, A, B, C#, D# & F whole tone scales	G	A	B	C#	D#	F
These scale tones can be used to solo over the following chords						
G7♭5 or G7#5 -	Root	9th	3rd	♭5th	#5th	♭7th
A7♭5 or A7#5 -	♭7th	Root	9th	3rd	♭5th	#5th
B7♭5 or B7#5 -	#5th	♭7th	Root	9th	3rd	♭5th
C#7♭5 or C#7#5 -	♭5th	#5th	♭7th	Root	9th	3rd
D#7♭5 or D#7#5 -	3rd	♭5th	#5th	♭7th	Root	9th
F7♭5 or F7#5 -	9th	3rd	♭5th	#5th	♭7th	Root

NOTES: The chords in the left column can be improvised over using the whole tone scale shown.

From the chart you can see how all chords contain notes that relate to tones which are the same in all the other chords within the matrix. This is why the whole tone scale can be used over all of these chord choices.

The 2nd scale consists of the six remaining notes and chords as listed on the chart below.

WHOLE TONE SCALE 2

Notes for G#, A#, C, D, E & F# whole tone scales	G#	A#	C	D	E	F#
These scale tones can be used to solo over the following chords						
G#7♭5 or G#7#5	Root	9th	3rd	♭5th	#5th	♭7th
A#7♭5 or A#7#5	♭7th	Root	9th	3rd	♭5th	#5th
C7♭5 or C7#5	#5th	♭7th	Root	9th	3rd	♭5th
D7♭5 or D7#5	♭5th	#5th	♭7th	Root	9th	3rd
E7♭5 or E7#5	3rd	♭5th	#5th	♭7th	Root	9th
F#7♭5 or F#7#5	9th	3rd	♭5th	#5th	♭7th	Root

NOTES: To reiterate the opening remarks made at the top of this page. In all cases, as can clearly be seen on the left, the notes that both scales address are the root, third, flattened fifth, sharpened fifth, flattened seventh and ninth; that is all.

In each case, the scale notes shown can be played over all the chords (or enharmonic equivalents) shown in that particular table.

The working out of the above and the point of this theory is actually very simple. What all this boils down to is that as dominant chords move through the cycle, the scale choice can only be one of two scales; whole tone scale number one or whole tone scale number two; binary indeed in its own way.

WHOLE TONE SCALE 1   WHOLE TONE SCALE 2   WHOLE TONE SCALE 1   WHOLE TONE SCALE 2
A7#5   D7♭5   G7#5   C7♭5

From a physical playing perspective, this would mean that if we had a motif that was constructed from scale form one and the next chord was a fourth away, the shape is simply moved up or down a fret (semi-tone) on the fretboard for the notes to be "in" for the new chord.

Here are two examples using the chord progression shown on the last page. It probably goes without saying that the progression itself sounds quite dissonant but it serves our purposes well.

In the first example, the initial idea is stated in bar one. This exact same line is taken up the neck chromatically as the chord progression moves through the cycle chord by chord. Each time the initial idea or "motif" is restated up a semitone, note how all the notes are within an alternate whole tone scale.

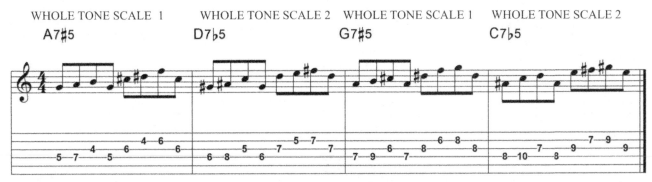

Regardless of where you are on the neck, this simple idea works every time. You are not confined to chromatic movement up the fretboard. In this next example, the idea moves backwards and forwards by just one fret. The notes played are all relevant to the scale and the chord they are played over.

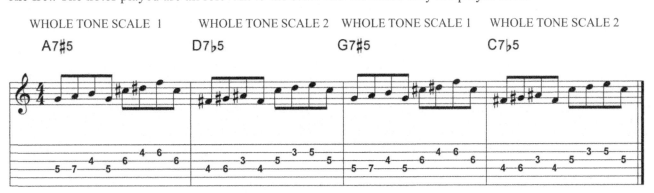

As also covered in chapter three, flat five substitution means that the chord values can change, however, the actual lines still make musical sense. I have not changed the notes to enharmonic equivalents to suit the chords the line is playing over for clarity of comparison when studying the examples below with those above.

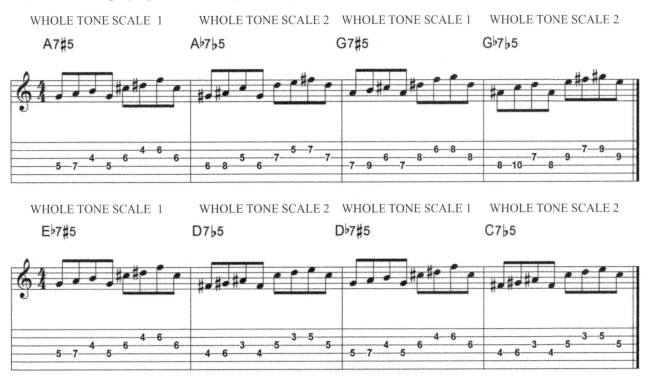

DO YOU REALLY KNOW YOUR TRIADS?

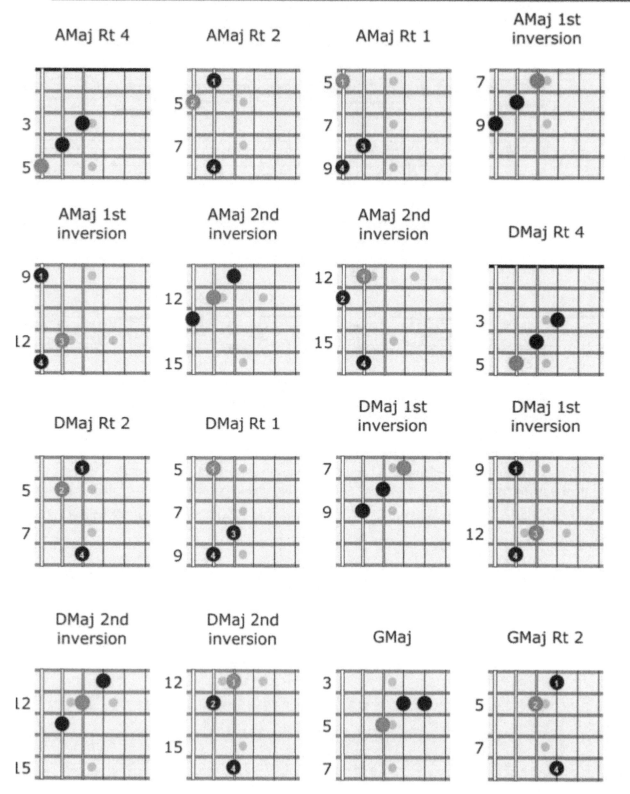

Augmented arpeggios root - 1st & 2nd inversion
note - where no fingering is shown obvious multiple fingerings are possible

AMaj Rt 4   AMaj Rt 2   AMaj Rt 1   AMaj 1st inversion

AMaj 1st inversion   AMaj 2nd inversion   AMaj 2nd inversion   DMaj Rt 4

DMaj Rt 2   DMaj Rt 1   DMaj 1st inversion   DMaj 1st inversion

DMaj 2nd inversion   DMaj 2nd inversion   GMaj   GMaj Rt 2

Augmented arpeggios root - 1st & 2nd inversion Page 2
note - where no fingering is shown obvious multiple fingerings are possible

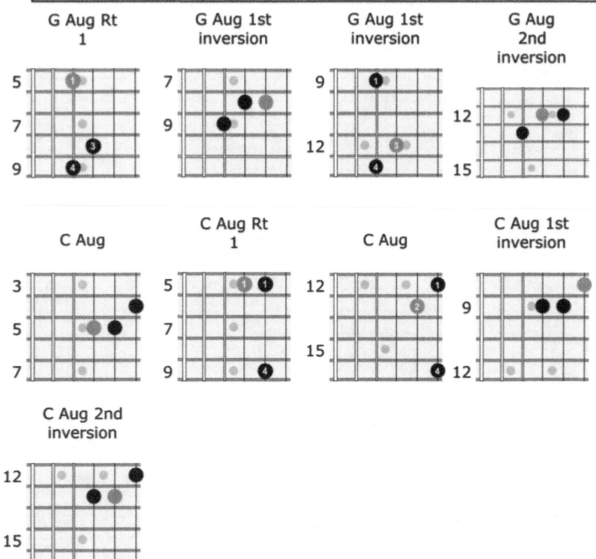

G Aug Rt 1

G Aug 1st inversion

G Aug 1st inversion

G Aug 2nd inversion

C Aug

C Aug Rt 1

C Aug

C Aug 1st inversion

C Aug 2nd inversion

Augmented chord (triads) in root, 1st & 2nd inversion
note - fingering are shown however in most cases multiple fingerings are possible

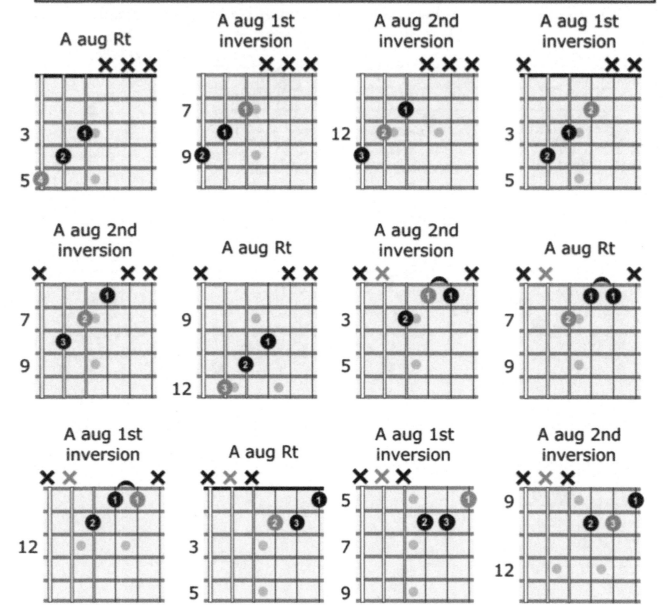

ALTERED VOICINGS & AUGMENTED/DIMINISHED CHORDS

Some of the altered dominant chords that we would want to play are only available through the use of polychords created from augmented (aug) and/or diminished (dim) triads.

First of all, let's look at a harmonised whole tone scale which, in this case, starts from the note "C". The resulting chords are shown directly above the music notation (row B).

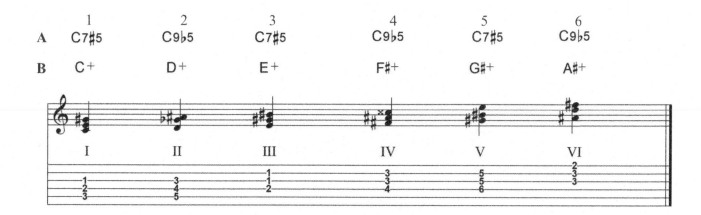

The chord symbols above the augmented chords (row A) are the resulting chord names if the augmented chords were played over a C dominant seventh chord (no fifth, for obvious reasons). Please note that chords I, III and V are all seven sharp five. The chords in position II, IV and VI, are all named C9 due to the presence of the 9th in the chord, the note "D". These chords are more or less a seven flat five chord and will be used for that chord type with only form number II being used.

It's a subtle difference between the overall sound of a nine flat five and a seven flat five chord but, for most practical purposes, all the above chords can be whittled down to the first two examples as shown below. A nine flat five will be played for a seven flat five. The proviso to this last point being that if you do wish to hear and play a pure seven flat five sound you need to play a chord or arpeggio that omits the 9th.

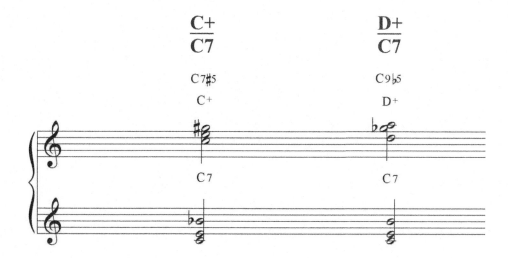

The examples shown in the next section are created using the two examples shown above. The examples will demonstrate the use of augmented sounds within single line ideas.

As with the whole tone scale, the diminished scale can also be harmonised. Below is a three note harmonisation of the C diminished scale. The chord symbols that these diminished chords generate are predicated on the triadic diminished voicings being played over a C dominant seven chord. Once again, many players may wish to learn each of these resulting polychord options as shown in line A, however, I limit myself to the results given in position II/2.

	1	2	3	4	5	6	7	8
A	C7♭5♯9	C7♭9	C13♭9♯11	C7	C13♯11	C7♭9	C13♭9	C7♭9
B	C°	C♯°	D♯°	E°	F♯°	G°	A°	B♭°

The reason for only considering position II/2 is most of the other results are either covered by more obvious and useful polychord options or the results themselves are duplicates of what is already available here.

For example, positions I and III are both offering up chord symbol results that we covered in chapters two and three. C dominant seven with a flattened fifth and a sharpened ninth can be played by a C7 chord with a minor triad a minor third higher played on top, E flat minor. The thirteen flat nine/sharp eleven (flat five) chord in position III is new but by playing a major triad played from the flattened fifth of the dominant chord we get almost the same effect. In this particular case, C seven flat five/flat nine would be played by a C7 chord with a G flat major triad on top.

Position IV is a straight dominant seventh result, there is no need to consider it. The position V chord is the same as a II_7 over a I_7 chord which we have discussed. Position VII is the same as VI major over a I_7 chord so that has also been covered as well.

By all means, if you wish to learn these extra polychord possibilities then be my guest. In the end, learning what works for you as an individual is what matters. I felt that this duplication was not worth the effort and kept to what I had originally learned after studying the options.

It should be noted that for the most part, the root of the C7 chord will more often than not be omitted when playing the above voicings.

This should be spelt as a D flat note, but I have left it as the enharmonic equivalent due to the initial triad being a C sharp diminished.

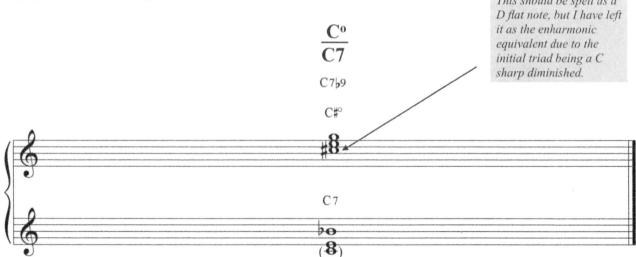

SUMMARY OF MATERIAL COVERED IN THIS CHAPTER

- Explanation of how symmetrical harmony works for both diminished and augmented chord types.

- How altered chords can act and be moved in the same way as diminished chords.

- That players can use the diminished idea of repeated chords in single line playing.

- That there are only two whole tone scales that address all related chords.

- That single line ideas can move up and down by semitones, both as a progression moves round the cycle as well as when the chords move chromatically.

- Explanation of the chords that matter within the harmonised augmented and diminished scales regarding polytonal structures.

GET THE DOWNLOAD PACK WHICH SUPPORTS THIS PUBLICATION

1. Use a QR code reader and point at box below to go to the GMI online store.

2. OR paste this URL in a browser and then follow the download instructions:

https://gmiguitarshop.com/collections/jazz-guitar-products/products/upper-voicings-synonyms-slash-voicing-download-free-for-book-owners

3. OR go to https://gmiguitarshop.com and use the search area at the top right of the website and search "Upper Voicings" and you'll see the download.

At Checkout Use The Code (*don't* include the dashes)

- JAZZSYNONYM -

To Get The Download For Free

WHAT IS INCLUDED?

- Video introduction and explanation from the author Ged Brockie.

- mp3 files of all denoted musical examples. All section 2 mp3 files include a discussion of the music played in that specific file.

- Backing and demo tracks of the section 3 solos for you to play along with.

- A PDF to help you memorise the upper structure chords.

PLEASE NOTE: The download is compressed by a utility programme named WINRAR which is commonly used by PC owners. If your PC does not see the compressed file, search "WINRAR DOWNLOAD" in your favourite browser to be directed to the main WINRAR website.

If you have a Mac computer, tablet or cell phone use a search engine to find "opening WINRAR files on a Mac". There are many sites and Youtube videos offering easy to follow ways on how to do this. A link is also placed at the bottom of the download page on the GMI website.

Most computers will be able to view/extract the contents of packed files without the need for extra software.

SECTION 2

A LICK LIBRARY OF IDEAS

This section is given over to solo improvised single line examples for a range of chord forms as detailed below. Specific arpeggio examples for you to practise. These example lines will predominantly be constructed over II - V - I chord progressions, both major and minor. As well as this, example chords for use in backing the line ideas are also provided.

- This is not a definitive listing of ideas but it will certainly help you create your own licks. You can build up your library of memorised musical phrases using the single line ideas presented in this section. I have not included the root note in the second octave for most diagrams to help the upper structure "breathe" within the context of the overall chord structure.

- Arpeggio patterns are offered in seven positions and many of them will be difficult or technically obtuse. I included these patterns to help with visualisation of the upper structures. Use as many as you find useful. I have not included the root note in the second octave for most diagrams to help the upper structure musically "breathe" within the context of the overall chord structure.

- Each of the chord elements covered contain chord diagrams for the line ideas, arpeggio patterns, up to three line examples for each chord category with comments regarding style, technique etc.

- No key signatures were added and as a general rule, either the accidentals will follow the direction of the line (ascending sharp, descending flat) or will relate to the chord alteration regarding flat/sharp 5th and 9th tones.

- I have not added any dynamic marking to allow you to interpret as you wish. I would suggest, as a general rule, that as a line ascends it will get louder and as it descends it will get quieter.

- I did not include chord shapes on the same page as the lines because I wanted to include chord diagrams at a larger scale. This separation also enabled the line examples to be provided in both music and TAB, and include comments on a single page. Chord symbols above the musical examples and the chords given in diagrammatic form beforehand are just one set of potential choices from many possibilities.

- Tempo instruction has not been provided to allow you, the player, to decide what tempo works best based on your own technical proficiency and knowledge. You can listen to the audio recordings of each line (provided in the free download) as a guide. The tempo of the recorded examples is given in the respective appendix list.

- For the most part, I have not included fingerings or position markers. The TAB will help if more clarity from a technical standpoint is needed regarding these elements. Having said that, there are some fingerings provided where I felt that it was important for you to know what I consider the most proficient way to play a specific line. You may find other ways to finger a specific line which works better with your technique.

LICK LIBRARY CONTENTS

MAJOR POLYCHORDS

CMaj9, CMaj13, C6/9

CMaj7♭5, CMaj7♯5, CMaj9♯11, Cmaj13♯11, CMaj7♭9♯11,

MINOR POLYCHORDS

Amin♮7, Amin9♮7

Amin9, Amin11, Amin13

DOMINANT POLYCHORDS

C9, C13

C7♭5, C7♯5, C7♭9, C7♯9, C7♭5♭9, C7♯5♯9, C7♭5♯9, C7♯5♭9

C9♯11 *Note: Ninths with a sharpened 5th are not represented*

C13♯11, C13♭9 *Note: Thirteenths with a sharpened 9th are not represented*

MAJOR LICKS

CHAPTER 5

Maj9

$\dfrac{\text{IIImin}}{\text{IMaj}}$

LICKS

CHORD FORM IDEAS - Major 9 shapes

Lick Idea #1

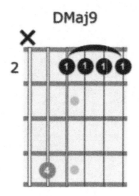

Lick Idea #2

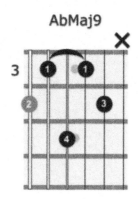

Lick Idea #3

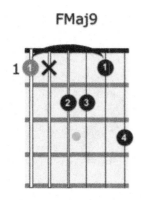

CMaj9 - C Major arpeggio with an E minor seven triad acting as the upper structure which results in the aformentioned arpeggio.

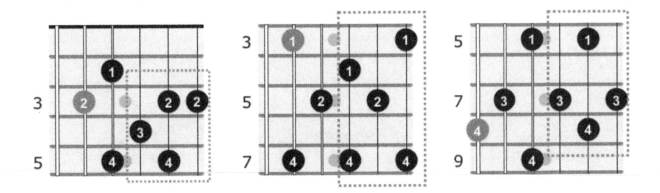

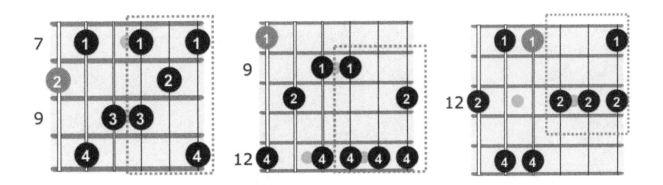

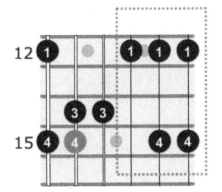

LICK IDEAS

I've included a variety of different time signatures for the licks in this section.

In these three examples the major ninth is outlined by simply playing a chord diatonic to the original key, in this case chord III of the respective scale.

You will find that this repurposing of existing arpeggios within a diatonic key centre can result in effective melodic ideas being brought to the fore.

In this second example I have deliberately delayed the introduction of the line to create some expectation and rhythmic tension. The use of the triplet figures brings an excitement to the line and the three over two at the end stretches the ideas out from a time perspective.

The line starts with a major seven arpeggio which helps define and centre the tonality of the melodic idea at an early stage.

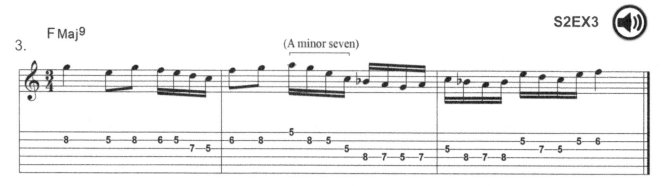

The final idea is not particularly difficult but does hold interest towards the end of the line. The A minor arpeggio in the middle of the second bar outlines the F major nine chord. From then on, there is a sequential pattern that moves over the three four bar line leading to the end of the lick.

The idea at the end is reminiscent of a hemiola device which is often used in classical music to move the music from triple to duple metre.

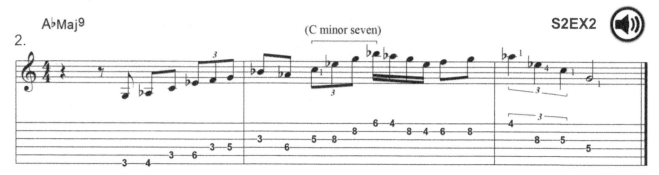

Maj13

III7sus4

I Maj

LICKS

CHORD FORM IDEAS - Major 13 shapes

Lick Idea #1

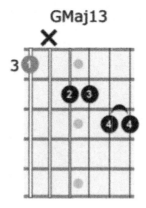

Lick Idea #2

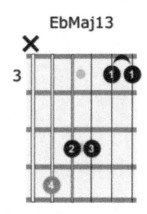

Lick Idea #3

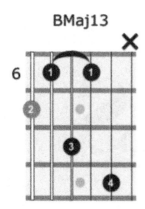

CMaj13 - C Major arpeggio with an E seven sus 4 acting as the upper structure which results in the aformentioned arpeggio.

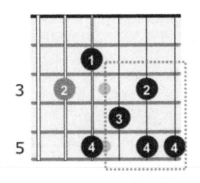 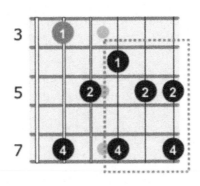 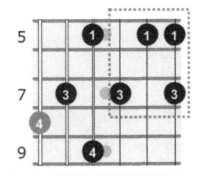

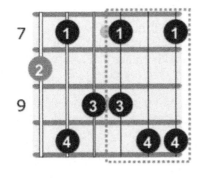 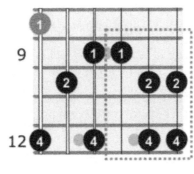 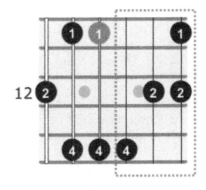

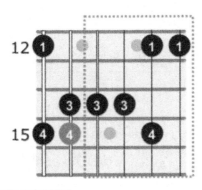

LICK IDEAS

The first idea begins with the mixing of linear scalar figures with arpeggios. There is also a position change to contend with so it may take a little practice to perform effectively.

When faced with a difficult passage mistakes can happen. I generally find that mistakes occur due to a build up of pressure that develops after a difficult technical challenge. The point at which the playing breaks down is the "straw that breaks the camel's back". Often, the actual problem that needs to be addressed is earlier in the musical passage.

If you find yourself continually making mistakes on a specific line at the same place, check back to see how you are handling the technical challenges up to that point. Once addressed, it may surprise you that your later mistakes suddenly disappear.

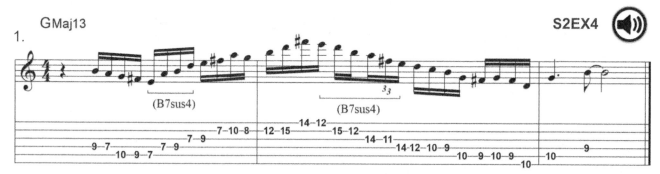

Line two will hopefully fall under the fingers relatively easily. One challenge to be mindful of when substituting a III₇ sus4 chord is that physically you will be playing notes that are not only on adjacent strings but the same fret. These specific chord types and the lines that can be played over them are a gateway to performing modernistic consecutive fourth and fifth interval melodic lines.

Seven sus(pended) four chords and their underlying arpeggios create an open sound which offer a refreshing change from consecutive third interval ideas. They are well worth practising and developing across the neck from a technical and musical point of view.

In the third example there is a pick up note played on the "+" of four. This note is pulled-off on to the first part of beat one in bar one. A chromatic approach tone (D natural) is used at the end of bar one which sets up the prolonged bar long use of the D sharp suspended fourth chord which outlines the major thirteenth.

6/9

$\frac{\text{II}_{\text{sus4}}}{\text{I}_{\text{Maj}}}$ LICKS

CHORD FORM IDEAS - Major 6/9 shapes

Lick Idea #1

C6/9

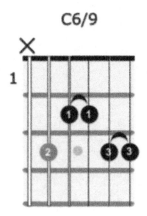

Lick Idea #2

D6/9

Lick Idea #3

F6/9

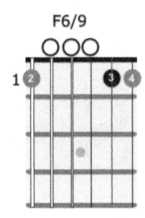

C6/9 - C Major arpeggio with an D sus 4 acting as the upper structure which results in the aformentioned arpeggio.

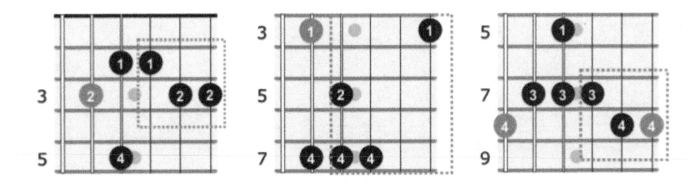

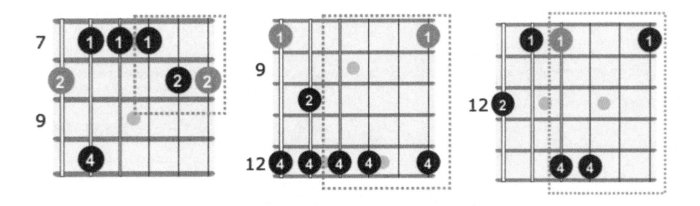

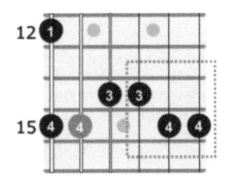

Note: Due to limitations in the chord/ scale/arpeggio software, it has not always been possible for the dotted box to only include the Dsus4 notes. The notes in Dsus4 consist of D - G - A.

LICK IDEAS

Six nine chords are based on the concept of quartal harmony as opposed to tertiary harmony which the majority of our other ideas are derived from. It may seem a little odd, however, that I actually heard lines that emphasise a quintal harmonic background (harmony based on fifths) when looking to create ideas around these chords. This can be heard in this first idea for you to learn.

I've added all the fingering to the line because it could prove a little confusing at first and this will help you get the idea under your fingers much faster as it crosses the entire fretboard.

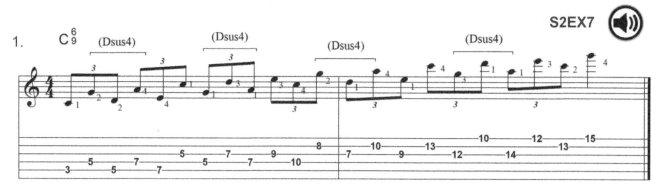

In this second line a distinctly pentatonic feel is evident and it is a line which could be played in a whole host of musical styles, not just jazz.

As stated in other line comments, this type of musical idea moves the sound away from a purely linear and tertiary based foundation and is created around a fourth-based concept which includes some awkward same fret/different string movements.

In many ways these ideas are harmonically vague and can be used in many different musical scenarios so I would encourage you to try playing these and other such ideas over as many diverse harmonic backgrounds as you can create.

Finally, we can hear and play a musical line that is itself based on P4th intervals over an F six nine chord which as stated above is itself constructed from intervals of a perfect 4th. I was tempted to use a B natural note in the 2nd and 3rd beats of the first bar but decided against it. If you decide to play a B natural it will enhance the angular and modern sound and you will be playing an F lydian mode idea in 4ths...nice!

Maj7♭5

VII

II sus4

I

I Maj

LICKS

CHORD FORM IDEAS - Major 7♭5 shapes

Lick Idea #1

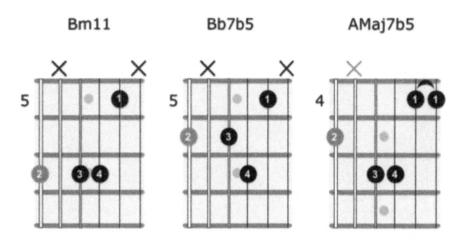

Bm11   Bb7b5   AMaj7b5

Lick Idea #2

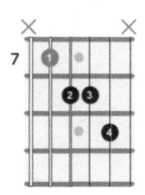

EMaj7b5

Lick Idea #3

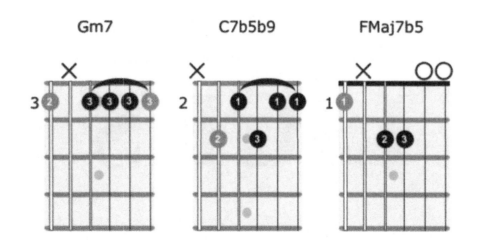

Gm7   C7b5b9   FMaj7b5

CMaj7b5 - C Major arpeggio (no 5th) with a Bsus4 acting as the upper structure which results in the aformentioned arpeggio.

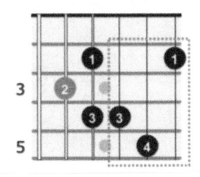

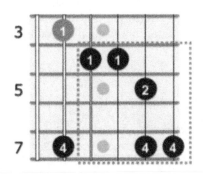

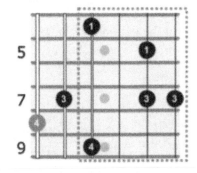

Note: not that useable.

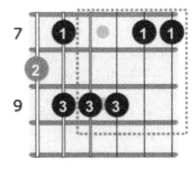

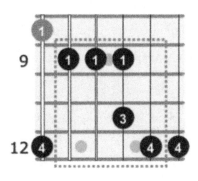

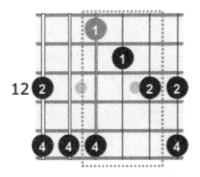

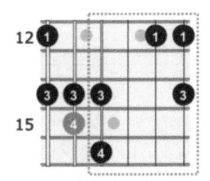

Note: not that useable.

LICK IDEAS

This first line starts with a flurry of chromaticism over the B minor seven chord leading into a flat five arpeggio which is restated at the lower octave over the B flat seven flat five chord.

The idea that that follows in the last two bars over the A major seven flat five chord is based around a melodic contour which also includes a repeated rhythmic figure. This starts off fairly easy to execute in the third bar but the final bar includes a cross-string technique which facilitates the large interval leaps. So, watch out for this.

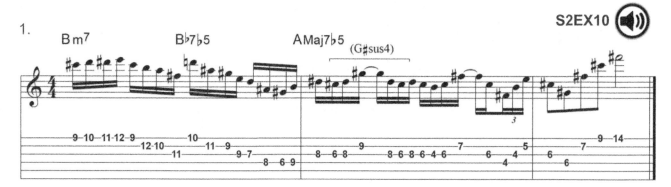

The second lick presented is more modern in its construction. It has more jumps and angular lines as opposed to the previous lick which has more third based ideas and chromatic movement, especially at the beginning. Lick number two does have commonality with idea number one in the use of sequence.

Using sequences within jazz, and in other styles of music, is a way of creating an underlying fabric that binds ideas together. In the lick above, this concept is used in bar two, in lick two it is heard yet again in bar two.

By including ideas that make use of the "sequence" concept you will create solos which are more bound together rather than just a collection of disparate ideas.

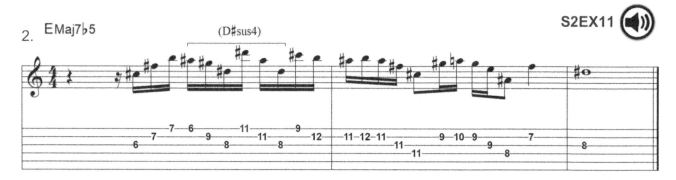

Lick number three is a simple melodic line which includes the use of altered tones over the C seven altered chord to reflect some of the alterations found in that chord symbol. A "C7 flat five, flat nine" chord would consist of a G flat major triad over a C dominant seven. The flat five and flat nine tones have been included in the line as mentioned. The line is continually ascending, at least in the sense that its general direction is up.

Maj7#5

IIIMaj / IMaj

IMaj

LICKS

CHORD FORM IDEAS - Major 7 5 shapes

Lick Idea #1

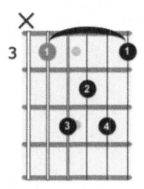

CMaj7

Lick Idea #2

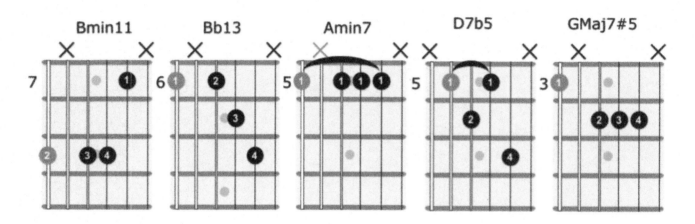

Bmin11   Bb13   Amin7   D7b5   GMaj7#5

Lick Idea #3

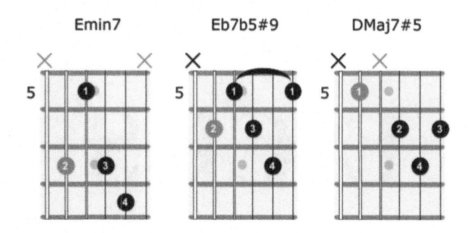

Emin7   Eb7b5#9   DMaj7#5

CMaj7#5 - C Major arpeggio (no 5th) with an E Major acting as the upper structure which results in the aformentioned arpeggio.

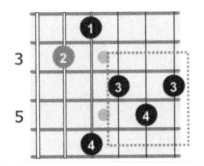

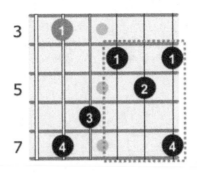

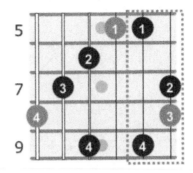

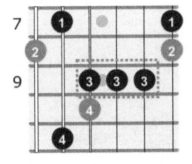

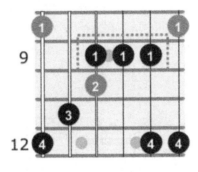

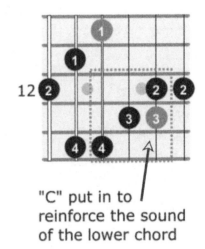

"C" put in to reinforce the sound of the lower chord

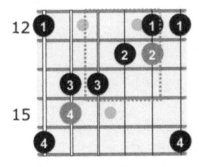

LICK IDEAS

In lick number one I outline a technique that I frequently use, especially on rideouts (the end of songs) where there is a sustained "I" major chord. In almost all the lick examples given I have emphasised the upper voicing within the line to give proof of concept. In this case, I am superimposing an arpeggio (a III major) over a I major that is not altered.

For me, this works really well sonically, but it may not be to everyone's musical taste. I felt I needed to include this idea so that you understand it's not just a case of this goes over this, this goes over that. It is up to the individual to use and experiment with the ideas presented, even if it goes against the grain or rules as stipulated. *If it sounds good to you, use it irrespective of musical rules.*

Next, a more traditional example with a flat five substitution (B flat thirteen) taking place for a (probable) E seven chord in bar one. The line includes a lot of rhythmic interest and may cause problems going into double time between beats two (triplet) to beat three (semi-quavers) in bar two.

In the final example I have made use of a melodic contour in each bar. It begins with an interval leap of a 6th and is followed by a linear ascending line.

The E flat half step/whole step scale is used over the E flat altered dominant, although this specific chord type is dealt with in greater detail in chapter seven.

Finally, in bar three, I have not just played the respective arpeggio note for note against the chord to emphasise the point, but split the chord tones over the bar with other notes being used as a bridge.

Maj9#11

LICKS

CHORD FORM IDEAS - Major 9♯11 shapes

Lick Idea #1

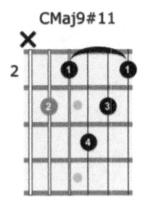

Lick Idea #2

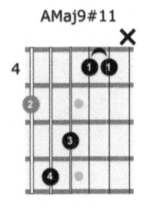

Lick Idea #3

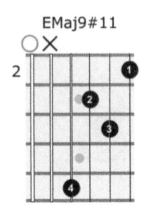

CMaj9#11 - C Major arpeggio with a B minor triad acting as the upper structure which results in the aformentioned arpeggio.

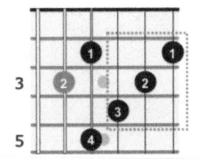

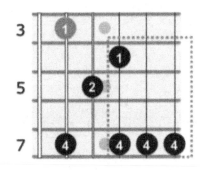

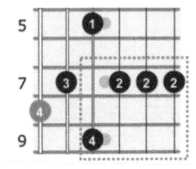

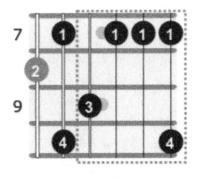

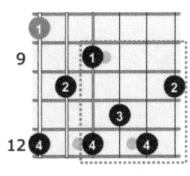

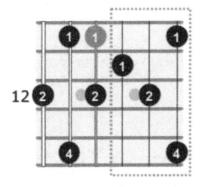

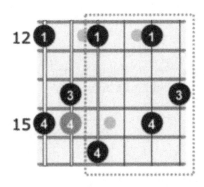

LICK IDEAS

Extended runs over the same chord voicing is a skill you definitely want to develop. This will no doubt already be in your musical DNA, however, if you are not that used to mixing arpeggios, then the following will definitely be of use in helping you build up your understanding and musical ideas.

In lick example one, an interweaving of C Major and B minor ideas is shown as well as direct use of the arpeggios given on the previous page.

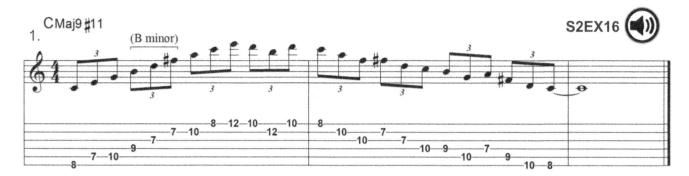

The second example has a funk flavour to it and this is reinforced by the nature of the lick opening. The G sharp minor arpeggio is also an outline of G sharp pentatonic minor. Pentatonic minors a semitone below major chords are an often used concept that creates an altered flavour in the line.

Also of note is the use of rhythm, in this case triplets that are used repeatedly to create a sense of structure within the line. You will find that rhythm is one of the best ways of creating a "story" that has a thread running through it when soloing.

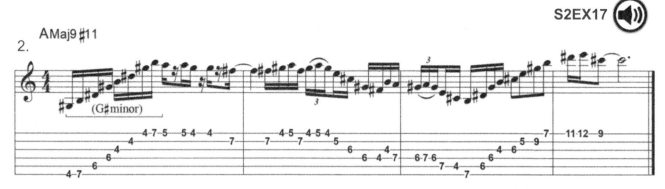

Again, idea number three is relatively simple but it does have a lovely open sound to it which the arpeggio patterns organically create through their interval structure. Hopefully you can see and hear how upper structures can really change the musical reality of a line.

Maj13#11

IIMaj / IMaj

LICKS

CHORD FORM IDEAS - Major 13♯11 shapes

Lick Idea #1

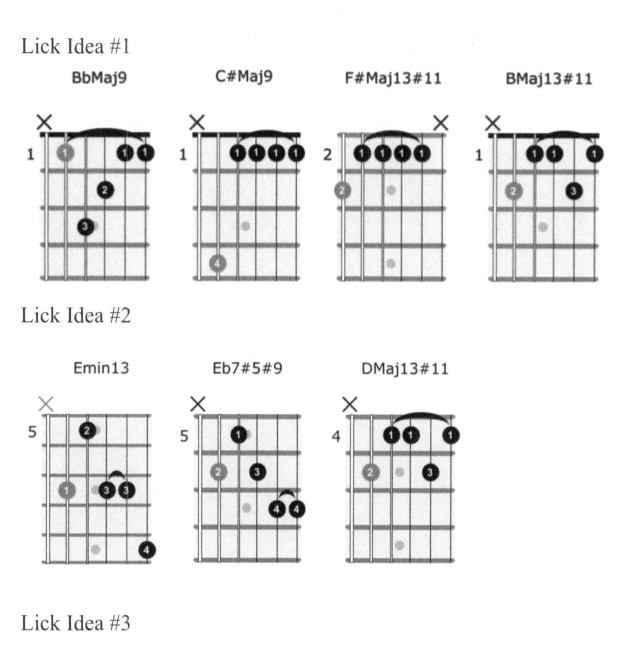

BbMaj9   C#Maj9   F#Maj13#11   BMaj13#11

Lick Idea #2

Emin13   Eb7#5#9   DMaj13#11

Lick Idea #3

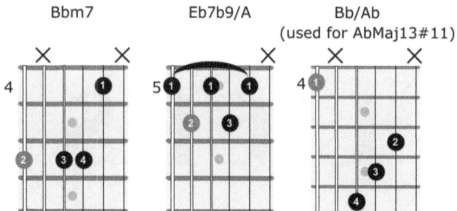

Bbm7   Eb7b9/A   Bb/Ab
(used for AbMaj13#11)

CMaj13#11 - C Major arpeggio with a D major triad acting as the upper structure which results in the aformentioned arpeggio.

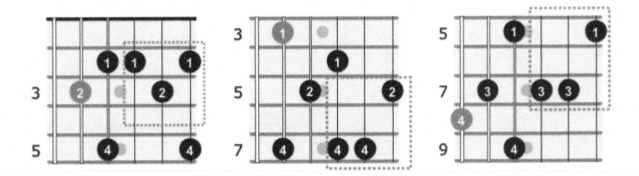

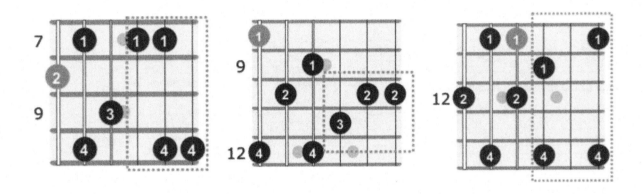

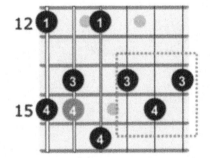

LICK IDEAS

Lick number one is a favourite cliché heard in many jazz guitar solos and certainly one of my best loved licks. It uses pull-offs with downward consecutive down-strokes with the pick on each beat.

To get the most out of this idea, try playing it all over the neck and change the basic concept o reflect the harmony underneath. Regarding the harmony, this is a simply I - VI - II - V - I turnaround where apart from the I chord, all the other chords have a major chord placed via a flat five substitution of the original chord. The last three chords are therefore utilising the "alternate cycle".

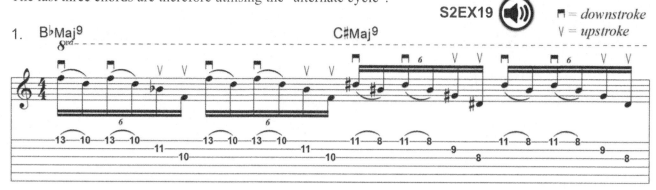

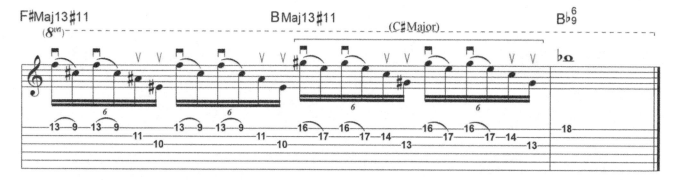

Lick number two is a relatively simple line that outlines the altered major chord. Two points; the first is that the sharp five/sharp nine chord is outlined using the A major triad as pointed out in the last section and later and second there are accent marks offset to create an internal rhythmic propulsion within the line toward the end.

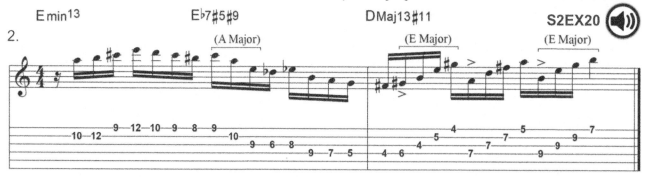

The final lick may prove relatively tricky for some as the second bar includes a lot of lateral movement with the same finger used (finger one). As always, only practice over time will eventually pay dividends.

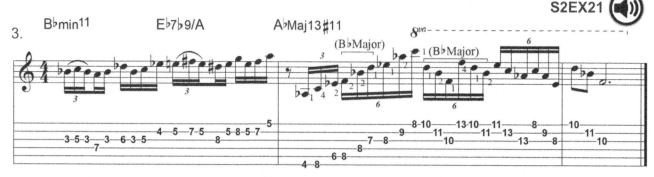

Maj7♯9♯11

LICKS

CHORD FORM IDEAS - Major 7♯9♯11 shapes

Lick Idea #1

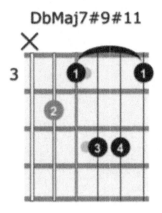

DbMaj7#9#11

Lick Idea #2

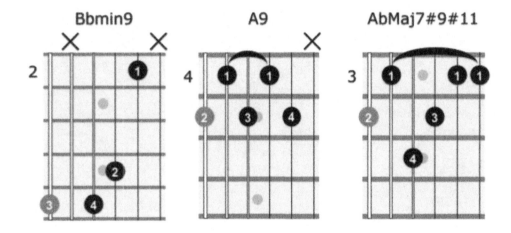

Bbmin9   **A9**   **AbMaj7#9#11**

CMaj7#9#11 - C Major arpeggio with a B Major acting as the upper structure which results in the aformentioned arpeggio.

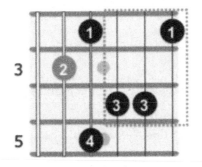
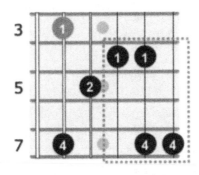
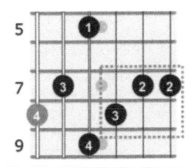

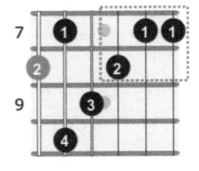
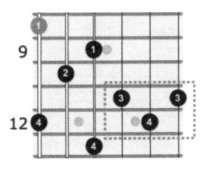
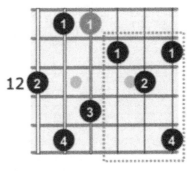

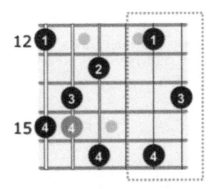

Note: not that usable.

LICK IDEAS

I have only included two examples for this upper voicing because it may sound more than a little odd to a lot of people and will probably not be to the musical taste of most. I decided to include it as I really love this sound and can be quite fascinating when used sparingly, and at an appropriate musical moment.

The stacking of a major triad over another major triad one semi-tone above gives a very complex, dark and rich sound which I primarily use for endings where I look to create a musical cadence that is mysterious and dark leaving, musically speaking, a question in the air.

As we are considering this D flat chord form primarily from an upper voicing perspective, it's simple enough to understand; an amalgam of D flat with an upper structure of C major above giving the mouthful of a chord symbol as shown below.

From a linear scale perspective, one of the best tools available to improvise over this chord would be to play a harmonic minor scale from the 6th degree which is named a lydian ♯2.

To example lick number one. Other than the use of the C major triad, you'll notice I have included a hemiola in beats two and three of bar two which consists of the triads D flat and C major.

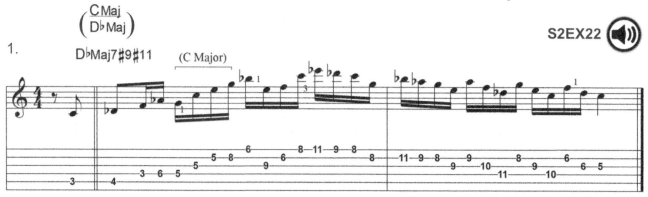

Harmonically, example lick two includes an A9 chord which is acting as a flat five substitute for an E flat dominant seven. This creates chromatic movement in the bass.

Regarding the voice leading of the chords shown at the beginning and heard in the mp3 file for this idea, the melody note moves up by a minor third from chord to chord. This idea also reinforces the continuity of sound and it's important to realise that this concept makes use of contrary motion. That is, the motion of melody and bass moving in opposite directions relative to each other as explained within the first section of this book.

Melodically, a B flat minor nine arpeggio is outlined via a D flat major seven arpeggio in the first bar which then moves to a chromatic idea connecting with the second bar. The A dominant nine chord for the first half of the bar is based around 5th intervals to create an open, less linear sound.

Finally, the idea ends with a simple initial statement of a G major triad over the A flat chord.

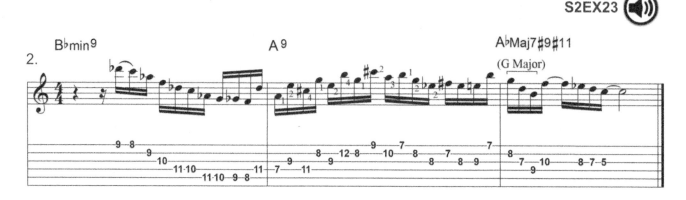

MINOR LICKS

min9

Vmin

Imin

LICKS

CHORD FORM IDEAS - minor 9 shapes

Lick Idea #1

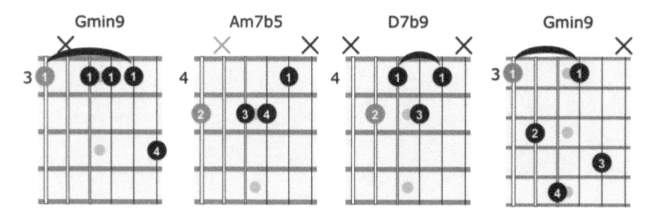

Gmin9   Am7b5   D7b9   Gmin9

Lick Idea #2

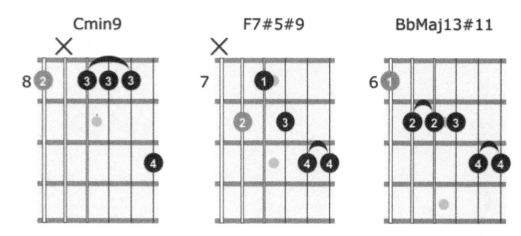

Cmin9   F7#5#9   BbMaj13#11

Lick Idea #3

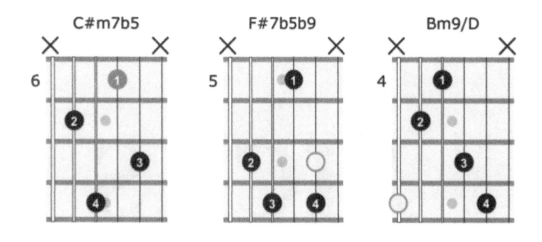

C#m7b5   F#7b5b9   Bm9/D

Amin9 - A minor arpeggio with an E minor acting as the upper structure which results in the aformentioned arpeggio.

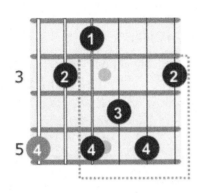 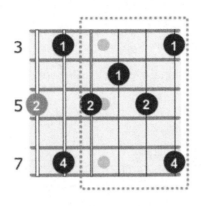 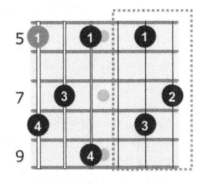

Note: not that usable.

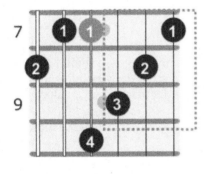 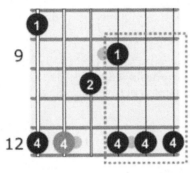 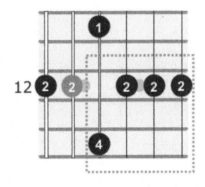

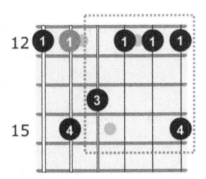

LICK IDEAS

Again, I've used different time signatures in the following licks, hopefully you will find them both interesting, and challenging.

The obvious point to make about this first lick, which is quite straight forward in how it has been constructed, is that it is an almost continual flow of eighth notes. Playing constant eighths and subdivisions of this, depending on tempo, is a really great way to get your "chops" together as a player.

The only other point is that there is the occasional chromatic note added in to make connections smooth.

I have been quite meticulous with regards the picking in the next lick to help you play this with the minimum amount of discomfort. Some of the picking may be at times counterintuitive, but for me this is the best solution.

The slurs over specific note groupings where no picking stroke are present indicates that you should execute the notes with a pull-off. A rallentando is also employed in this line taking effect from the second beat of the second bar as the consecutive B flat and C major arpeggios are played outlining the major thirteen sharp eleven chord.

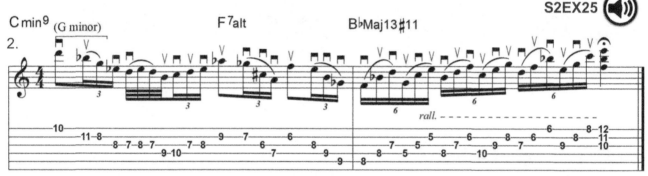

Lick idea number three is another line that makes use of melodic contours. Note how the line starts high, then moves down in leap before ascending for the rest of the bar.

The chords employed and shown two pages earlier may surprise or even confuse some of you. To be clear, a bass note would be needed to perceive these chords as notated. Yet again, synonyms are used to create different and perhaps new ways of expressing routine progressions. For example, the F sharp altered chord is represented by a C7/E which when analysed against an F sharp produces the flat five and nine tones.

min11

$$\text{♭VIIMaj} / \text{Imin}$$

CHORD FORM IDEAS - minor 11 shapes

Lick Idea #1

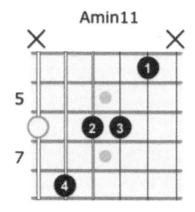

Lick Idea #2

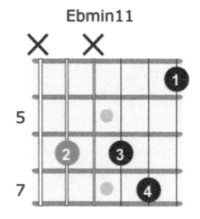
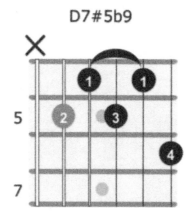
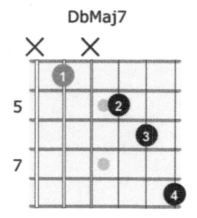

Lick Idea #3

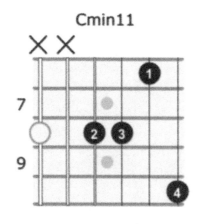
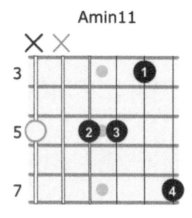

Amin11 - A minor arpeggio with a G major acting as the upper structure which results in the aformentioned arpeggio.

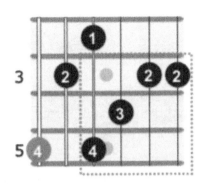

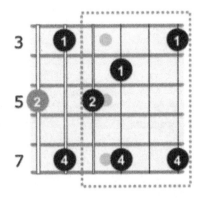

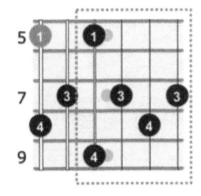

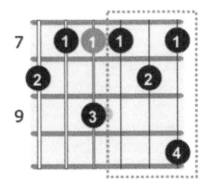

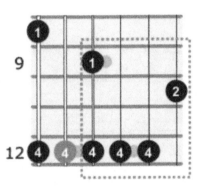

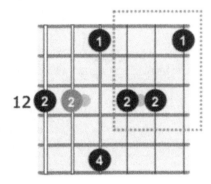

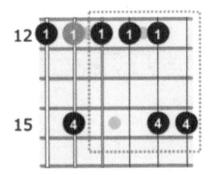

LICK IDEAS

One technique that made a big difference to my understanding of how to improvise was that of targeting. The basic idea is that a fundamental tone such as root, 3rd, 5th etc., is the desired location and you play the notes either a half or whole step around until played. You can get away with many supposed "outside" notes as long as you resolve to the target tone. There are quite a few examples of this and chromatic approach ideas within this first minor 11 idea.

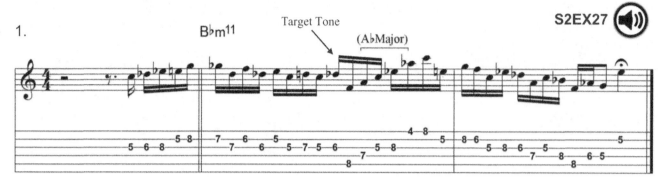

The second idea consists of a II - V - I in D flat major. The V chord has been substituted by a D seven altered chord which is the flat five substitution for A flat seven. Accordingly, the sharp five/flat nine chord consists of a tri-tone (for D7) with an E flat minor triad on top as is shown.

Here is a modal idea where a C Dorian scale over the C minor 11 (B flat major tonal centre), leads to an A dorian mode over A minor 11 (G major tonal centre). I deliberately stayed away from chromaticism in this idea to keep it diatonic and to let the upper voicings shine through.

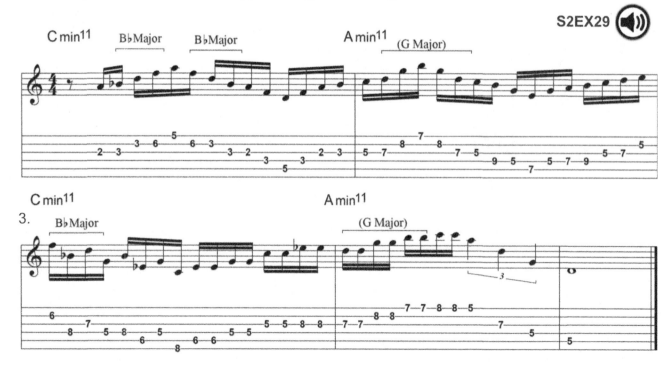

min13

$$\frac{\text{IImin}}{\text{Imin}}$$

CHORD FORM IDEAS - minor 13 shapes

Lick Idea #1

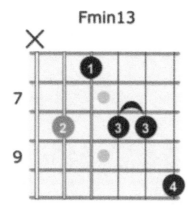

Fmin13

Lick Idea #2

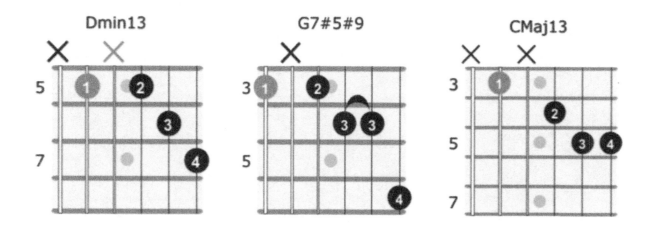

Dmin13   G7#5#9   CMaj13

Lick Idea #3

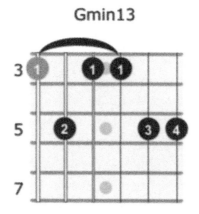

Gmin13

ARPEGGIO PATTERNS

Amin13 - A minor 7 arpeggio with a B minor 7 acting as the upper structure which results in the aformentioned arpeggio.

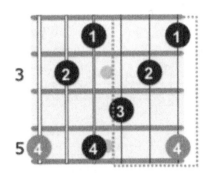

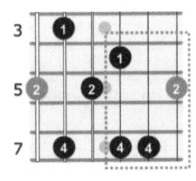

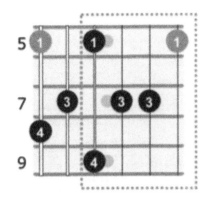

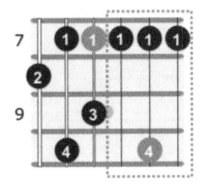

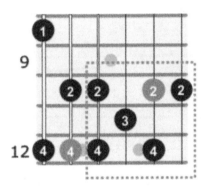

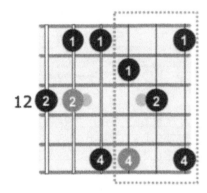

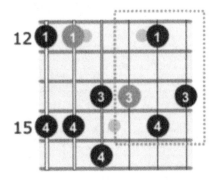

LICK IDEAS

This polychord concept is as simple as it is powerful and is probably one of my favourite upper voicing sounds that I use. A minor seventh arpeggio is superimposed over another minor seventh arpeggio. The superimposed arpeggio is a tone higher than the original chord which creates the minor thirteenth sound. For example, a G minor seven would be played over F minor seven.

In this first idea, a pentatonic form is used to begin with and the idea continues in bar two with a bluesy ending.

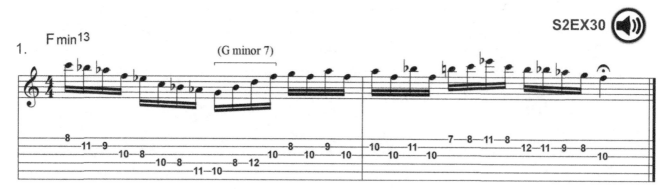

You can see how the concept works within a II - V - I in C major in lick idea number two. Watch out for that quick slide upward to catch the F note at the thirteenth fret. Other than that, this idea should be plain sailing, but still sound very effective.

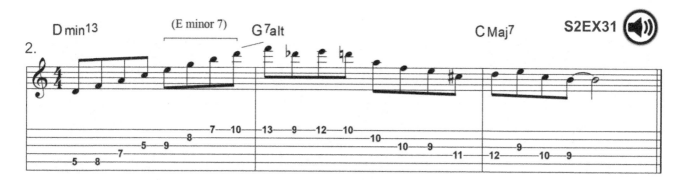

I thought I'd end the thirteenth ideas list by playing over a six eight time signature to mix things up a little as well as moving between the two minor arpeggios as shown below. Being able to do this over the neck really opens up a lot of melodic possibilities for players.

min♮7

Vaug
Imin

CHORD FORM IDEAS - minor natural seven shapes

Lick Idea #1

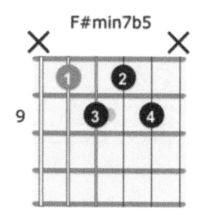 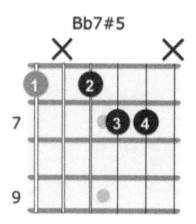 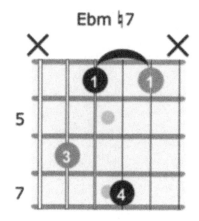

Lick Idea #2

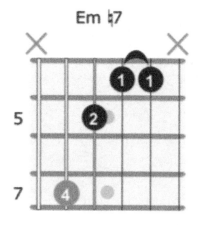 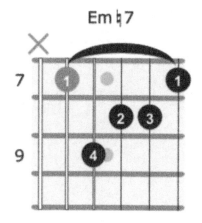

Lick Idea #3

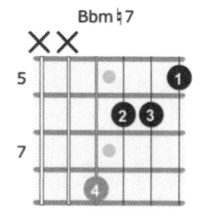 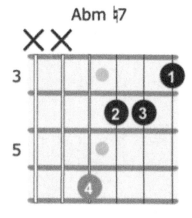

ARPEGGIO PATTERNS

Amin ♮7 - A minor arpeggio with an E augmented triad acting as the upper structure which results in the aformentioned arpeggio.

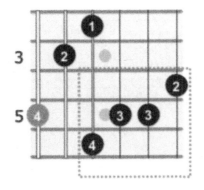

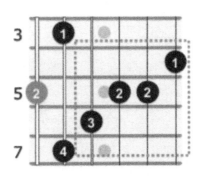

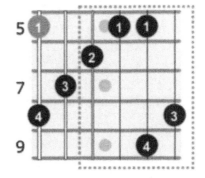

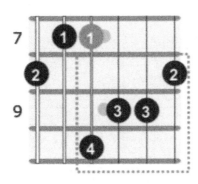

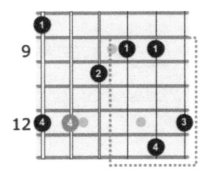

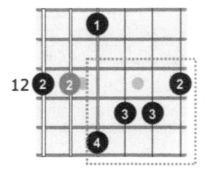

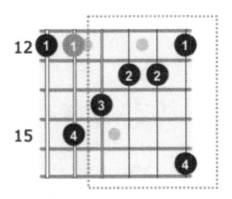

LICK IDEAS

Something a little bit different with lick number one which is in three four time. It is fairly self explanatory. Watch out in bar three where fingerings are stipulated for best execution.

1. **S2EX33**

Idea number two includes single line and unison octave playing. I am a big fan of Wes Montgomery and Wes was instrumental in bringing octave playing to the forefront of mainstream jazz guitar improvisation and also demonstrating just what was possible with them.

You may well find the single line idea in octaves which begins this idea quite challenging to begin with. As always, begin slowly and build your speed up as accuracy increases.

2. **S2EX34**

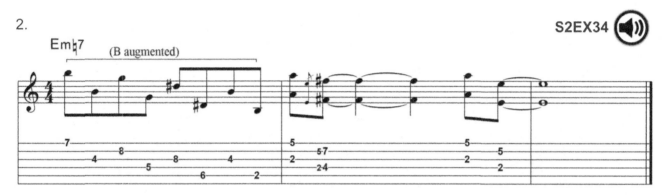

Lick idea number three includes part of a chord sequence that is central to the well known jazz standard "Nica's Dream" by Horace Silver. Below I play an idea over the major/minor chords in five four to keep things interesting.

Again, this line should be self-explanatory in how it has been constructed, but I would like to bring your attention the heavy reliance on the triplet throughout which gives the line it's distinct feel.

3. **S2EX35**

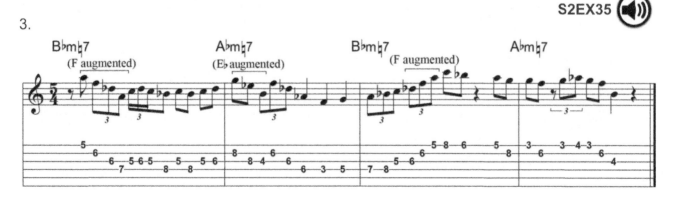

min9♮7

VMaj
―――――
Imin

CHORD FORM IDEAS - minor nine natural seven shapes

Lick Idea #1

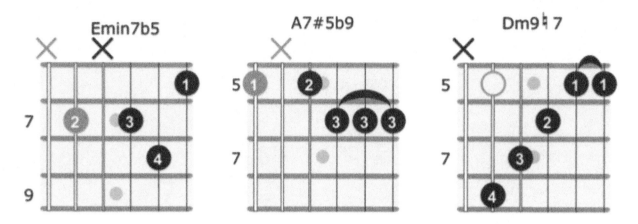

Lick Idea #2

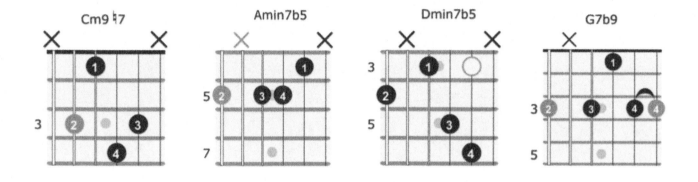

Lick Idea #3

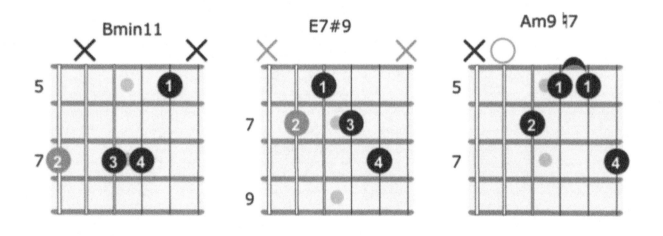

ARPEGGIO PATTERNS

Amin9 ♮7 - A minor arpeggio with an E major acting as the upper structure which results in the aformentioned arpeggio.

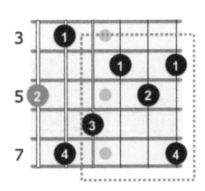

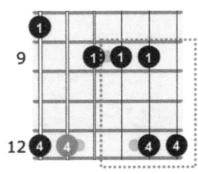

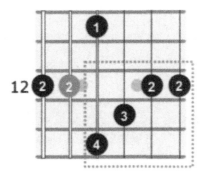

Note: not that usable

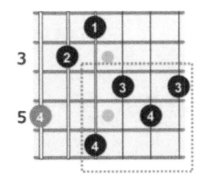

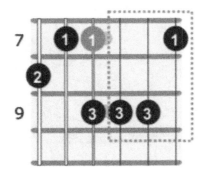

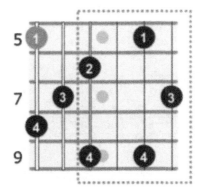

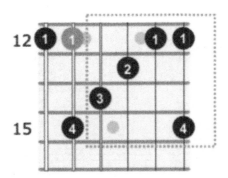

LICK IDEAS

A II - V - I in the key of D minor. The technically challenging thing about idea number one is that the movable form in the second bar outlining an A major triad actually starts on the "+" of beat two. You may find this a little awkward to get round physically to begin with as it offsets the usual execution of this movable arpeggio form in terms of the rhythmic placement.

Also of note in this line is the C minor arpeggio outlined in bar one over the A seven flat five/sharp nine chord. This actual chord type is outlined later in this section and was highlighted in the dominant seven chapter in section one.

S2EX36

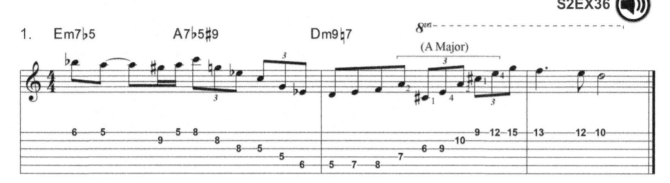

Next, a deceptive lick idea that looks a lot more frightening than it actually is. The tempo is slow and you'll find that your fingers fall into this with little effort. Note the lower chromatic neighbour tones that outline the C minor arpeggio played over the A half diminished chord in bar one.

The underlying progression is a I - VI - II - V in C minor. The first bar is harmonically drawn from C melodic minor and the second bar from C harmonic minor.

S2EX37

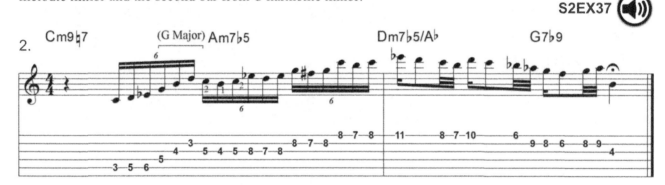

Lick idea number three starts off with a pentatonic idea played over the B minor eleven chord. The way the harmony is laid out is quite deceptive as it would initially suggest a major progression, however, it resolves to minor. I put this idea in for this reason just in case you haven't come across this type of harmonic device before.

S2EX38

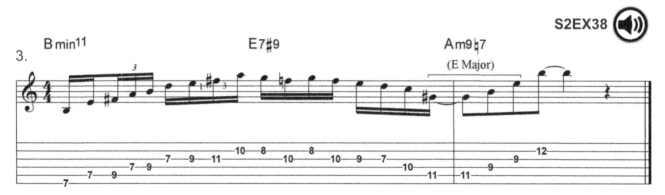

178

DOMINANT & ALTERED LICKS

CHAPTER 7

9th

$$\frac{V_{min}}{I_7}$$

LICKS

CHORD FORM IDEAS - 9th shapes

Lick Idea #1

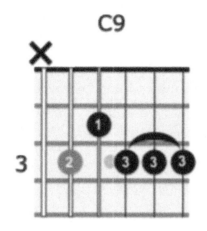

Lick Idea #2

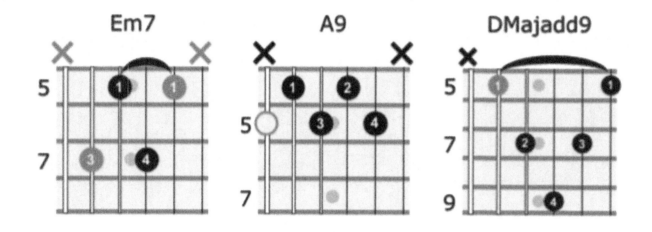

Lick Idea #3

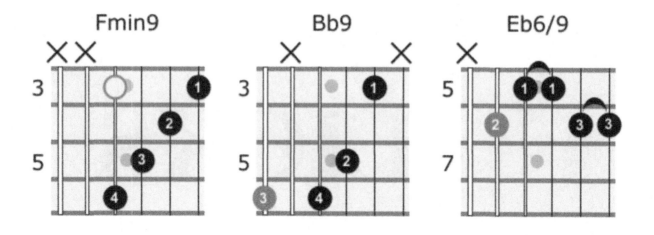

ARPEGGIO PATTERNS

C9 - C7 arpeggio with a G minor triad acting as the upper structure which results in the aformentioned arpeggio.

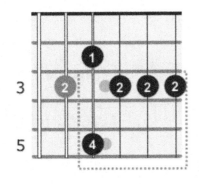
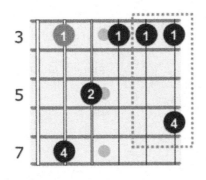
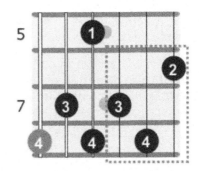

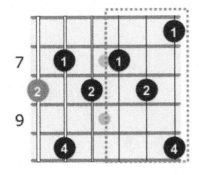
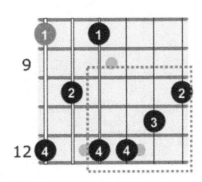
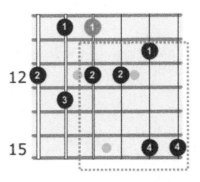

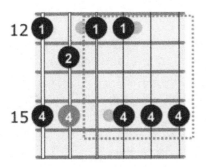

LICK IDEAS

I love playing altered sounds over straight dominant chords. Here you can see several of the concepts I use on a regular basis when improvising. Firstly, in lick one, the G minor arpeggio appears not once but twice as shown, however, on the second showing it's a G minor seven arpeggio. Although the F natural from the minor seven arpeggio could be thought to clash with the C9 as the F is the 11th tone, the ear hears it as part of a chromatically descending line and it does not negatively stand out.

Also worth consideration is the use of an F sharp to an F in beat four of the first bar. This technique is called "targeting" where a note is outlined by playing notes around it before actually playing the target tone. The target tone in this case is actually the E note which is the first note in the second bar.

Targeting also takes place around the B flat note which is played on the first sixteenth of beat two, second bar. It should also be observed that a D major arpeggio is being superimposed over the C9 in this second bar which creates the sound of a thirteen sharp eleven chord.

Here, in lick idea two you have a classic rhythmic idea that starts off this line over the E minor seven chord. The line is not that tricky to play and is all played on one position of the guitar neck.

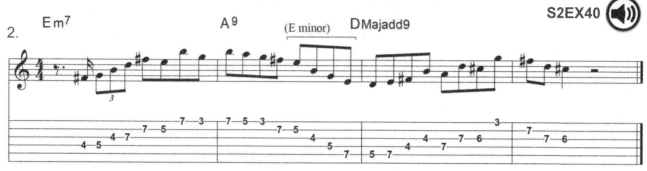

Another rhythmic idea starts of this last lick idea but this time it's eighth notes that set up a constant sixteenth note pattern over the B flat nine chord.

To end, I've played a quartal-harmony based six nine chord (a chord constructed from forth intervals) which has gives less of a frenetic ending and uses extended tones of the E flat scale in the last bar.

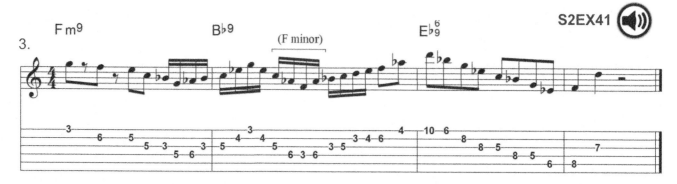

184

13th

$$\frac{VImin}{I_7}$$

LICKS

CHORD FORM IDEAS - 13th shapes

Lick Idea #1

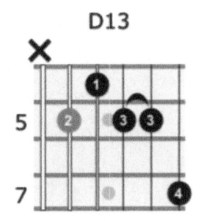

Lick Idea #2

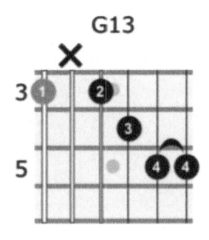

Lick Idea #3

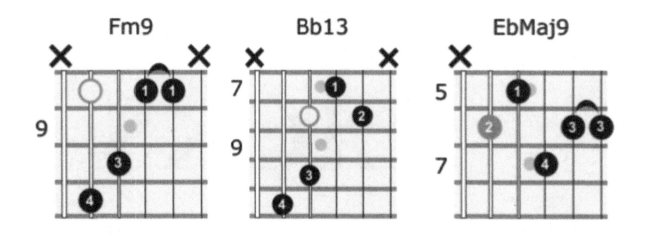

ARPEGGIO PATTERNS

C7(13) - C7 arpeggio with an A minor triad acting as the upper structure which results in the aformentioned arpeggio.

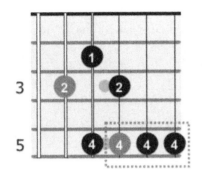

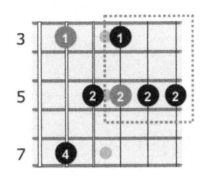

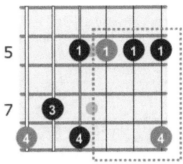

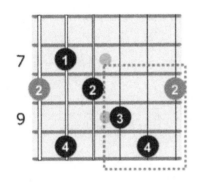

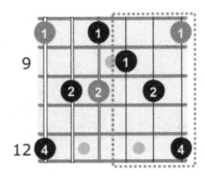

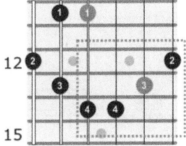

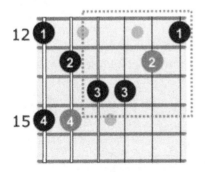

LICK IDEAS

The thirteenth chord ideas are another chance to stretch out a bit when it comes to more bluesy sounding ideas and more time can be taken to develop ideas.

The minor triad based on the 6th degree of the dominant seventh (mixolydian) scale tone means that for the example below, a B minor triad is played over the D dominant seven chord. This polychord is definitely worth pursuing, however, it's not the strongest of triadic overlays, just be aware of that. The B minor tones related to D seven for example mean that the B is the 6th or 13th tone, but other tones are just doubling what is already in the D chord; B is the 3rd of D and the F sharp is the 3rd.

That being said, it's still a useful tool in our armoury of polychords and the lines below should back this point up. Here is the lick idea number one.

Lick two is difficult for various reasons. The notes and where they are played is difficult in itself but allied to that is the triplet feel that goes through the entire lick. This, as with the last lick idea, is an effective blues sound extended over the time.

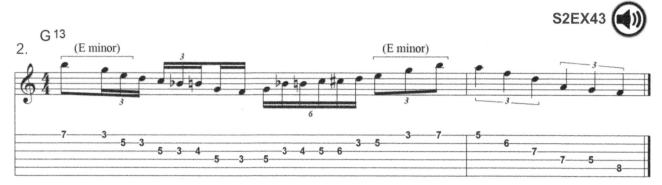

The final idea is played over a II - V - I progression and I've placed it high up on the neck. There are other places that this idea could be played "in position" or, indeed, played over several positions on the neck so experiment to get the most out of it.

By the way, if you are not sure what that symbol on the last note is called it's a fermata and it means to prolong the note (or chord) longer than the time and tempo of the song would normally allow. Sometimes referred to as a pause.

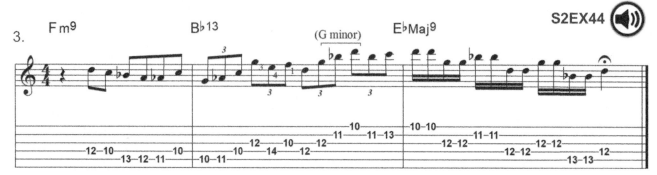

188

7♯5/9♯11

LICKS

CHORD FORM IDEAS - 7#5 and 9#11 shapes

Lick Idea #1

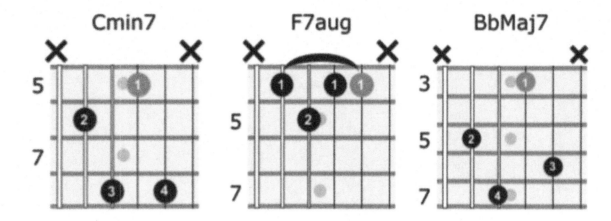

Lick Idea #2

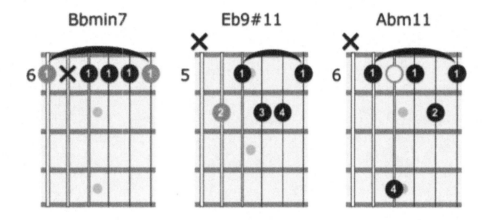

Lick Idea #3

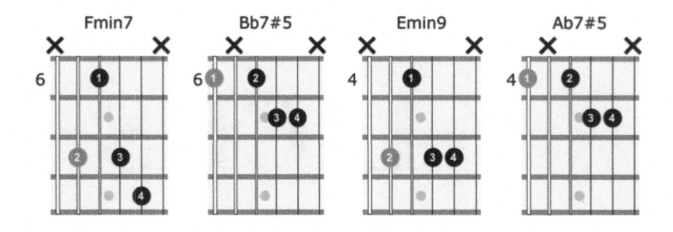

C7#5 arpeggios. C7#5 is a C7 arpeggio (no fifth) with C+ on top.

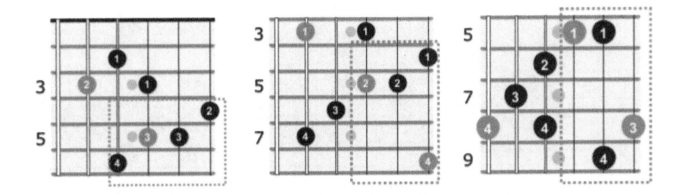

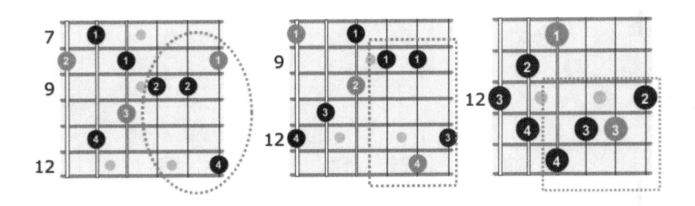

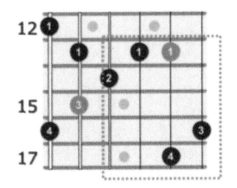

C9#11 arpeggios. C9#11 is a C7 arpeggio (no fifth) with a D+ on top.

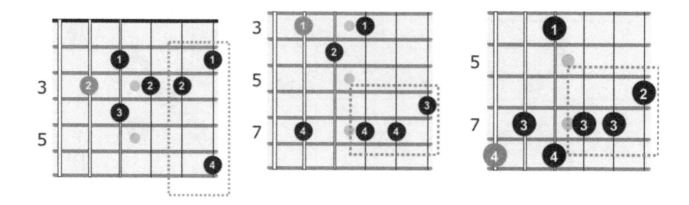

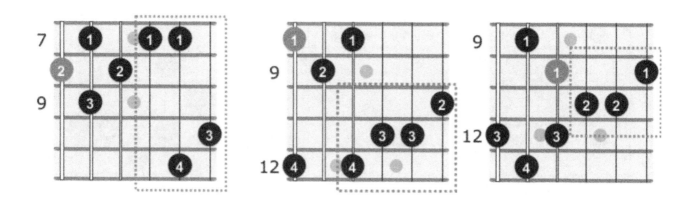

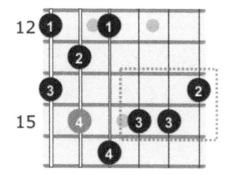

LICK IDEAS

As you'll find when playing the lick ideas below, there is a lot of similar shapes and patterns when augmented lines are introduced. There is also a lot of adjacent string movement which necessitates a strong ability to roll across same fret/different string combinations.

I've injected some momentum in the opening to this first idea by delaying the first note by half a beat and then going straight into a triplet. The first note is also a chromatic lower neighbour tone to the first note played in the triplet, "G".

The triplet idea is continued in the second bar with the rhythm in the first two beats of bar one being repeated.

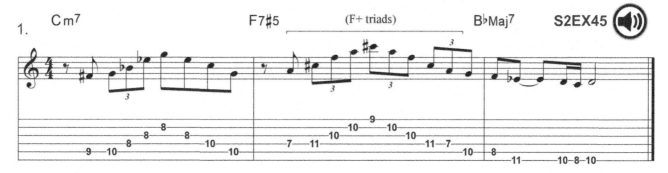

I thought I'd mix it up slightly with the second lick. First of all, it's in six eight time so it's best to feel this in two with each beat equalling a three eighth notes. The opening bar is a minor arpeggio which is often more difficult technically to play. Basic arpeggio triads often contain many consecutive notes are found on adjacent strings, as in the last example, whereas extended triads have multiple notes found on the same string. The second bar contains an augmented triad but I've displaced the notes to add some interest.

The final bar does not resolve to major as you may expect, but minor. The final chord is A flat minor seven. It's an interesting ending which emphasises a B major seven (enharmonic spelling to what is actually notated) resulting in an A flat minor nine sound.

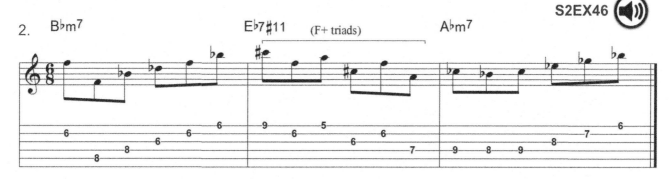

Once again, I've gone with something a little different in this final line which has consecutive II - V's. First in E flat major then in D flat major. Hopefully you see how the whole tone scale and augmented arpeggios can be combined to create lines of a unique quality and interest.

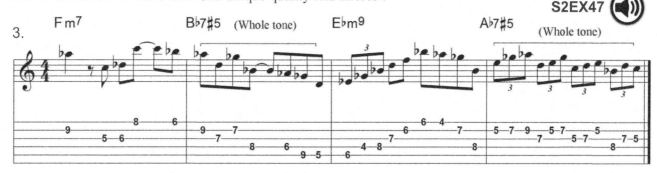

7♭9

#Idim
—
I7

LICKS

CHORD FORM IDEAS - 7♭9 shapes

Lick Idea #1

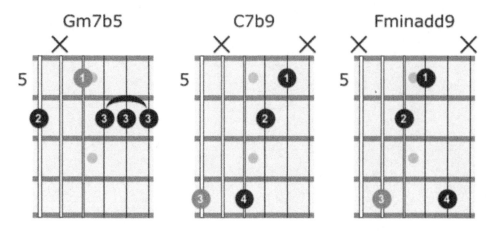

Lick Idea #2

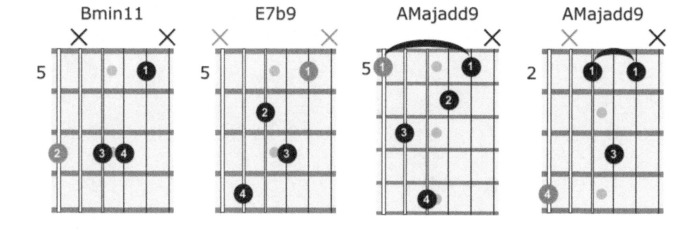

C7b9 - Seven positions of the C7 arpeggio with a C diminished triad acting as the upper structure which results in the aformentioned arpeggio.

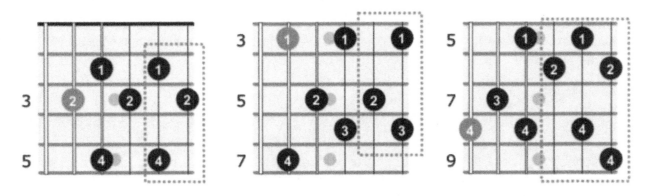

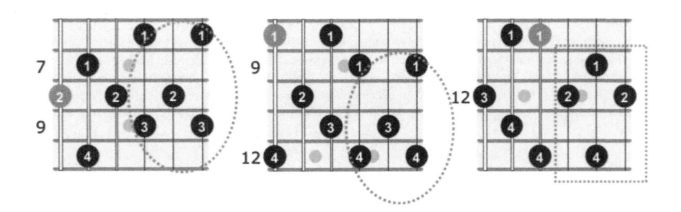

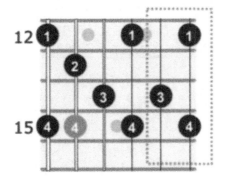

LICK IDEAS

Only two licks are given in the flat nine category. The emphasis here is placed on knowing your basic diminished triads. From my own experience, when faced with learning diminished chords, I went straight to the diminished seventh arpeggios and didn't look much at the diminished chord/arpeggio in triadic form.

Below in lick example one you can see a triadic diminished arpeggio being used to outline the C seven flat nine chord. Make use of the "Do You Know Your Triads" within chapter four, section one which details diminished triad chords.

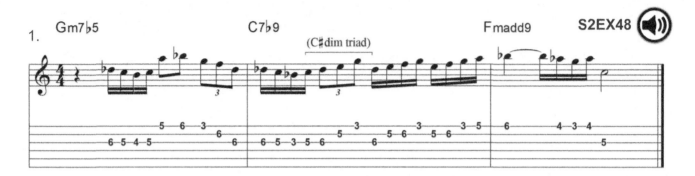

Idea number two starts out with a B melodic minor idea over the II (B minor) chord. This scale choice adds a tension over what would usually contain the more neutral sound of B dorian mode. In the second beat of the second bar I've added a device on guitar which I feel is reminiscent of a sound that Michael Brecker favoured i.e. the restating of notes. In bar three you'd be forgiven for thinking that it looks incredibly complex, however, after study you'll realise the note choices are based around lower chromatic neighbour tones. These chromatic neighbour tones are created within a triplet figure which repeats itself for the duration of the entire third bar.

The final bar is less frenetic. Should you want to continue with the sixteenth note patterns and make this lick your own, the last bar would be a great place to start.

7♯9

♭IIIMaj / I7

LICKS

CHORD FORM IDEAS - 7♯9 shapes

Lick Idea #1

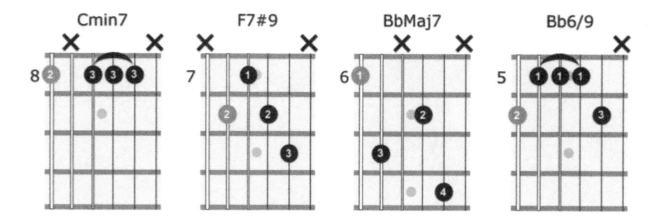

Lick Idea #2

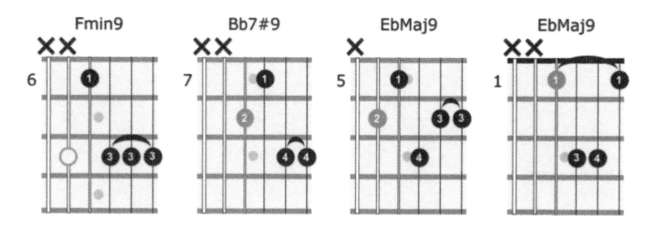

Lick Idea #3

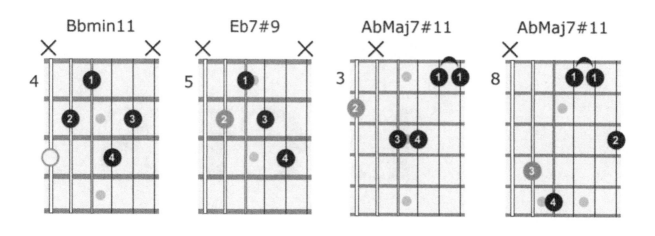

ARPEGGIO PATTERNS

C7#9 -   Six positions of the C7 arpeggio with an Eb major triad acting as the upper structure which results in the aformentioned arpeggio.

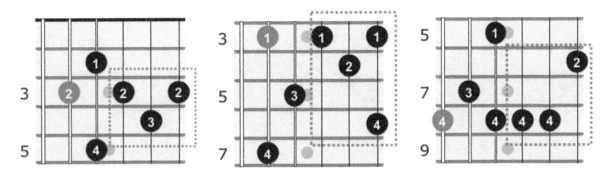

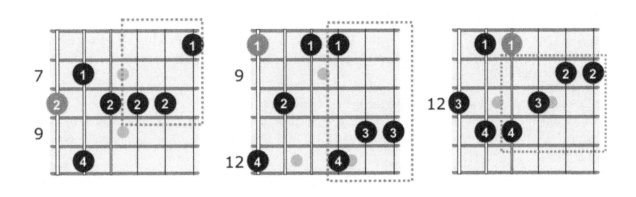

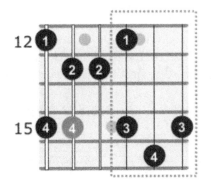

LICK IDEAS

You may well have found the seven sharp nine arpeggios rather difficult to play. There is definitely something about certain arpeggio combinations that are more difficult to play that others. As one of the more "common" altered dominant chords used, however, it's absolutely worth learning.

This first idea begins with an E flat major seven arpeggio played with a triplet to give the line a rhythmic kick to begin. From there, some chromatic line work is followed by the upper structure major triad which is a minor third (three frets) higher than the root of the dominant to give that distinctive sharp nine sound.

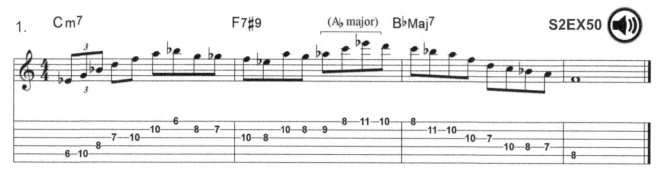

This next lick is played in one position throughout; third position. If you are unsure about positioning on the guitar neck, here is a simple rule. The fret that your second finger of your left hand (if you play right handed) is over, minus one. This will be the fretboard position you currently occupy.

To be in third position for this lick idea, your second finger would have to be over fret four. The reason fretboard positions are understood in this way is due to the practice of first finger stretching to lower frets whilst the rest of the hand stays in the same position. The activity of stretching finger one does not constitute a change in fretboard position.

The line itself is fairly straight forward, with a syncopated approach to the third bar - the high "G" note being held over. Notice again that although a B flat seven sharp nine chord is played, the actual chord symbol simply states "alt" for altered. This allows the player to decide how to treat the chord regarding note choice.

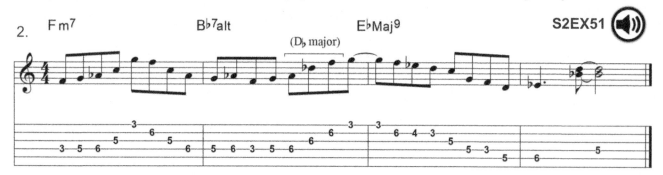

This line has been TAB'D out to make you move around a bit. The idea over the altered A flat major chord may cause some technical challenges. The melodic idea brings together 4th/5th interval jumps along with the stressing of a lydian sound complementing the A flat major chord. The triad played against the E flat seven chord is a G flat major resulting in a sharp nine sound.

b5#9

$\dfrac{\flat\text{III}\text{min}}{\text{I}_7}$ LICKS

CHORD FORM IDEAS - 7♭5♯9 shapes

Lick Idea #1

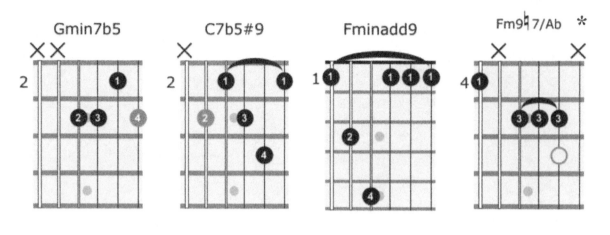

Lick Idea #2

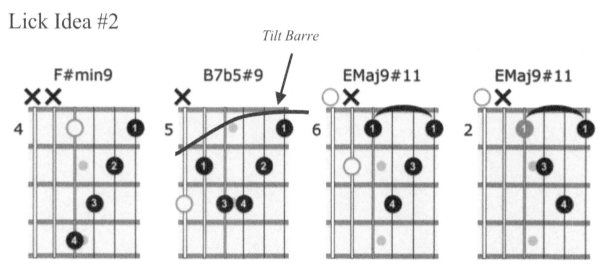

Lick Idea #3

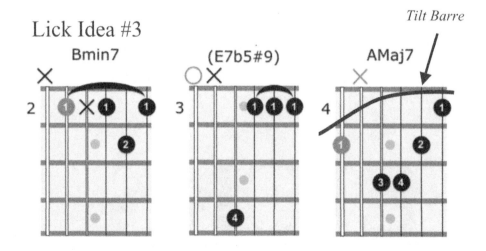

* *This chord is probably more commonly known as "A flat major seven with a sharpened fifth" but due to relative major/minor relationships - can be used as shown here for an altered F minor chord.*

ARPEGGIO PATTERNS

C7b5#9 - Seven positions of the C7 arpeggio with a Eb minor triad acting as the upper structure which results in the aformentioned arpeggio.

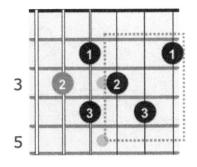
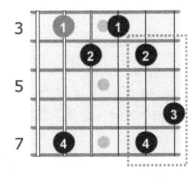
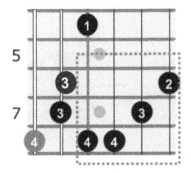

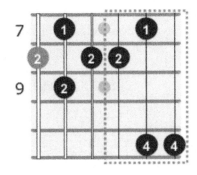
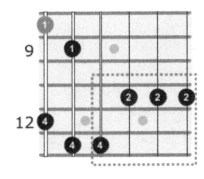
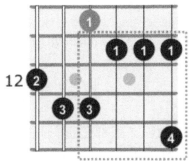

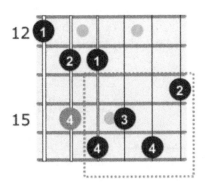

LICK IDEAS

Simple is best in many cases and that is exactly what you get over the first chord of lick number one. The G half diminished uses a descending A flat major scale which many will hear and relate too as the G locrian mode.

In the second bar I again have made efforts to move you around the fret board instead of just sticking in one position. If you find that this makes visualisation of the line more difficult then by all means work the line out in one position where all the notes can be found.

The last two bars pick up from the first bar with a descending scale, F harmonic minor.

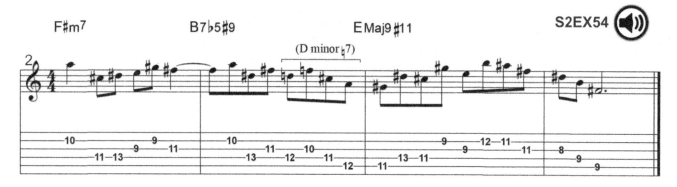

I really enjoyed playing lick number two. Perhaps it was something about the openness of the intervals in the second bar. The dominant seventh with the flat five and sharp nine is outlined by a D minor chord. You will see, however, that I have included the natural seventh (C sharp) for a crunch minor second interval. Another example of breaking the rules to suit my own musical taste.

The line continues into the third bar with a raft of perfect fifth intervals. This, in my opinion, helps emphasis the modernistic sound conjured up by the modal lydian idea at the end of the line.

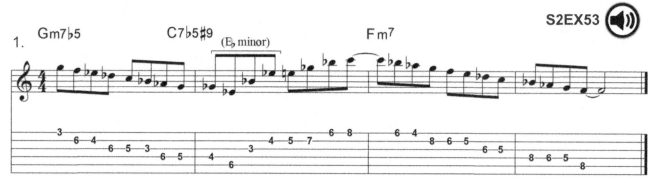

The final example again has you moving across the fretboard but this time downwards. Nothing much needs to be said about this line that hasn't been covered in the text above other than there is a bit of stretch for the chord at the very end over the A major seven, so watch out. By the way, the chord which will now sound with this chord overlaid at the end is A major nine.

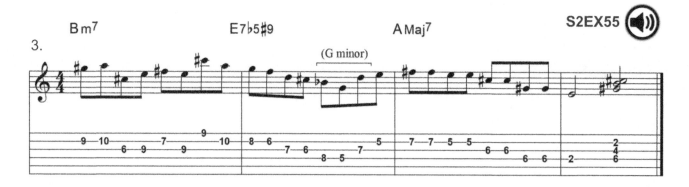

206

#5♭9

♭IImin / I7 LICKS

CHORD FORM IDEAS - 7#5b9 shapes

Lick Idea #1

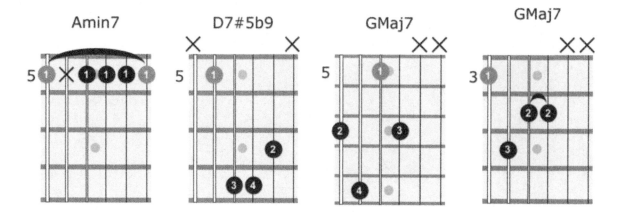

Amin7   D7#5b9   GMaj7   GMaj7

Lick Idea #2

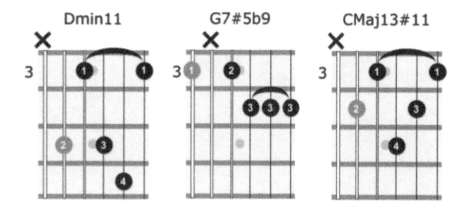

Dmin11   G7#5b9   CMaj13#11

Lick Idea #3

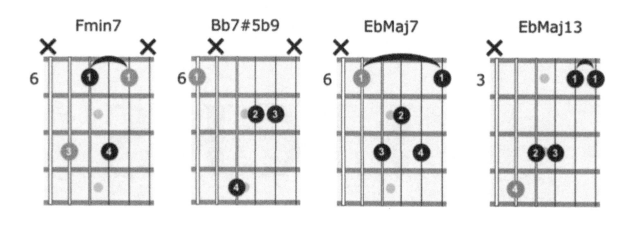

Fmin7   Bb7#5b9   EbMaj7   EbMaj13

ARPEGGIO PATTERNS

C7#5b9 - Seven positions of the C7 arpeggio with a D♭ minor triad acting as the upper structure which results in the aformentioned arpeggio.

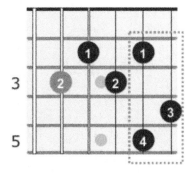

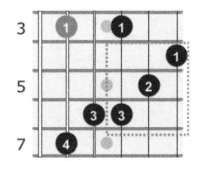

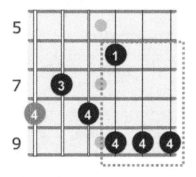

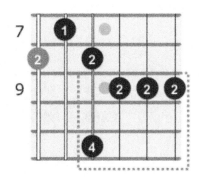

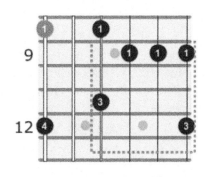

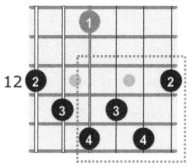

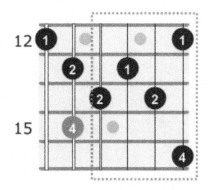

LICK IDEAS

If you have a look at the first two bars of the first line below, you will see how the line rises and falls, rises and falls. The third and fourth bars follow a similar if less pronounced shape. This is a good example of a melodic contour. This melodic contour idea is probably one of the simplest that can be created. Melodic contours are a great way of "sculpting" your musical ideas with an underlying shape in mind.

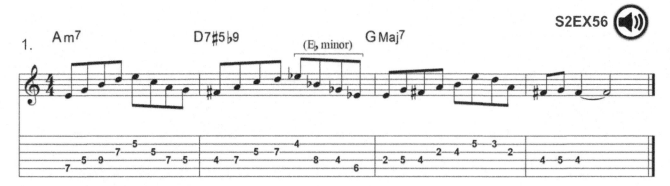

Although these lines are predominantly used to highlight the polytonal nature of extended and altered chord forms, they're also a good vehicle in introducing concepts to the improviser such as the melodic contour idea above. In this idea the use of intervals is prominent throughout.

The first bar intervals are primarily based around a perfect and augmented fourth. As the line progresses the intervals change predominantly to thirds and are a good example of chords being superimposed upon the extended and altered C major structure.

The chords superimposed over these last two bars are A and B minor in the third bar with C and D major in the last bar. Note the linkage of these four chords; relative major and minor. A minor to C major and B minor to D major. The D major over C major idea was covered in chapter one of section one of this book.

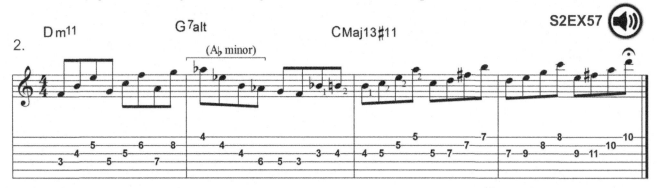

This last line is relatively straight forward. Notice how I approach the second beat note in the first bar by a chromatic half-step. You will find that in most improvised musical scenarios you can approach chord tones from a half-step above or below and it will make musical sense. It's all about taking the listener's ear on a journey from dissonance to a point of resolution.

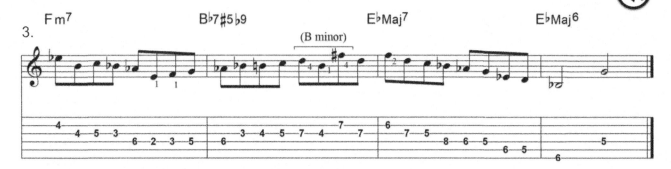

7b5b9

$$\frac{\flat V \mathrm{Maj}}{I_7}$$

LICKS

CHORD FORM IDEAS - 7♭5♭9 shapes

Lick Idea #1

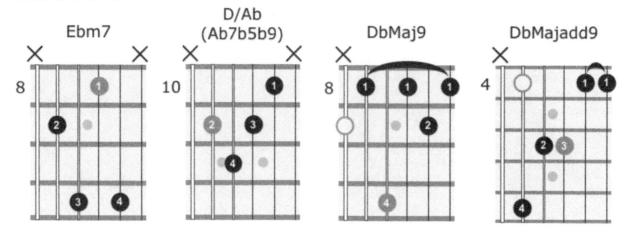

Lick Idea #2

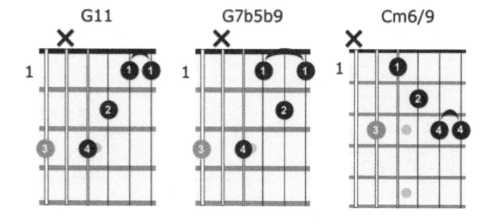

Lick Idea #3

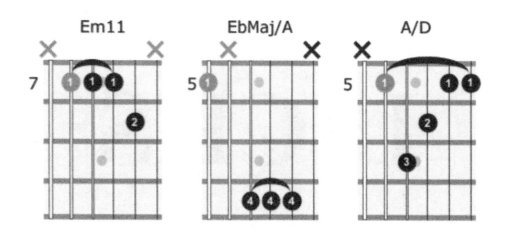

ARPEGGIO PATTERNS

C7b5b9 - Seven positions of the C7 arpeggio with a Gb major triad acting as the upper structure which results in the aformentioned arpeggio.

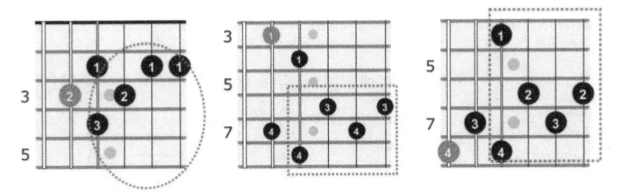

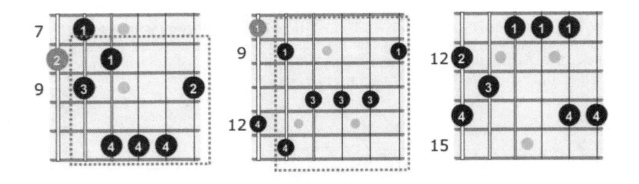

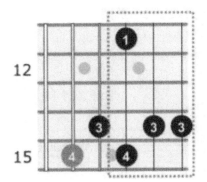

LICK IDEAS

If you have read and studied section one of this book then you'll be well aware of how a dominant flat five/flat nine chord is constructed. Here are three examples for you to learn and ultimately edit to your own liking.

In the first bar and a half of lick one, a melodic contour, initially of three scalar notes descending is played. This idea carries on in a similar way until the D major triad played at the end of bar two. I like how the line is descending in form whilst ascending overall until the flat five arpeggio is played. The line ends again with some wide intervals of 4ths and 5ths descending for an open sound.

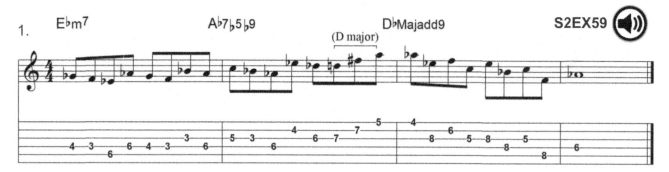

In lick idea two the G11 chord at the beginning could be thought of as F major with a G in the bass. The notes played over the G11 chord are collectively "A pentatonic minor" scale; one to remember for other such situations (play a minor pentatonic built on a note a tone above the 11th root).

The G7 altered chord is led into by a sharp nine note ("A" sharp en-harmonically spelt B flat), has a D flat major triad all the way through the rest of the bar with the D flat leading as a chromatic approach tone to C minor six nine. I have fingered the third bar in a perhaps surprising way. This is because fifth intervals are often played laterally across the neck and this fingering echoes that fact.

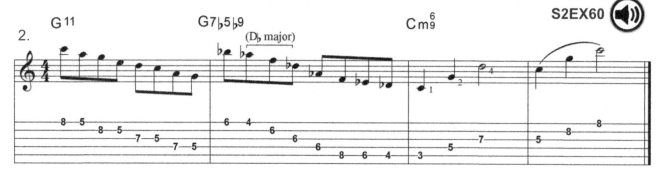

This line which is in the tonality of D major, can be played at several places on the neck. However, I deliberately placed it in seventh position to utilise and show how different neck areas should always be a consideration when working on solo ideas. Try and let all the notes ring together over the last two bars. For a change, the slash voicing is shown as well as it's usual chord symbol alternative in brackets.

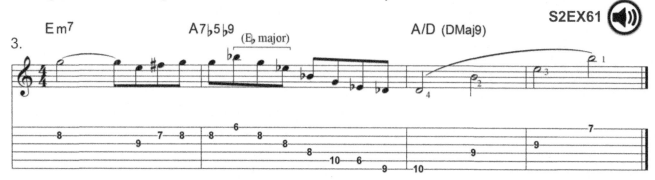

7#5#9

$$\dfrac{bVIMaj}{I_7}$$

LICKS

CHORD FORM IDEAS - 7♯5♯9 shapes

Lick Idea #1

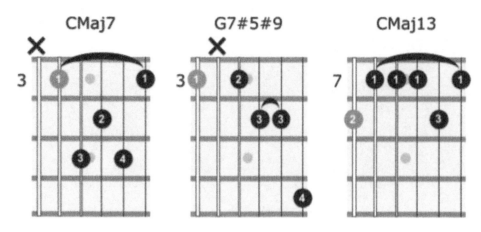

Lick Idea #2

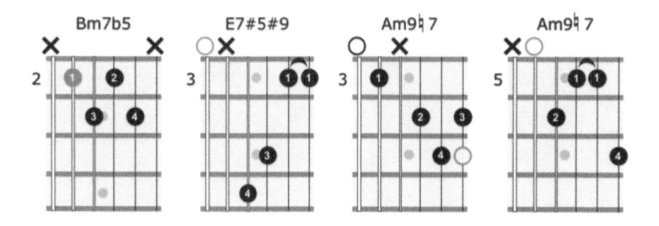

Lick Idea #3

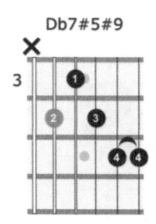

ARPEGGIO PATTERNS

C7#5#9 - Positions of the C7 arpeggio with an Ab major triad acting as the upper structure which results in the aformentioned arpeggio.

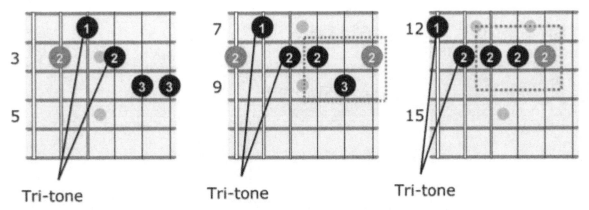

These top three arpeggio patterns include the tri-tone that we would wish to define sonically for #5#9 chords. Due to the limitations of the guitar, it is not always possible to include the 3rd & b7th. The shapes below often dispence with the b7th to facilitate in position playing whilst retaining a flavour of the sound of #5#9 chords.

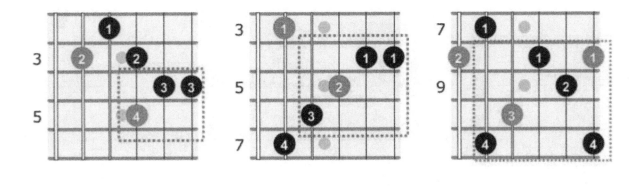

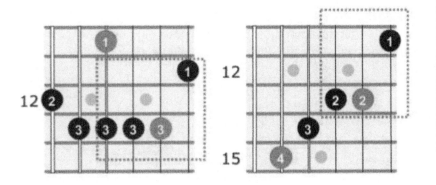

NOTE: Of course, if you feel this is really ruining the sound of the sharp five/sharp nine, then by all means add the flattened seventh to all of these arpeggios.

In this specific case, the note you will be looking to add is a B flat note to the last four forms shown on this page.

LICK IDEAS

We start our sharp five/sharp nine lick ideas with something a little different. The chord progression simply swings between chord I and chord V then back to chord I again in C major. I have kept to the enharmonic equivalents over the sharp five sharp nine chord, however, keep in mind this is a simple E flat major triad you're playing. The written notes can sometimes make things look harder than they actually are.

The fingering here is important and I've added in as much as is needed to play this idea securely. Notice how I have played chromatic notes over the C major chord at the end of the line. The sharpened fifth is a note I often use over I major chords and the F sharp emphasises a lydian sound.

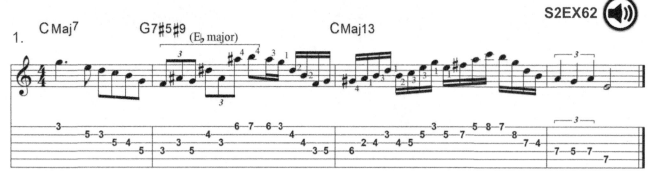

Another slight departure in lick number two being it's in a minor key. The line moves around the neck quite a bit starting off in first position but ultimately ending up in position five.

I always feel there is a certain tactile satisfaction when moving between positions on the neck. This makes sense regarding fingering and creating physical momentum within the line. This feeling comes around bar two with the hammer-on from the G to the G sharp note and the notes that come immediately after. There are many places this line could be played on the neck from bar two onwards.

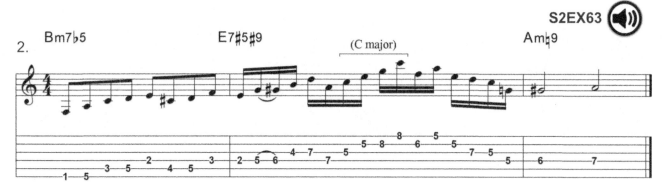

Again, for anyone who has really worked through section one, lick idea number three will not be a surprise. I've basically lifted what I played back then but re-figured the line by using a new melodic contour.

Instead of having the motif up then down etc., I've set the contour as up, down, down, up, up, down, down and finally up. Through this little change, new life can be breathed into an idea to give it a fresh new sound.

13♭9

$$\frac{VIMaj}{I_7}$$

LICKS

CHORD FORM IDEAS - 13♭9 shapes

Lick Idea #1

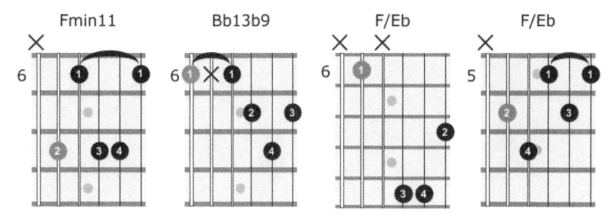

Lick Idea #2

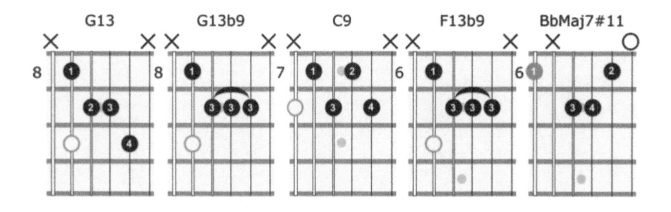

Lick Idea #3

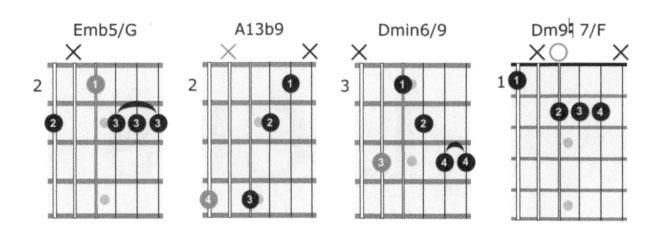

ARPEGGIO PATTERNS

C13b9 - Seven positions of the C7 arpeggio with an A major triad acting as the upper structure which results in the aformentioned arpeggio.

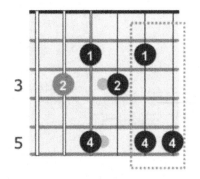

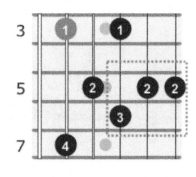

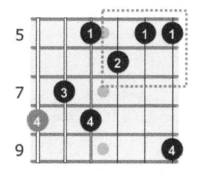

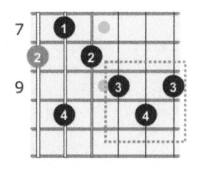

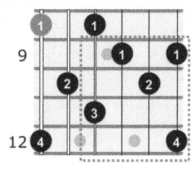

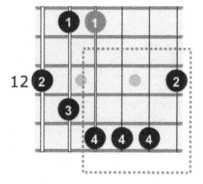

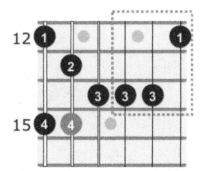

LICK IDEAS

As stated in the arpeggios page, this chord's polytonal structure consists of a dominant seventh with a major triad based on the dominant seventh's sixth tone. In bar two of the first lick a B flat seven with a G major triad on top is shown. What I have played in the second bar is a simple meld of these two triads played one after the other, coming down the inversions. Keep this salient fact in mind when fingering and learning the line as it will help when visualising what you are doing.

The first bar includes a quick jump up the neck to get that high G and F note but you'll find the connection to the first note of the second bar fairly easy. I finished the line off by using another polychord combination. I have added the chord symbol for clarity. Again, I'm simply moving up the two triads one after the other. A rhythmic hemiola effect for the rest of the bar is present.

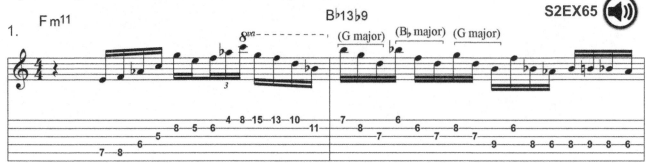

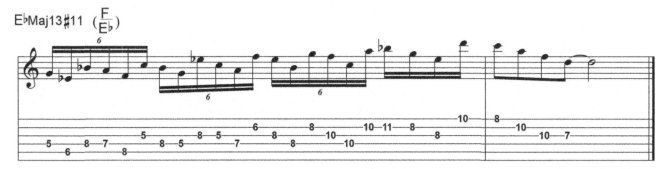

If you have worked through section one, this second lick idea will not come as a surprise. I've used what I played back in the section 1 examples but re-figured the line by using a new melodic contour.

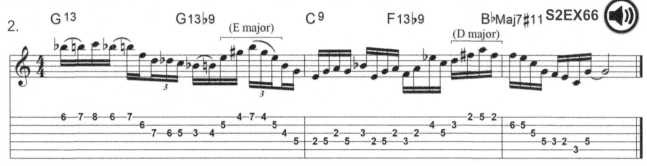

In the final idea in this chord category you can see that I have simply played a non-linear arpeggio of F sharp major over the thirteen flat nine chord. This II - V - I in the key of D minor would be a good candidate for memorisation and then altering to suit your own musical taste.

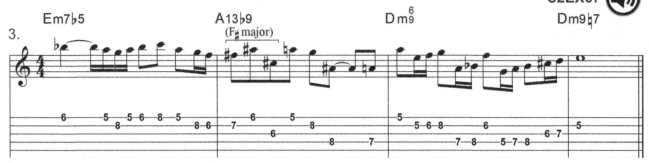

13#11

LICKS

CHORD FORM IDEAS - 13#11 shapes

Lick Idea #1

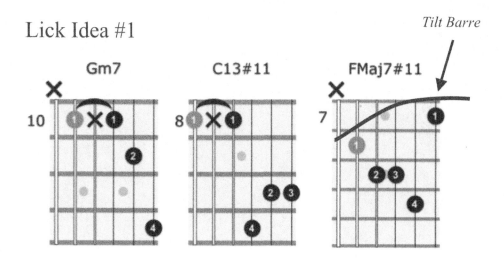

Tilt Barre

Lick Idea #2

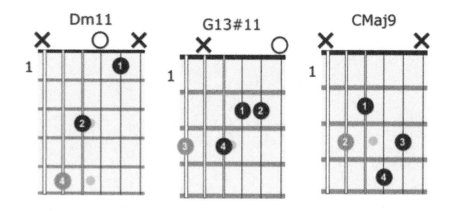

Lick Idea #3

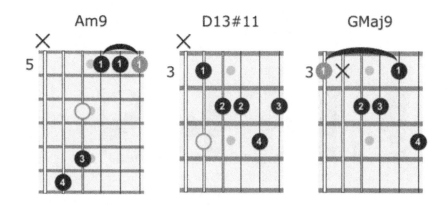

ARPEGGIO PATTERNS

C13#11 - Seven positions of the C7 arpeggio with an D major triad acting as the upper structure which results in the aformentioned arpeggio.

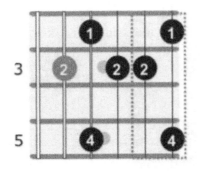
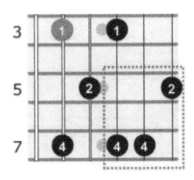
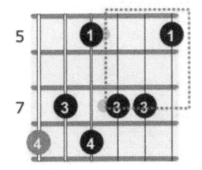

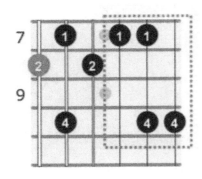
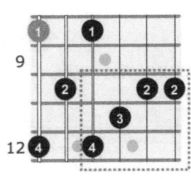
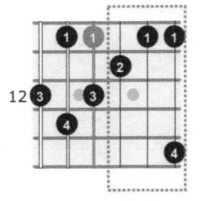

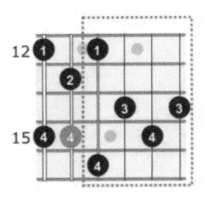

LICK IDEAS

The 13 sharp 11 sound is created over altered dominant chords by playing a major triad that is a major 2nd interval up from the root of the dominant chord. I have labelled these chords in brackets within each dominant seventh bar.

I have deliberately moved the line physically around the fretboard to allow you to play in more than one position across the neck. From a melodic/harmonic perspective, note the B natural note in the penultimate bar over the F major sharp eleven chord.

Also observe that the C dominant seventh has "alt" beside it. As mentioned earlier, this stands for "altered" and is often seen on chord charts as a matter of course.

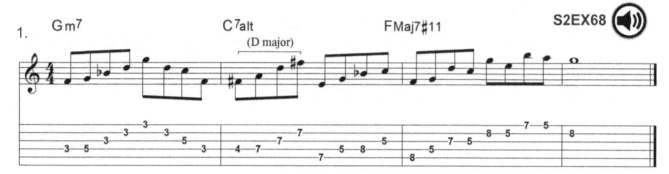

The opening bar of lick number two contains the arpeggio, descending, of an F major seven chord. Synonyms are again at work here. Any major seven is equivalent to the chord's relative minor ninth; in this case D minor nine arpeggio. The V bar (second bar) includes several large interval leaps of a fifth to give a modern intervallic sound. This idea is continued into the I chord, C major in bars three and four.

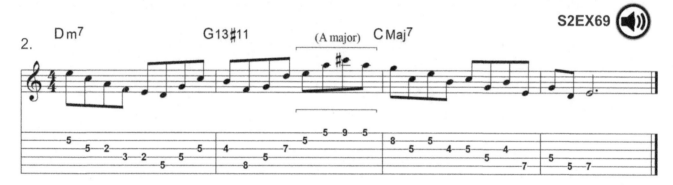

For the most part, this line consists of a more linear, that is, scalar approach. It's only when we get to the chord superimposition of the E major arpeggio over the D7 chord that the line has more leaps.

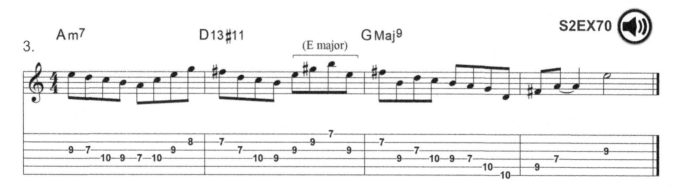

SECTION 3

CHORDAL IDEAS & COMPLETE SOLOS

You will now put the ideas and concepts found in earlier sections to use by learning these complete solos with chordal ideas included. I found that one of the best ways to learn chord sequences was to understand, see and hear them as part of an actual jazz standard rendition. So, what you'll find on the pages that follow are three chord sequences that have a lot in common with three very popular standard tunes. I have also provided chords to "comp" over the sequence and complete solos; I'm sure you will find this a real help.

The chord progressions detailed here are offered in mp3 format as part of your free downloads to play along and practise with. Details of how to get this free download can be found at the end of section one. This free download is an important consideration because it will enable you to get the most from this book.

- The names of the songs are made up but are close to the song names that the progressions represent. If you can't work out what the original song is, ask a seasoned jazz player, they're sure to know.

- Each example goes round one complete sequence of the form which is AABA in the first two solo examples to keep things simple. Just to be clear, each A section is eight bars long as is the B section - making up a thirty two bar form in total. In the third song, which is still AABA, section A is sixteen bars long as is section B making a total of sixty four bars.

- All chords used within the staff and TAB section are also shown in large size at the end of each example solo for easy reference and to check fingerings. Upper structure formula and the original chord symbol are also included for analysis and memorisation purposes. Finally, I've added notes with examples shown of what I consider important melodically and harmonically.

THE THREE SOLO EXAMPLES THAT FOLLOW

1. I Can't Hear A Thing!

2. The Day We Renamed Night

3. Whose Dream Is This?

Song #1

"I Can't Hear A Thing!"

CHAPTER 8

Song #1

"I Can't Hear A Thing!"

Comparative Analysis of the Harmony...

REMARKS ABOUT "I CAN'T HEAR A THING".

This first song is a medium tempo thirty two bar AABA form jazz standard. The way in which the information and ideas are offered for this specific song will be the template for the other two songs also found in this section.

ANALYSIS

I have carried out three analyses; comparative, melodic and harmonic for all solos. Please note that when carrying out these analyses, I have not addressed each bar of music, rather, I have focused on specific bars that include musical interest or relevance to the subject matter.

The comparative analysis enables you to view the chord symbols and the chords actually played, along with the upper structure formulae and the resulting chords that were then used (due to said formulae). I would encourage you to study and understand what is going on at this point before you then move on to the notated solo. A comparative analysis is included with each song included in this book.

SOLOS

I thought long and hard about the notated solos in this section, specifically around what would be best for you, the reader, and player, to learn from. On the one hand, lifting ideas directly from other sections of this book, especially section two, would allow you to hear them played in a chord progression from a song which you could then use in other similar compositions. This approach, however, ran the risk of the finished solo sounding contrived and not that musical. On the other hand, I didn't want to solo over the chord progressions and possibly miss a chance to really feature some of the ideas presented in this book. So, as what usually happens, I went for a comprise in the middle ground.

The solos are improvisations, however, I predominantly created them over four/eight/sixteen bar phrases with an eye on what I played and altered accordingly as needed. I also needed to ensure that the lines brought out certain aspects that I felt would only really be appreciated within the performance context. I feel I have struck the correct balance and I hope you concur.

The melodic and harmonic analysis of the solo for each title will help you use any ideas you like in your own improvisations where possible. Finally, I have included all the chords played in large format so there can be no mistakes with fingering or position.

One last point. I'd like to clarify that the Roman numerals found in the comparative analysis relate to the respective I (one) chord in any one specific structure and *do not* relate to the tonal centre (key) of the song.

I CAN'T HEAR A THING!

I CAN'T HEAR A THING! Cont…

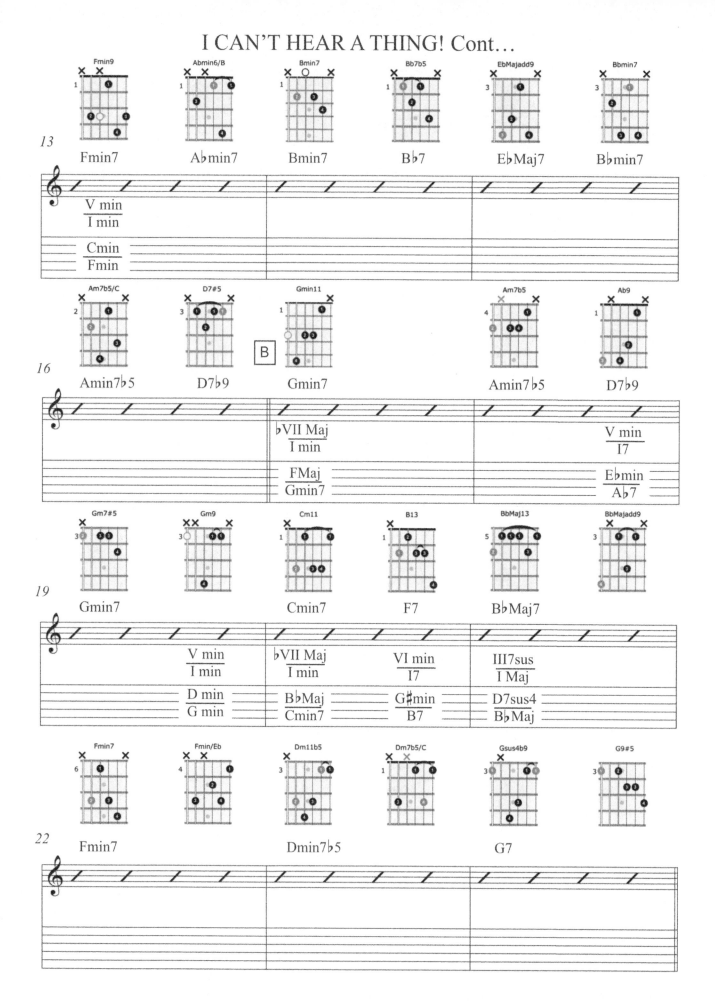

236

NOTE: * = no fifth present in the lower chord due to the alteration taking place in the upper structure voicing.

Song #1

"I Can't Hear A Thing!"

Notated Solo...

I CAN'T HEAR A THING! IMPROVISED SOLO

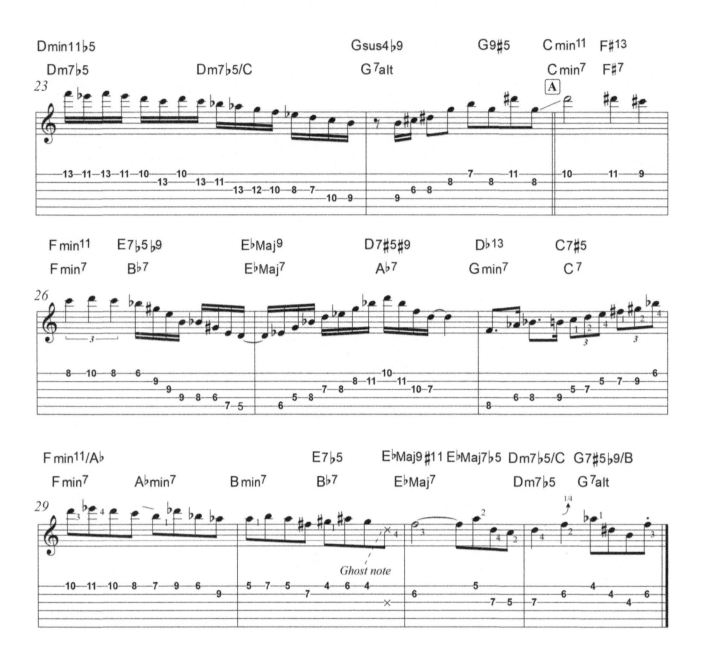

Song #1

"I Can't Hear A Thing!"

Melodic Analysis of the solo…

I CAN'T HEAR A THING! MELODIC ANALYSIS…

BAR 1: Simple outline of the notes found in the chords being played. The line starts off with a rhythmic jazz cliché which gives propulsive impetus to the line.

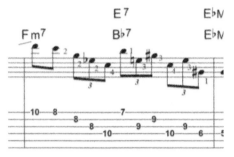

BAR 2: Both chords are superimposed with other chord tones to create rich melodic lines. A "C minor nine" arpeggio is played over the F minor chord (giving an equivalent sound of F minor thirteen). Then an E major triad, which eventually includes an augmented fifth, outlines the substituted E seven chord for B flat seven.

Note: that although an E dominant seven is played, the trained ear will no doubt hear an artefact of the originally predicted harmony which was B flat dominant seven (II - V). With this original chord harmony in mind, the E major triad outlines a B flat seven flat five/flat nine chord with a polychord formula of flat V Major over I dominant seven. This substitution makes use of tri-tone substitution as outlined in section one, chapter three.

BAR 3: Line brings out the important tones. A melodic sequence has been used. Note the use of the note "D" on the downbeat of beat three which is the first beat of the new chord. This "D" note is the sharp eleven of A flat dominant nine.

In time, these sounds and responses to sounds become an automated response and it's up to the improvisor to choose the sounds he/she feels most appropriate for the musical situation at hand.

BAR 4: The anticipation of the sharp five before the C altered dominant is played. This anticipatory technique is commonly exercised by players.

BARS 5 - 6: Double-time line over the chords. Harmony is outlined and the important notes are brought out.

Note that I'm treating the minor chords as Dorian throughout (II minor).

An interesting harmonic movement takes place at this point in the song.

The harmonic movement in bar five is based around symmetrical harmony with minor seven chords moving up by minor third intervals.

The composer then uses a downward chromatic movement where a B minor seven is being utilised (I assume) as a flat five substitution for F dominant seven. This chord leads smoothly to the B flat dominant seven. Consider how the composer has invigorated what is basically a well worn II - V progression with a re-imagined harmonic touch.

BARS 7 - 8: In bar seven the "A" note brings out the sharp eleven even although it is neither notated in the chords or played in the harmony. This is definitely worth trying from time to time to mix things up in terms of how melody and harmony interact with each other.

Bar eight includes an augmented idea that is based around the whole tone scale. If you are new to these types of sounds and ideas, take a close read of chapter four in section one which covers this area of how symmetrical scales and harmony can be used.

BAR 9: The sixteenth run over the F sharp 11 chord is F sharp Mixolydian with an additional chromatic tone, C natural.

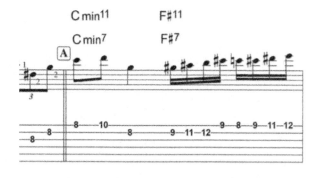

BARS 11 - 12: In bars eleven and twelve, the rhythmic figure used over the E flat major chord is then repeated as the line moves through the D altered chord which is substituting for the A flat dominant seven.

Using repeated rhythmic ideas like the one shown opposite helps to bind disparate melodic ideas and concepts as they move over changing harmonic foundations.

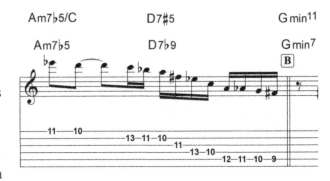

The listener will be more likely to perceive the solo from a more unified standpoint as a whole even though at times there may be little linkage between chordal structures.

In bar twelve the B flat major triad outlines the polytonal nature of a thirteen flat nine chord. The formula of this chord would consist of VI major over I seven, hence we have a B flat major triad played which is chord VI in relation to D flat.

Note that this upper voicing of B flat major over D flat thirteen flat nine, now results in a melodic line that is diatonic to the *original* notated chord symbol. This is an example of the circular nature of music theory and practice.

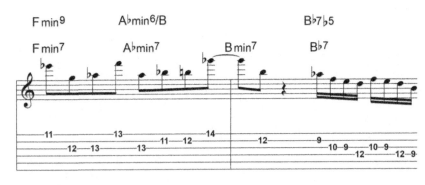

BARS 13 - 14: Threading my way through the chords as they come thick and fast in bar thirteen. When chords move quickly and are not diatonic to each other look for tones that are common to both chords; the one being left and the one you are about to play over. If you can approach your improvisations like this, you will create line ideas that tie together more. Hopefully that makes sense in light of the sounds presented in bar thirteen. In bar fourteen, there are various ways to describe the descending scale, but a locrian natural sixth or II degree of the harmonic minor scale ("A" in this case) would probably be the simplest explanation.

BAR 16: This bar is a good demonstration of how a harmonic minor scale works over a minor II - V progression.

There is a chromatic approach note used in the fourth beat of the bar (the A flat note), but other than that, it's G harmonic minor scale all the way.

The II chord of G harmonic is A half diminished (as shown). The fact that the chord is a first inversion makes no difference to the chord's functionality within the progression. The V chord in G harmonic is D dominant seven. Although not an altered dominant within the harmonised diatonic scale, the altering and addition of the fifth and/or ninth is perfectly acceptable if not desirable when looking to create a strong harmonic gravity as the progression moves towards chord I *(see diagram on page 104).*

BARS 17 - 18: In the first bar shown in the graphic below, the chord being played behind the line is G minor seven. The the first two notes of the phrase are found within the chord and the last three notes chromatically move down until the fifth of G minor seven is played and held over the bar line. The next bar's harmony is an A minor seven flat five chord (chord II in the key of G) moving to an altered D dominant seven. An A flat nine chord was played instead of the D seven which is a common tri-tone (flat five) substitution technique as explained in chapter three.

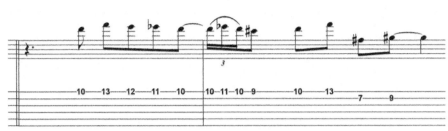

The use of the sixteenth triplet at the beginning of bar one highlights the flat five of the minor II chord and the C sharp note is a chromatic approach tone to D. The last two notes in bar eighteen (F sharp and G sharp) are the flat seven and root of the substituted chord (A flat nine). I have spelt these two notes from a musical notation perspective in relation to the chart's initial chord which was the aforementioned D7.

Although a large amount of words are sometimes needed to describe what has happened musically, the fact is, I heard this idea and played it as the chords moved by. This is the skill that you need to develop more than any other; the ability to hear and play melodic ideas against a moving harmonic background in real time.

BAR 19: A triplet figure that is played out in one position. The G minor seven with the sharpened fifth was played to back up the melody. This is a tricky sound and needs to be handled with care. I feel that the line that is played works. However, it's up to the individual to decide what works for them regarding the sonic pallet that one creates and chooses from.

BARS 20 - 21: This line is easier to play than it looks. You will find that the fretboard notes fall easily under the fingers until the need to move and play the descending Lydian idea in bar twenty one.

The B thirteen is a flat five substitute for F dominant seven and I've used a C whole step/half step diminished scale (part of) to outline this chord.

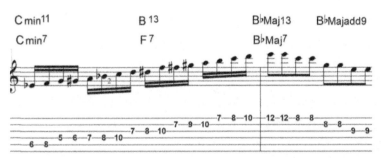

Over the B flat major chord I play a C major triad (Lydian sound) with the notes doubled up (II major over I major).

BAR 22: This short bar has been included for analysis as it includes a chain of 4ths in melodic form and is often referred to as quartal harmony.

The second half of the bar has four consecutive notes that are not based on tertian (tertian, tertial - take your pick), harmony. Tertian harmony is harmony that is based on the intervals of the 3rd, both major and minor. The majority of people on planet earth at this time have been exposed to tertian harmony from the womb and although quartal harmony has been used heavily from the end of the 19th century, it's still very much fringe for many musicians.

Quartal harmony is based on intervals of a 4th (both perfect and augmented). In my opinion, quartal harmony sounds very modern and reminds me of an urban culture and landscape. Perhaps paradoxically, it's quite nomadic in that it has no real defined root or harmonic centre and is an excellent way to infer individualism and the breaking down of traditional social structures.

A whole book could be written on the subject of quartal harmony; but suffice to say it's an area of music that is well worth exploring in depth and in its own right.

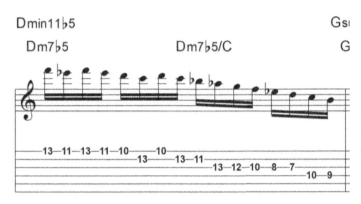

BAR 23: This idea is based around D Locrian mode (tonal centre of E flat major) in sixteenths with the chords giving movement in the bass.

BAR 24: Last bar of the B section before the song repeats the A section for the third and final time. The line over the G suspended four with a flattened nine can be explained in several ways. One would be to think of the idea as based around an A flat minor with a natural seven arpeggio.

From a scalar perspective, the G sus four flat nine can be played over using the G phrygian mode (E flat major from the 3rd degree) or, if this chord is resolving up a fourth, as in this case, use a C harmonic minor starting from the harmonic minor's 5th degree. The name of this mode is a phrygian dominant. This second scalar option can potentially help emphasis the V - I cadence point more effectively with the now present B natural note.

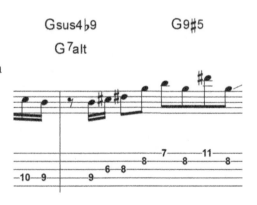

If you are interested in finding out more about these modes, then please look up my book "Scales You Can Use!".

The last four eighth notes outline the augmented quality of the G dominant nine chord with a raised fifth.

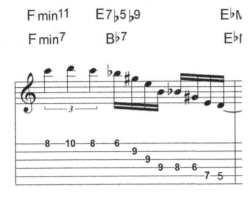

F min¹¹   E7♭5♭9   E♭M
F min⁷   B♭7   E♭

BAR 26: The E dominant seven with a flat five/flat nine is substituting for the B flat dominant seven chord. Remember, the reason for this is to create chromatic movement which is achieved with the F moving down to E and reaching its harmonic destination of E flat major in the next bar.

On closer inspection, you will see that the line that is played over the dominant chord in this bar draws both from the altered dominant and the original unaltered dominant and results in a whole tone feel towards the end of the bar.

BARS 27 - 28: The held common fundamental tone over the bar line is a common technique used by jazz players and one that I would encourage you to practise and employ within your playing, if you do not do so already.

E♭Maj⁹   D7♯5♯9   D♭13   C7♯5
E♭Maj⁷   A♭7   G min⁷   C⁷

This concept creates a
unity of sound and a point of melodic/harmonic stillness over moving chord progressions.

An E flat major seven arpeggio is played and you will need to carry out a positional change to then play the second half of the bar which is a B flat major arpeggio played over the D altered dominant. The B flat major chord is the flat VI in relation to the D dominant root and automatically provides all the tones needed for the sharp five/sharp nine voicing.

A pedal tone of sorts is used in the next bar, bar twenty eight, with a whole tone run played over the C dominant seven including the sharp five which is commonly heard and used.

BARS 29 - 32: I play a melodic contour over these two bars which is more about the sweetness of the sounds it creates rather than the crunchiness of sounds that have come before.

These two bars lead to the final two of the solo where the sharp eleven is brought out in the E flat major chord. In the final bar last chord a flat II over I seven is used. That is a G seven with a sharp five/flat nine outlined by playing an A flat minor arpeggio.

F min¹¹/A♭   E7♭5   E♭Maj9 ♯11
F min⁷   A♭min⁷   B min⁷   B♭7   E♭Maj⁷

Ghost note

Song #1

"I Can't Hear A Thing!"

Harmonic Analysis of the solo....

I CAN'T HEAR A THING! HARMONIC ANALYSIS…

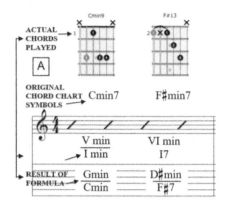

BAR 1: Substitution of F sharp dominant seven for F sharp minor seven. I felt that by playing the dominant seventh instead of the minor seven it would give the progression more impetus and movement without negatively affecting the melody line. The melody is not actually played but was a consideration.

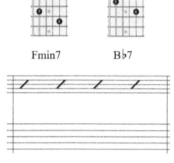

BAR 2: E dominant seven is a flat five substitution for B flat seven to create chromatic movement in the bass.

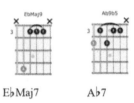

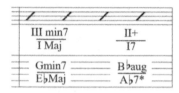

BAR 3: A dominant seven includes 9th extension for more colour and a sharp eleven to support the melody.

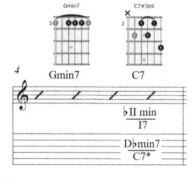

BAR 4: C dominant seven altered to create more dissonance and therefore movement in the progression. Other chords extended from the basic versions shown.

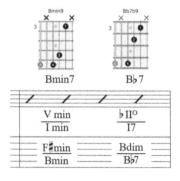

BAR 6: B flat dominant seventh chord altered with a flatten nine tone employed to increase tension of the V - I cadence which is completed in the next bar.

252

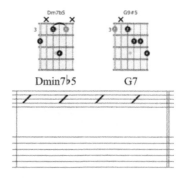

BAR 8: The D half diminished is played in inversion. The flattened fifth in the bass has voice leading in mind. Once again the dominant seventh chord, in this case G, has been altered with a sharpened fifth to increase the dissonance of the structure.

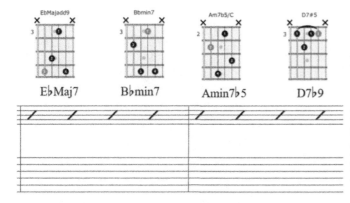

BARS 10 - 12: Extensions to the basic chords have been added as well as alterations as previously outlined (in the text) to increase the dissonance of the dominant seventh chords wherever possible. Bar ten and bar twelve see flat five substitutions used. E seven flat nine for B flat seven and D flat seven altered for G minor seven. This last substitution may seem odd as the original chord was not a dominant, however, this is common practice in flat five substitution. In this particular case, it sounded good to my ears so I went with it.

BAR 13: Bar thirteen has a second inversion F minor chord used. Playing this chord in this way enabled an interesting movement in the bass going forward with the A flat minor chord first inversion being used to dovetail nicely into the B minor seven using the same bass note for both. The movement neatly moves to the B flat note root in the B flat seven chord.

BARS 15 - 16: Synonyms at play in bar fifteen and sixteen. Making use of these chord forms is useful in creating alternate comping ideas. The B flat minor seven chord is often perceived as a D flat major six from a "guitaristic" physical chord shape perspective. In bar sixteen the A minor seven flat five chord is often considered as a C minor six. See the appendix for a list of synonyms.

253

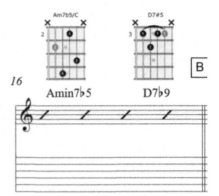

BAR 16: The D seven sharp five chord (which I preferred to a seven flat nine chord which was stipulated in the chord chart) in the second half of the bar is an often used form where the root is *not* in the bass. The tri-tone is formed from the flattened seventh and third in the lower chord and the chosen tones are built upon this foundation.

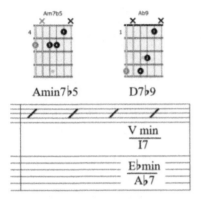

BAR 18: Flat five substitution taking place in the second half of the bar. A flat nine is substituting for the D seven flat nine chord.

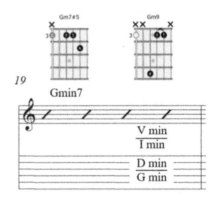

BAR 19: Used a minor seven with a sharpened fifth to support the melody on this occasion. The use of minor sharp five chords needs to be handled with care as it can be misleading. The original harmonic intent must be considered.

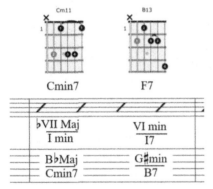

BAR 20: B thirteen being used as a flat five substitution for F dominant seventh. Again, this was to create chromatic movement in the bass.

BAR 22: Note the descending bass line present in these chords is created by making use of inversions to create the harmonic movement.

254

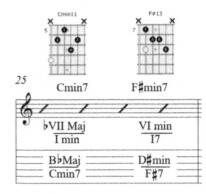

BAR 25: Again, a synonym being employed to create a C minor eleven sound by playing an E flat major nine chord. Re-purposing chord forms in this way can greatly extend the palette of sounds and shapes available to the guitarist in many different scenarios. You do have to take care, however, that the original harmonic progression does not get lost if the root movement is not referred to. This is especially pertinent and a serious consideration regarding voicing choice if no bass player is present.

BARS 26 - 32: For the most part, everything that takes place harmonically from bar twenty six to the end of the piece has already been described.

Note: I changed the sound of the E flat major seven chord in the penultimate bar by flattening the fifth. I did this as I consider this sound as quite dark and melancholic which acts as a contrast to upbeat or bright harmonies within songs.

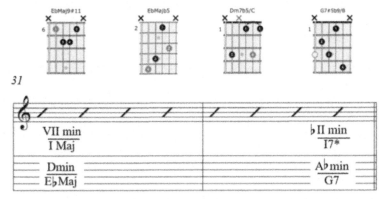

I understand that most will consider the lydian mode as the brightest of modes (in most occasions I do as well). Within this specific musical context, however, I consider and hear this sound as representative of a darker, lonelier emotion.

The last point is that the bass line is again utilising inversions to create a descending line.

Song #1

"I Can't Hear A Thing!"

The Chords Used In Large Format...

REFERENCE CHORDS FOR "I CAN'T HEAR A THING!" #1

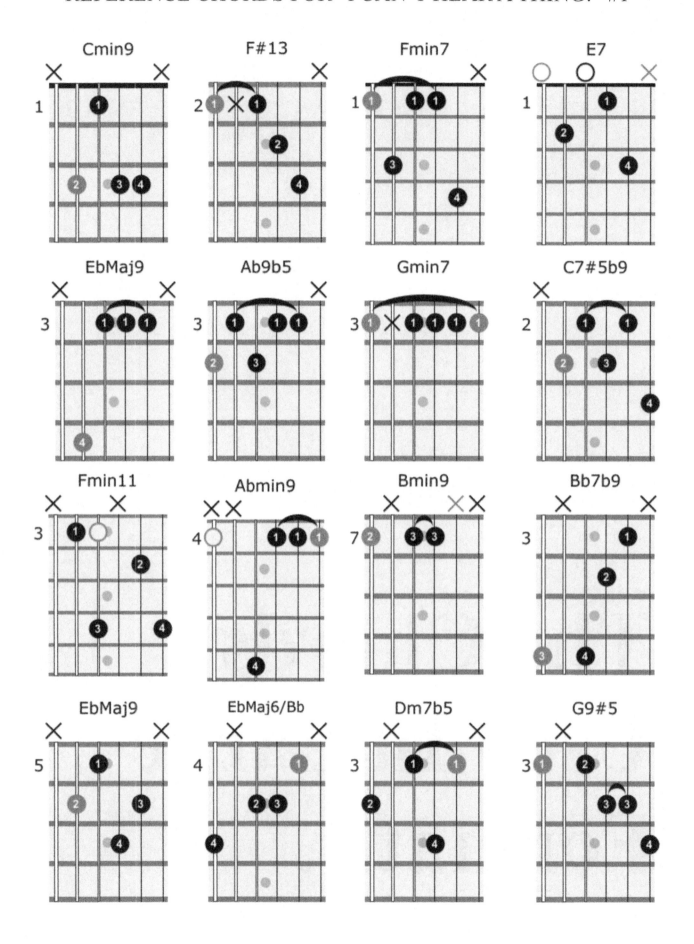

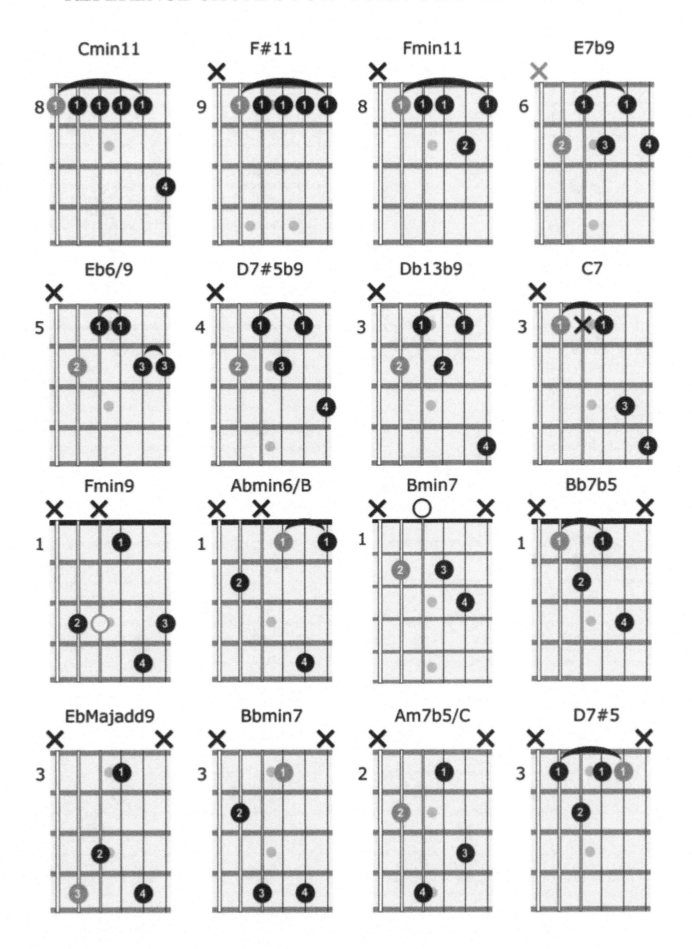

REFERENCE CHORDS FOR "I CAN'T HEAR A THING!" #3

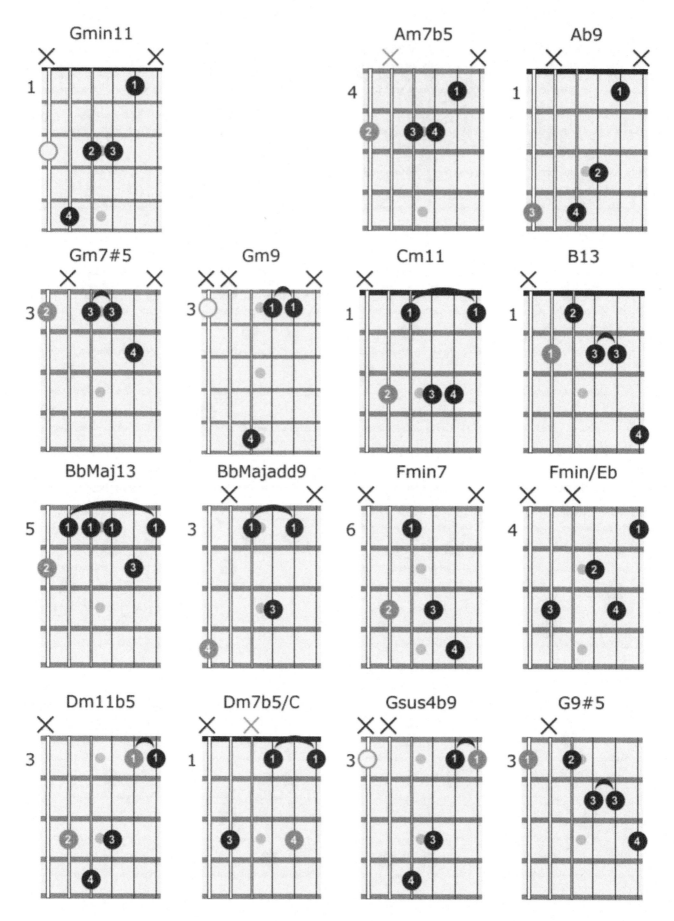

260

REFERENCE CHORDS FOR "I CAN'T HEAR A THING!" #4

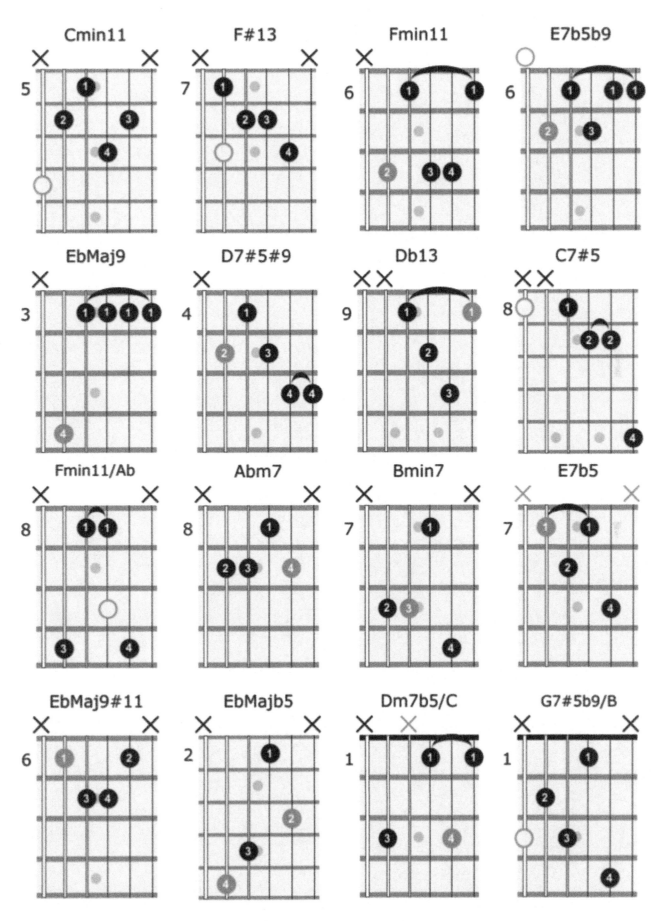

Song #2

"The Day We Renamed Night"

CHAPTER 9

Song #2

"The Day We Renamed Night"

Comparative Analysis of the Harmony…

REMARKS ABOUT "THE DAY WE RENAMED NIGHT".

This second song is a slow tempo thirty two bar AABA form jazz standard. I have tried to balance embedding ideas and chordal concepts shown in the previous song with other ideas; for example using the same chord form for different chords. This is shown in the very first bar.

I have also included examples of contrary motion in the harmony towards the end of the sequence. To darken the colour of voicings I use the sharpened fifth, for major sevenths and the natural seventh for minor chords.

The single line solo features wider intervals and a lot of ideas that move across the strings. Some of you will undoubtedly find this a challenge, but it's a good way of opening up the guitar neck laterally as opposed to always playing up and down in a horizontal fashion.

You will also find that due to the slower tempo, the solo sweeps around the neck a lot more than the last solo. I would urge you to isolate, modify and use any of the lines presented in these solo examples that musically speak to you, in your own solos.

THE DAY WE RENAMED NIGHT

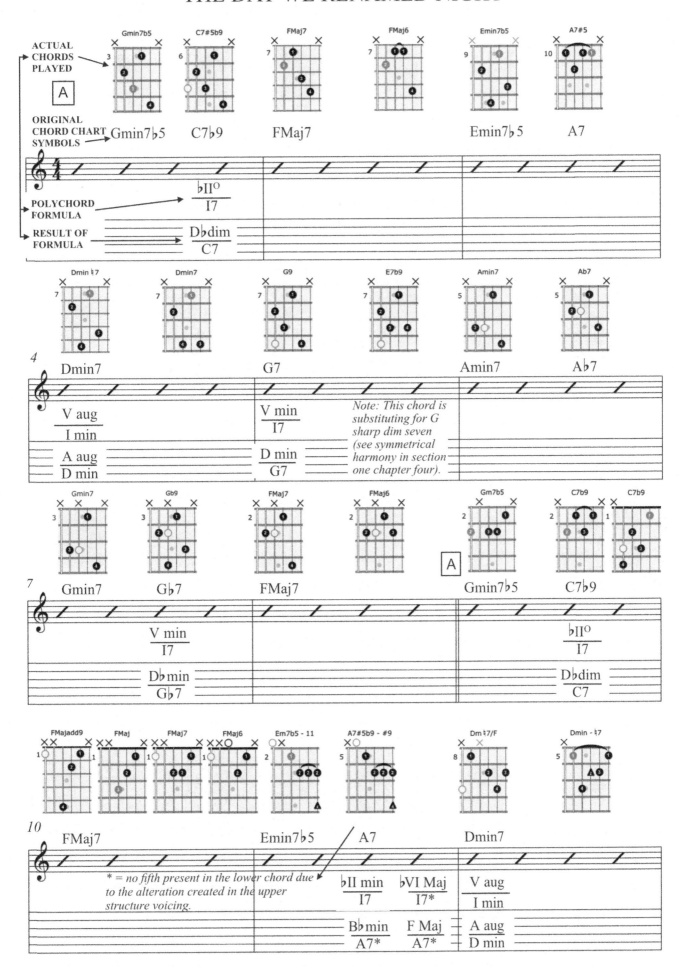

267

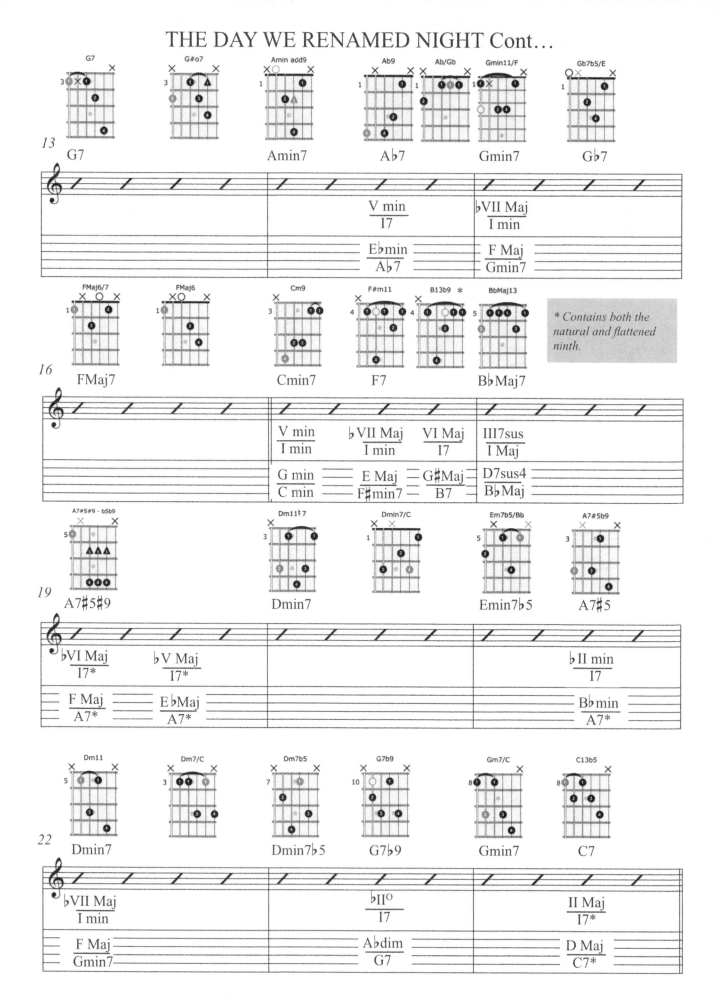

* Contains both the natural and flattened ninth.

THE DAY WE RENAMED NIGHT Cont...

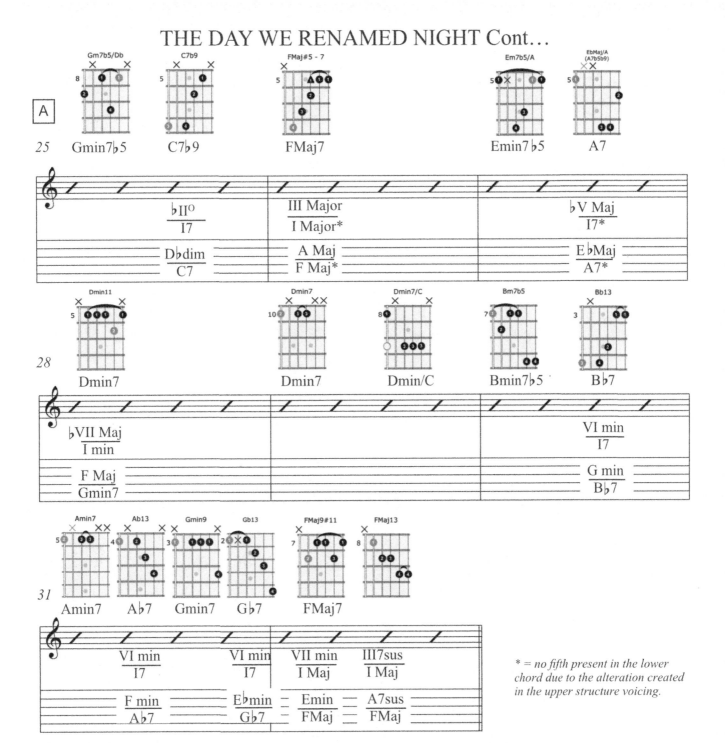

= no fifth present in the lower chord due to the alteration created in the upper structure voicing.

Song #2

"The Day We Renamed Night"

Notated Solo…

THE DAY WE RENAMED NIGHT

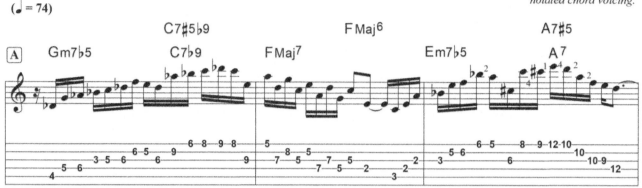

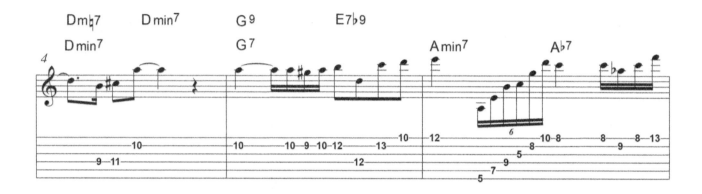

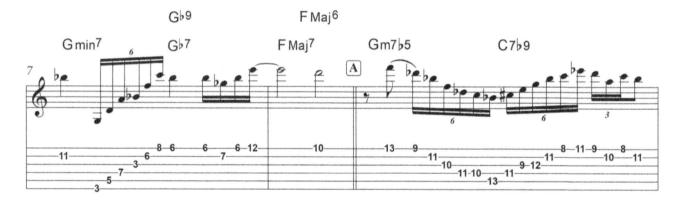

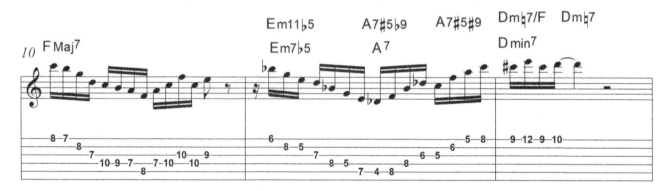

272

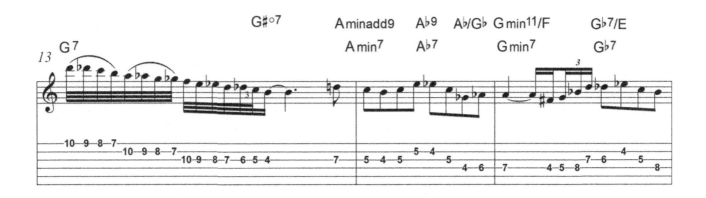

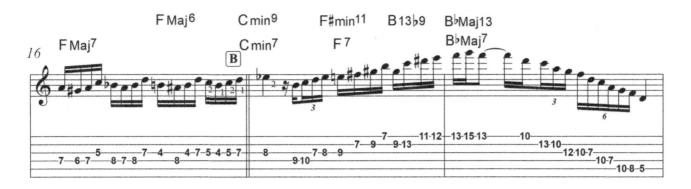

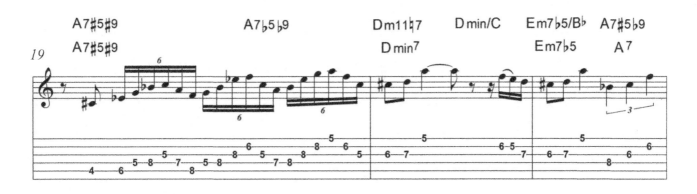

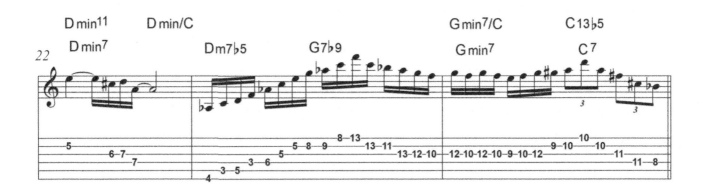

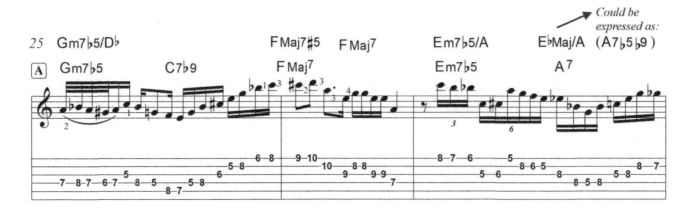

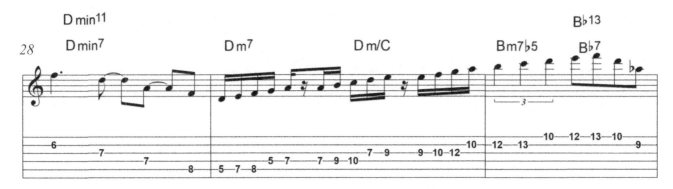

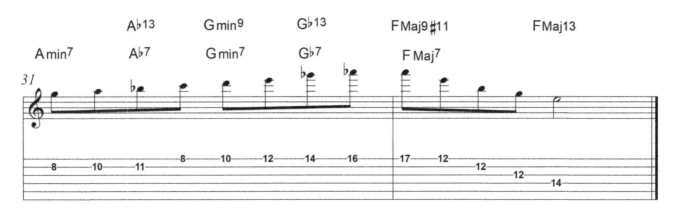

Song #2

"The Day We Renamed Night"

Melodic Analysis of the solo…

"THE DAY WE RENAMED NIGHT" MELODIC ANALYSIS...

BAR 1 - 2: The opening two bars are a II - V - I in the key of F major, however, the II - V is actually signifying a minor resolution that does not take place. This is a common harmonic technique in many songs from the time period that this song was written in. For example, the song "Night and Day" which is of similar vintage begins with D half diminished to G seven altered and a C minor chord is expected, but as in this example, the progression then moves to a major chord. A form of Tierce de Picardie where minor progressions resolve to major.

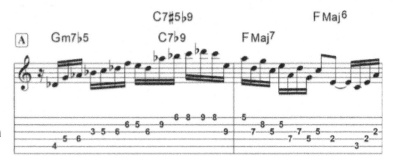

The opening bar notes can be thought of as being from the F harmonic minor scale with the song then resolving to F major.

The note leaps which are much in evidence make the line a little less linear, and dare I say more interesting? In the second bar I have gone for an open sound with fifth intervals defining the F major tonality.

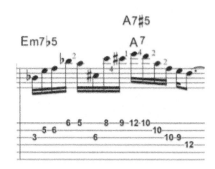

BAR 3: Bar three is a minor II - V progression which will actually resolve to D minor in the next bar. Again, and you will see this a lot in the solo, I have displaced notes by the octave to create interest in the line.

The augmented line idea over the A dominant seven augmented chord contains a D natural note which definitely does not help define the chord. I heard this D minor idea and played it over the chord and some would say that this is wrong. As the note passes by very fast it's, in my opinion, the intent of the musical idea that helps guide the ear through the passage.

BARS 6 - 8: These two bars make use of the ninth within the arpeggio and as such creates a chain of consecutive fifths across the bottom three strings. Playing consecutive fifths in this fashion opens up the fretboard to a lateral playing approach. Playing with a lateral approach fundamentally changes the note options available to you at any one point on the neck and helps change the way in which you hear the forward motion of the musical line.

You can also see another concept in action here that I employ - the use of sequence. I play the idea in A minor and then play the idea in G minor. Playing and repeating motifs in this way binds the melodic ideas together, creating a unity throughout the solo. This is stronger than playing a collection of unconnected musical ideas.

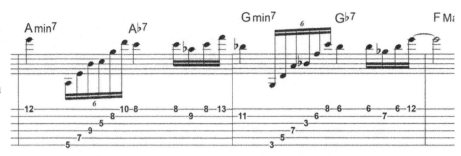

If you like the idea of using sequences in your playing, then learn the idea above and use it in different musical scenarios. This will help anchor the technique and concept within the musical library of ideas that you have at your fingertips.

BAR 10: You will hear in the audio and see in the notation the use of a II major chord arpeggio (G major) being played over the I chord (F major) to effect a thirteen sharp eleven sound. This is despite the fact that the chord symbol states a non altered F major seven. I played this because I heard it and thought it would work well. Keep in mind that you do not have to play exactly what the chord symbols stipulate when you are improvising. The best advice is to play what you hear regardless of any rules. Remember the old adage, rules are there to be broken. If you can hear what you want to play over the harmonic background you're playing against then play it. If we only play exactly as the chord symbols dictate, music will be all the poorer for it.

BARS 9 & 11:

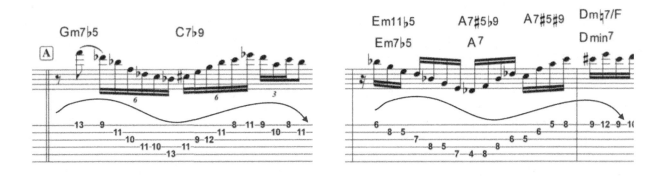

Above I have placed bars nine and eleven from the solo. The reason for this is to draw your attention to the same melodic contour that is present in both of the lines.

This melodic contour approach is not a conscious act as far as I'm concerned, but it is obviously happening when I create lines. When I was starting out trying to play guitar I was a big fan of the jazz guitar legend Ted Greene and Ted did have a lot to say about melodic contours. I worked away and tried to play the ideas and lines he presented in his books and although I didn't think that I made much progress at the time, it may be that more of his ideas rubbed off than I had at first thought.

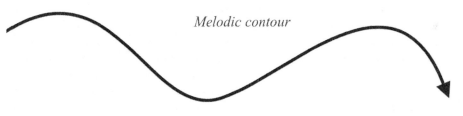

Melodic contour

If you look at the melodic shape within the solos presented in this section, you will see that it is possible to outline a wave shape, like that shown above, from the notated music. For me, it creates a natural ebb and flow within a solo. This is another useful idea that you can work to integrate into your playing style - if it chimes with you.

As to the content of the two bars; bar nine is fairly straightforward, outlining the minor II - V in arpeggio form. In bar eleven, the A seven with a sharp five/flat nine is outlined by a B flat minor arpeggio and the sharp five/sharp nine at the end of the bar is outlined by an F major arpeggio. These upper structures are documented in section two in their respective chord categories and at the end of the book in the appendix section.

BAR 13: This line may sound difficult to play but actually it's an almost complete chromatic run. If you have practised your chromatic scales but never found a place or reason to use them, then this example shows how they can be played to great effect within a solo.

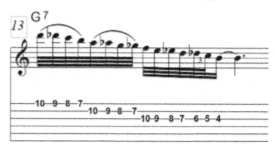

BAR 16: Here you can see, and hear by listening to the mp3 of the solo, one of my favourite melodic concepts that I picked up at some point.

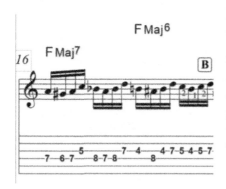

This idea has at its core an ascending line which is the first note of each of the four sixteenth note groupings. Around this first note a pattern that consists of a note down a half step, back to the first note, then a note a major or minor third higher. Due to the half step, non diatonic notes are used and it creates a strong joined together line that has a lot of interest within it.

BAR 17 - 18: I go into detail regarding the use of F sharp minor to B dominant altered chord substitutions in the harmonic analysis found later in this chapter. From a melodic perspective, the line played in this bar simply outlines this new harmonic reality.

If you are going to reinterpret passages of music with quite distant substitutions like those shown in this passage, unless you know the people you are playing with really well from a musical perspective, it would make sense to talk over such changes before playing them.

If, however, you are playing with seasoned professional players, they will hear these alternate changes and

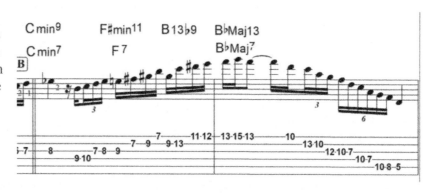

play accordingly so long as you are not mixing it up in a different way every chorus. Knowing when to spice things up but to not overdo it is part of maturing as a musician. In other words, don't feel you need to use every idea, lick or technique you know on every progression you play.

In bar eighteen I play an F major/D minor pentatonic scale. The substitution of pentatonic scales over static chords (both major and minor) is a great way to access coloured or altered tones in the second octave of a scale/chord relationship. By using pentatonic scales, your musical lines will sound fresh, open and not so linear as opposed to using diatonic scales all the time.

For example, here I have used (with regards major to major relationships) a major pentatonic based on the V of the I major chord (F major over B flat major). Another major pentatonic worth practising over chord I would be a major pentatonic based on the I chord's II degree. So, over B flat major you would play C pentatonic major. This will result in tones being automatically generated that are lydian in relationship to the original major chord.

Major triads based on the flattened sixth and fifth from the root of the dominant chord are woven together to create a strong altered line that reflects the alterations and dissonance taking place in the harmony.

Specifically, the altered A dominant seventh line is played over the harmony using the triads of E flat major (the root played from the flattened fifth of A seven) sounding a flat five/flat nine and F major (the root played from the flattened sixth of A seven) sounding a sharp five/sharp nine.

Also note that as I know the two chords are being used in combination I do not worry about playing the exact triad over the exact altered chord at the beginning. I begin the line with the third of A dominant to ground the line with respect to the harmony then play the E flat triad followed by the F triad and so on.

My advice is to try to take the whole soundscape into consideration and try not to be led by dogmatic rules all the time (even the ones you have read in this book). You do need to know various "rules" but as your musical and technical ability increase, allow your taste and musical sensibility to be the ultimate arbiter as to what is musically appropriate.

If you allow yourself this freedom now, in the future, if you ever hear recordings of yourself from this time on, you will be surprised at the ideas you came up with. You may also hear the unexpected with respect to following the convention and rules of music.

BAR 23: This is one of those occasions where you can not only play an extended line, but you get the chance to show off by playing across the neck. This line has a range of two and a half octaves and to facilitate it means playing laterally across the neck. To be shallow for a moment, audiences enjoy watching these flurries of creativity! Notice how the line starts on the flattened fifth.

Some points regarding this note choice. Firstly, consider the octave leap from the previous bar note which is a melodic feature of this solo and has already been commented upon in other parts of the solo. This continues the theme started earlier and helps to unify the solo. Secondly, the change in tonality from the D minor to the D half diminished is very pronounced and underlines to the listener that a significant change has taken place in the harmony.

Finally, I often play half diminished and the other chord structures that are synonyms of it from the flat five (in this specific chord's case). I like the sound and it gets away from playing arpeggios from the root all the time. Always playing from the root, to my ears anyway, becomes a little predictable. I also think that, for example, if this line was played over B flat nine, the idea sounds more "bluesy" being played from the flattened seventh, not playing the root and incorporating the ninth.

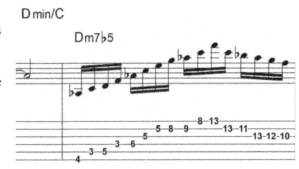

I want to make clear, this is a completely subjective observation and it is up to you to decide how you feel about these sounds and their interaction with the harmony surrounding them. You may enjoy the sound of these chords being defined in the line by starting from the root. It's not a case of what is wrong or right but what your musical taste and direction decides.

279

BAR 24: The first two beats of the bar are straight forward apart from the use of a chromatic bridging tone which connects the G natural note to the A natural on the third beat.

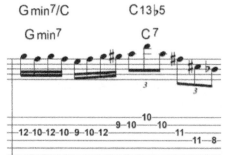

The C thirteen flat five chord is often expressed as a thirteen with a sharpened eleven. For both of these expressions you have a tri-tone of your chosen dominant seventh with a major triad one tone above its root as the upper structure.

By studying the first triplet and the first note of the second triplet you will see that is exactly what I played; a D major triad. Note the addition of further dissonance by my playing a C sharp note which is the flattened ninth.

BAR 25 - 26: The rather complicated rhythmic figure at the beginning of bar twenty five is not nearly as frightening as it looks when you take the tempo of the piece into account. It is, however, quite interesting as a study in the concept of target tones. The first note "A" is the target tone and all the other notes in the demisemiquaver pattern are, in this case, only a semi-tone away from this note.

For the record, targeted tones can also be approached using tones and do not have to be approached or left only by a semi-tone interval.

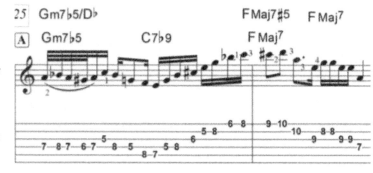

The C dominant seventh with the flattened ninth has a diminished arpeggio played over beat three which is common usage as explained elsewhere in chapter four of this book.

I played a major seven sharp five chord instead of a straight major seven in the recording and I emphasised this note at the beginning of bar twenty six.

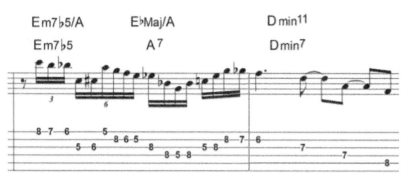

BAR 27 - 28: Once again I make use of the octave displacement idea in bar twenty seven. Contrary chromatic movement is presented as a mirror between the upper and lower notes within the octave in the opening beats of the bar. Note the use of a sextuplet in beat two.

The slash voicing states an E flat major over an A bass which infers the sound of an A dominant seventh with a flattened fifth/ninth. An E flat major triad is actually played at this point in beat three which then leads to a C minor triad which offers up a sharp nine, flattened fifth and flattened seventh tones. The G flat is again a chromatic bridge between the G immediately before and the F which is played at the beginning of bar twenty eight.

BAR 29: I've included this measure in the melodic analysis, not because it's especially difficult to play, but because it shows the power of rhythm and how it can make the mundane or commonplace more interesting.

I've been lucky enough to score several films and media projects and one thing that is used to create forward movement and propulsion is rhythm and that is what is happening here. It's a line that breaks up into five notes, then five notes then four. The notes played are from D Dorian and are ascending step wise. You can see that the rhythm then elongates in the next bar so it's an interesting effect.

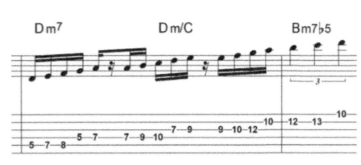

So, the message here is don't just think about the amount of notes, or the type of notes you play all the time. Think how rhythm can be utilised to infuse interest into linear scale ideas.

BAR 31 - 32: Here is an example of how to play over chromatic movement which can be very difficult especially at faster tempos than the solo presented here.

In many musical scenarios, when chords move by step up or down a semi-tone from a fundamental chord tone you often have a good chance of landing on a note that is diatonic or melodically significant to the new chord by simply moving by one fret (semitone) movement.

In the chart below I have listed "A minor seven" in the centre of the box. On the far left and right of the box is the chord A flat seven with it's tones shown in column beneath. The notes in the "DOWN A SEMITONE" and "UP A SEMITONE" display the resulting note's relationship to A flat seven if you move by a fret in either direction on the guitar neck.

A♭7	DOWN A SEMITONE		Am7	UP A SEMITONE		A♭7
A♭	IN	G♯/A♭ (root)	A	A♯/B♭ (9th)	IN	A♭
C	OUT	B(♯9)	C	D♯/E♭ (3rd)	IN	C
E♭	OUT	D(♭5)	E	F (6th)	IN	E♭
G♭	IN	F (13th)	G	G♯/A♭ (root)	IN	G♭

This is not a foolproof system, however, it will help you see that in most cases, the note that you want in the next chromatic chord shift is probably a semi-tone (or tone) away. Ultimately, it's not systems that will help in playing over chromatic progression, but your musical ear allied to what you know will happen if you move your fingers a certain distance on the fretboard.

Song #2

"The Day We Renamed Night"

Harmonic Analysis of the solo…

THE DAY WE RENAMED NIGHT HARMONIC ANALYSIS…

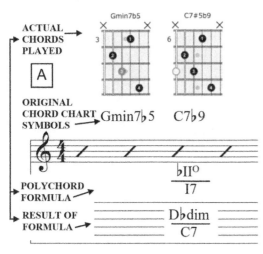

ACTUAL CHORDS PLAYED

A

ORIGINAL CHORD CHART SYMBOLS

POLYCHORD FORMULA

RESULT OF FORMULA

BAR 1: Here you can clearly see once again how a chord can be heard in different ways even although we are utilising the same shape. The same form is used to play both a G half diminished and a C altered dominant chord.

Although the chord stipulated in the chord symbol is a flat nine, I increased tension by also including a sharp five tone. Altering tones in this way is very much down to your own musical taste and knowing what is musically appropriate.

The relationship between these two chords is detailed in the appendix of this book, along with other common synonyms. The appendix will also allow you to see, at a glance, the upper voicing formula and the chords used for both harmonic and melodic use.

BAR 3: The first chord shown in this bar would often be considered a minor sixth chord, but on this occasion the chord functions as a half diminished with the root found on the 3rd string.

The A dominant seventh with a sharp five is played with the flattened seventh in the bass. The flattened seventh in the bass is a common device used all over the neck. Often the root is discarded with, but not on this occasion, being found on the second string.

Knowing where the root can be found in a voicing is useful for identification purposes when learning new chord forms.

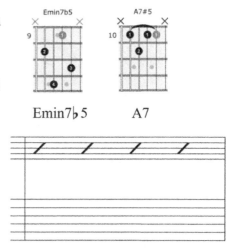

BAR 4: In bar four I played a minor chord with a natural seventh. I would like to emphasise that playing the minor chord with a natural and not flattened seventh was not done from any formulaic point of view, but simply from what I heard when playing through the sequence. Finger four is used to play the natural seventh and although it will be very uncomfortable for some to play, I see this as the result of "organic technique". I use this term when I play something that may be slightly different to what would usually be expected from a technical viewpoint, but is appropriate for the musical reality in hand. In this case, the natural seventh falls a semi-tone to the flattened seventh in beat three of the bar.

BAR 5: Notice that the G dominant ninth chord is using the same shape as was used in bar one for the two different chord functions found in that bar. This is the third different use of the same shape.

Although I placed a note under the E seven flat nine chord, it should be understood that the chord was not even mentioned in the original chord chart. The reason I played this diminished chord form here (which functions as a dominant seventh with a flattened ninth) is that it creates a V - I cadence to the next chord, A minor.

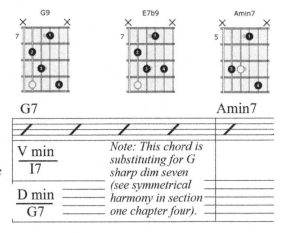

BAR 10: The thing to remember here is that the tempo is not that fast. This is an important consideration when it comes to creating movement in a line which is exactly why I played this.

It's not that I just want to play lots of chords. I felt that the moving line would enhance the music at this point and so it meant playing the appropriate chords as given.

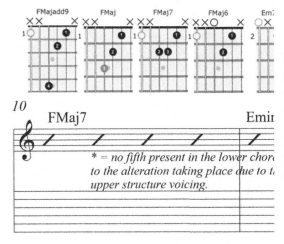

BAR 11: Perhaps stating the obvious, but yet again, exactly the same chord shapes are used for four different chord types.

What is perhaps less obvious is that this is an excellent example of how understanding the construction of heavily altered chords with respect to upper structures can aid you in your single line improvisations.

It's not always the case that you would wish to play only arpeggios over this minor II - V progression, but if you are looking to reflect the harmony in this way, make sure to memorise the upper structure formulas shown. There is a complete list of those covered in this book in the appendix found after this section.

The italic text which is partly seen in the diagram simply states that the fifth of the chord is not present due to the alteration already taking place within the chord structure.

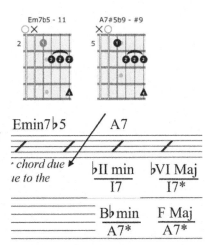

285

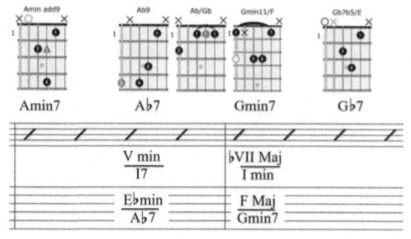

Amin add9 | Ab9 | Ab/Gb | Gmin11/F | Gb7b5/E

Amin7 Ab7 Gmin7 Gb7

V min	♭VII Maj
I7	I min

E♭min	F Maj
A♭7	Gmin7

BAR 14 - 15: The main thing to consider in this example is the inversions used and the resulting bass line of the progression.

The extended A flat seven chord, A flat nine on beat three, moves to an A flat with a G flat in the bass; this equals an A flat seven on the fourth beat.

The bass line has now travelled from an initial A note bass with respect to the A minor seven to A flat to G flat. This then continues through the chords with a third inversion G minor seven (F in the bass). The last viewable chord here is G flat seven. The flattened seventh of G flat seven, an E, is played in the bass which will then resolve smoothly to the F major chord in the next bar.

This is a good example of inversion theory in practice and shows how chords can take different routes through progressions and weave intricate new sounds over old themes.

BAR 17: There are a few subjects to discuss with respect to bar seventeen.

First of all, you may well have thought of the first chord shown as orientated more towards an E flat major than C minor chord. Although care does need to be taken, as a general rule, major chords can be employed as their relative minors and visa versa if the music's harmony is underpinned by fundamental tones.

As stated, if you have a bass player present, there will be no problem with this approach for most musical occasions and this concept opens up a new world of extended voicings available for use in your sound palette. Just be careful when playing solo guitar that the musical direction is not lost by never actually referring to the original key centre's root position chords. An overview of the general modulations taking place within the music must also be a consideration when considering using chord synonyms

Cm9 F#m11 B13b9 BbMaj13

B Cmin7 F7 B♭Maj7

V min	♭VII Maj	VI Maj	III7sus
I min	I min	I7	I Maj

G min	E Maj	G#Maj	D7sus4
C min	F#min7	B7	B♭Maj

In the second half of bar seventeen, moving backwards from the end of the bar, as so often is the case when analysing harmony, I used a flat five substitution. An altered B dominant seven was substituted for F dominant seven which in the first instance created chromatic movement; C - B - B flat.

I then, however, inserted the dominant minor of the B seven chord (F sharp minor) a beat before. This in effect creates a II - V progression based around the flat five of the original I chord (B flat major). The ear could expect this new II - V to resolve to this new tonal centre of E major, however, the resolution moves to the initial key of B flat with chromatic movement.

This "surprise" element to the listening experience, where the music goes somewhere that was not expected is something that musicians have been aware of and employed for centuries. A musician can use this technique for their own enjoyment, but it can also be thought of as a way of surprising and continually

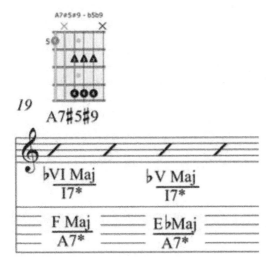

19

A7♯5♯9

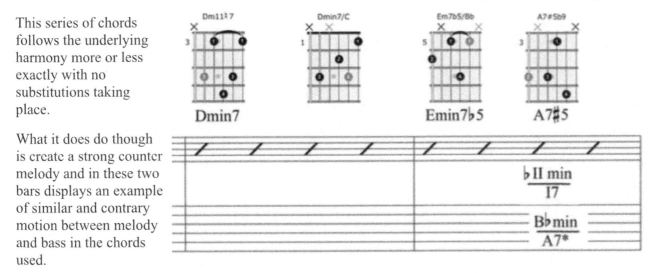

BAR 19: It took me a long time as a young guitarist to realise that although the dominant flat five/flat nine and sharp five/sharp nine chords sound like musical polar opposites, they are often played together and this is an example of this combination.

Invariably, to get the most out of this book you will need to not only understand but memorise the upper voicing formulae. I would urge you to start with these two examples and then build from there.

Use the layout of the guitar fretboard to pinpoint upper voicing triad root notes as a starting point in your studies. In this particular case, the root of the initial A seven is found at fret five string six and the upper voicing root notes are found on string five at frets six and eight. The chords that are used to create the more complex chords of flat five/flat nine, sharp five/sharp nine are E flat and F major respectively.

This visualisation of where roots are found in relation to the original chord root is an important step towards applying the musical ideas found in these pages. The movements you make with your hand in relation to specific harmonic stimuli will eventually become second nature and will "hear" them as options as you play.

BAR 20 - 21: These two bars set a musical chain of events that continues through to measure twenty four.

This series of chords follows the underlying harmony more or less exactly with no substitutions taking place.

What it does do though is create a strong counter melody and in these two bars displays an example of similar and contrary motion between melody and bass in the chords used.

In bar twenty up to the E half diminished we see similar motion, where the melody and the bass both are descending, but not in strict parallel motion. The E half diminished to A seven altered in bar twenty one displays contrary motion where the melody ascends by a half step and the bass descends by a half step.

Considering bar twenty one more, the initial D minor includes a natural seven that coloured the chord in a way that I specifically like, with an eleventh added for colour.

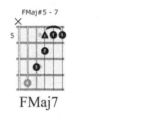

FMaj7

BAR 26: You're no doubt beginning to see a pattern in how I voice my chords! Here I initially include the sharpened fifth which I resolve later in the bar.

Note that this voicing can be viewed as a III major sitting over a I major chord. Remember, this knowledge can be applied for both single line playing as well as for harmonic application.

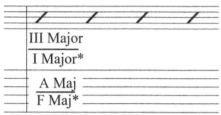

BAR 27: The first chord played is an E half diminished with the fourth in the bass which is crucially also the root note of the dominant seventh, if it were notated, that would lead us to D minor seven in the next bar.

In effect, I'm creating a pedal tone (although I accept a very short lived one) underneath the E half diminished to set up the movement to D minor in the following bar via its dominant. Furthermore, I play an E flat major triad in the second half of the bar which equates to A dominant seven flat five/flat nine.

This intrusion of the E flat over A bass helps define the cadential movement even although it was not present in the chord chart. It's up to the individual musician to decide what works best in any one musical situation.

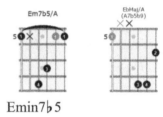

Emin7♭5

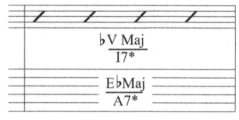

BAR 31 - 32: To end this song I play a series of chords which utilise flat five substitution to create chromatic movement in the bass. Also, it is important to state that the entire sequence makes use of contrary motion which is only broken up on the final chord where the F root stays in place for both chords, however, the melody continues to ascend.

So, the melody ascends and the bass descends for the entirety of bar thirty one.

The F chords were played up the neck to access the ascending melody which did not allow a low F note to be in the bass. The only other option would be to strum the chords, without the root, with the right hand then finger tap the F bass note at fret one at the bottom of the neck. This option would be a distinct possibility but would break the chordal flow somewhat.

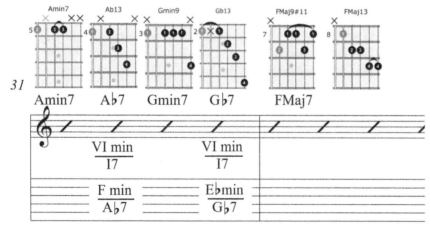

Song #2

"The Day We Renamed Night"

The Chords Used In Large Format...

REFERENCE CHORDS FOR "THE DAY WE RENAMED NIGHT" #1

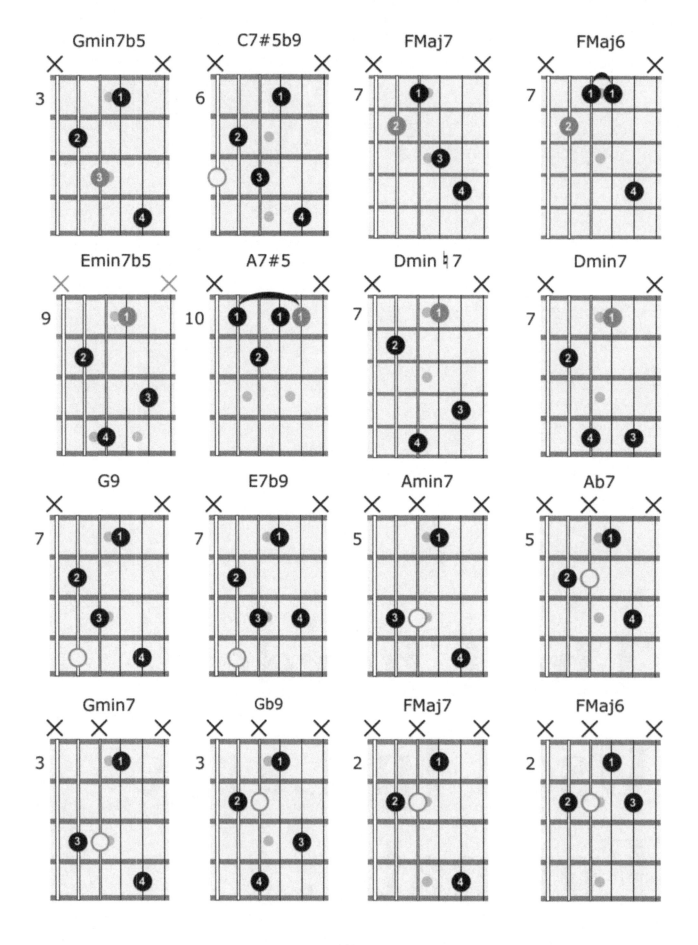

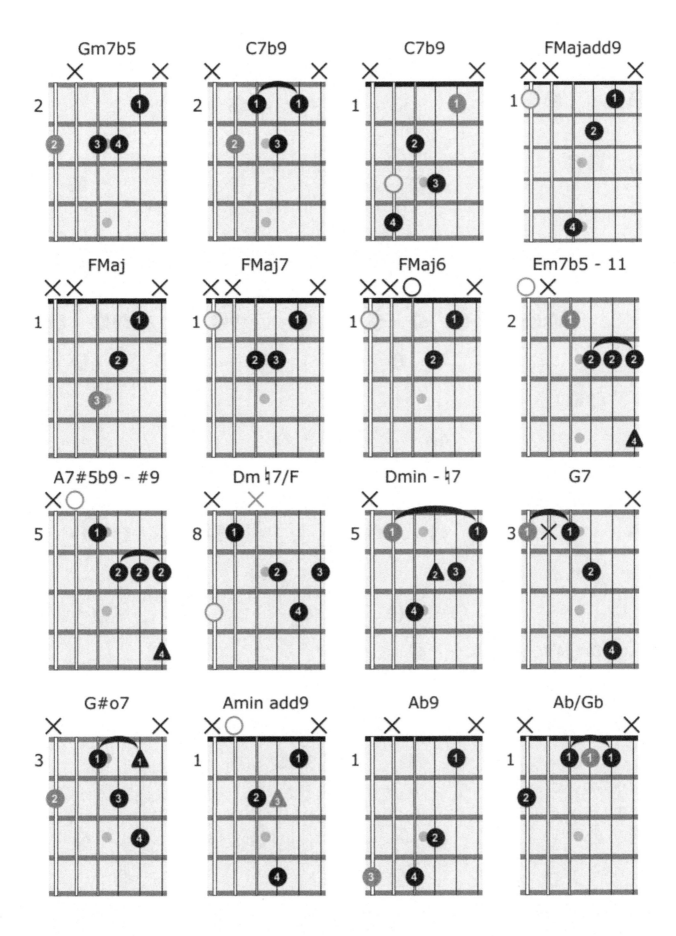

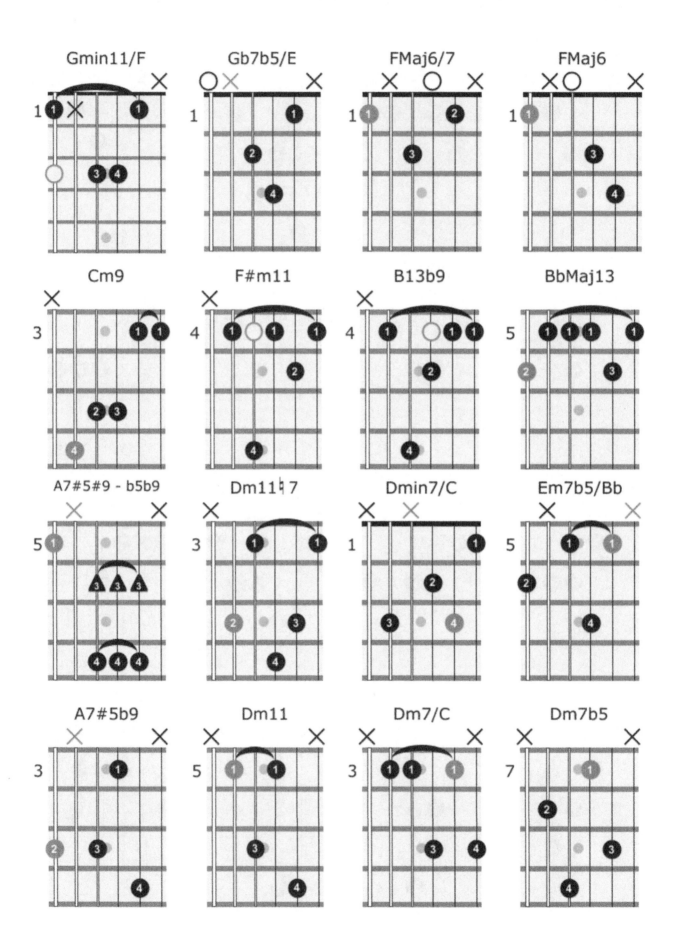

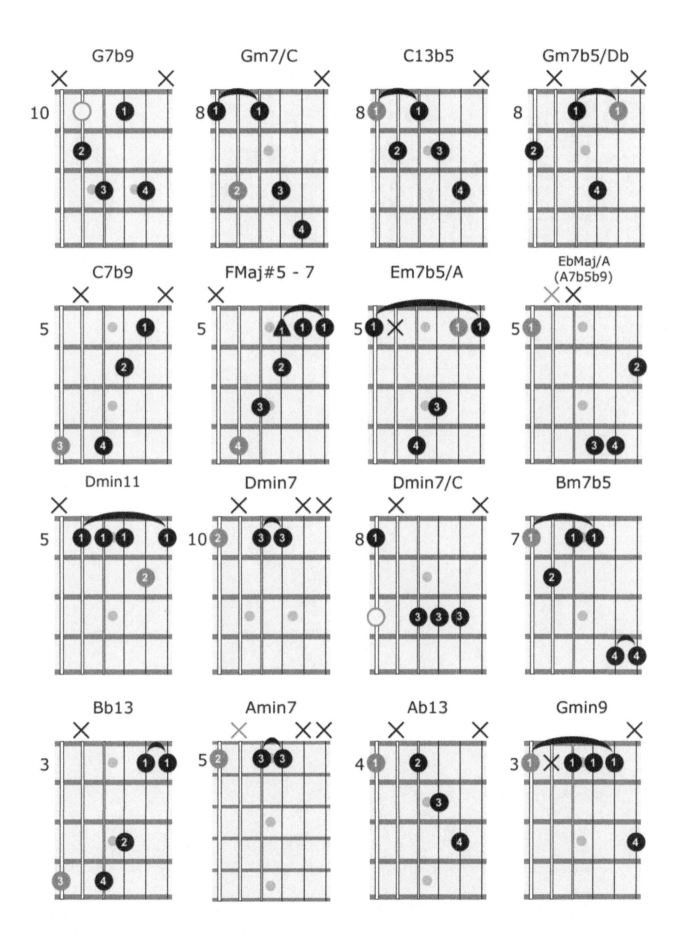

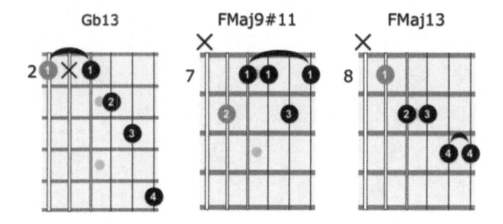

Song #3

"Whose Dream Is This?"

CHAPTER 10

Song #3

"Whose Dream Is This?"

Comparative Analysis of the Harmony...

REMARKS ABOUT "WHOSE DREAM IS THIS?".

In our final solo example we have a song that is AABA in form but with a difference. First of all, each song section is not eight but sixteen bars long. Secondly, the A section is played with a latin feel while the B section is played swing. Again, this is one chorus from a very well known jazz standard and if you don't know the original, here is a clue: Wes Montgomery played this very song on his European tour of 1965 and you can watch and listen to him play it live with a Danish rhythm section on Youtube.

This song is challenging in various ways. The changing feel of the song from latin to swing can present real difficulties. This song uses a predominance of minor chords with natural sevenths. The use of these chords is not that common in jazz compositions. The song progression includes chromatic II - V movement which again will provide a challenge to many who are not used to this kind of harmonic gymnastics.

I have incorporated some of the melodic and harmonic ideas as found in section one within this example without making the solo sound too contrived. This solo and the chords played will be a challenge for many of you, but with hard work you will ultimately find it worth the effort.

WHOSE DREAM IS THIS?

ACTUAL CHORDS PLAYED →

Bbmin9♮7   Bbmin♮7   Bbmin9♮7   Bbmin9♮7   Abmin9♮7   Abmin♮7

A

ORIGINAL CHORD CHART SYMBOLS → Bbmin♮7   Abmin♮7

POLYCHORD FORMULA →	$\dfrac{\text{V Maj}}{\text{I min}}$	$\dfrac{\text{V aug}}{\text{I min}}$	*Note: I've stated the polychord formula and result only once for each different iteration of the first two chords to prevent the pages becoming cluttered by repeating the same information.*	$\dfrac{\text{V Maj}}{\text{I min}}$	$\dfrac{\text{V aug}}{\text{I min}}$
RESULT OF FORMULA →	$\dfrac{\text{FMaj}}{\text{Bbmin}}$	$\dfrac{\text{F aug}}{\text{Bbmin}}$		$\dfrac{\text{EbMaj}}{\text{Abmin}}$	$\dfrac{\text{Ebaug}}{\text{Abmin}}$

Abmin9♮7   Abmin♮7   Bbmin♮7   Bbmin9♮7/Db

4

Bbmin♮7

Ebmin11   Ab13b9   Abmin9/11

7

Eb min7   A b7   Abmin7

$\dfrac{\text{bVII Maj}}{\text{I min}}$	$\dfrac{\text{VI Maj}}{\text{I7}}$	$\dfrac{\text{VII Maj}}{\text{I min}}$
$\dfrac{\text{Db Maj}}{\text{Ebmin7}}$	$\dfrac{\text{FMaj}}{\text{Ab7}}$	$\dfrac{\text{Gb Maj}}{\text{Abmin7}}$

Db9   Db7b9   Db7#5#9 (A/F)   GbMaj13   BMaj13   B6/9   BMaj13#11

10   Db7   GbMaj7   GbMaj7

$\dfrac{\text{V min}}{\text{I7}}$	$\dfrac{\text{bII}^{\text{O}}}{\text{I7}}$	$\dfrac{\text{bVI Maj}}{\text{I7*}}$	$\dfrac{\text{III7sus}}{\text{I Maj}}$		$\dfrac{\text{III7sus}}{\text{I Maj}}$	$\dfrac{\text{IIsus4}}{\text{I Maj}}$	$\dfrac{\text{II Maj}}{\text{I Maj}}$
$\dfrac{\text{Abmin}}{\text{Db7}}$	$\dfrac{\text{Ddim}}{\text{Db7}}$:	$\dfrac{\text{AMaj}}{\text{Db7*}}$	$\dfrac{\text{Bb7sus}}{\text{Gb Maj}}$		$\dfrac{\text{D\#7sus}}{\text{BMaj}}$	$\dfrac{\text{C\#sus4}}{\text{BMaj}}$	$\dfrac{\text{C\#Maj}}{\text{BMaj}}$

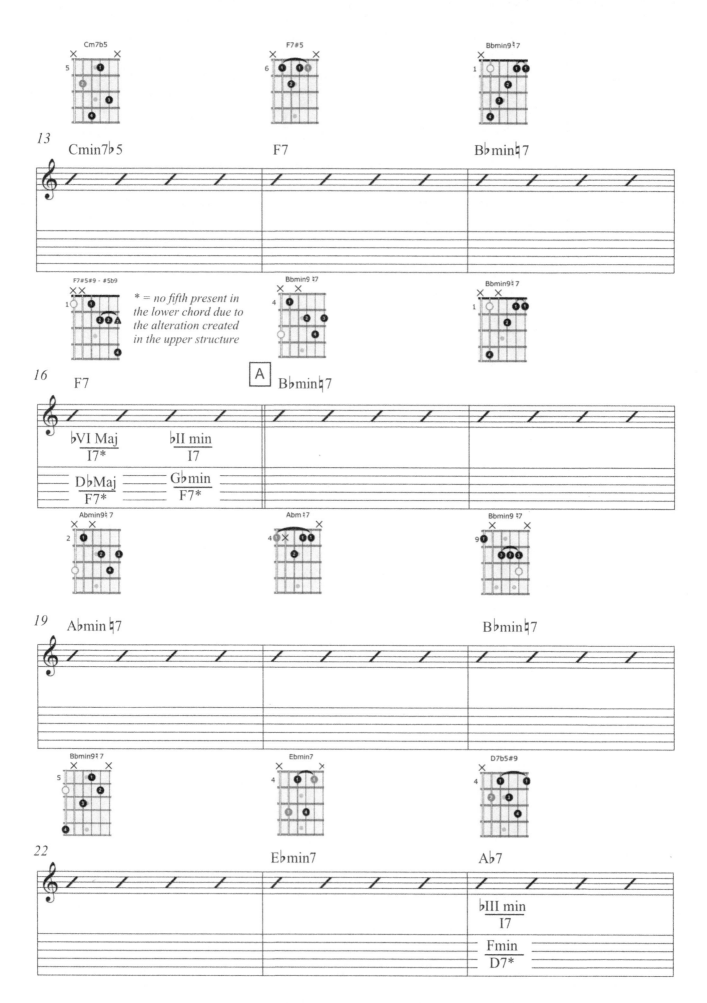

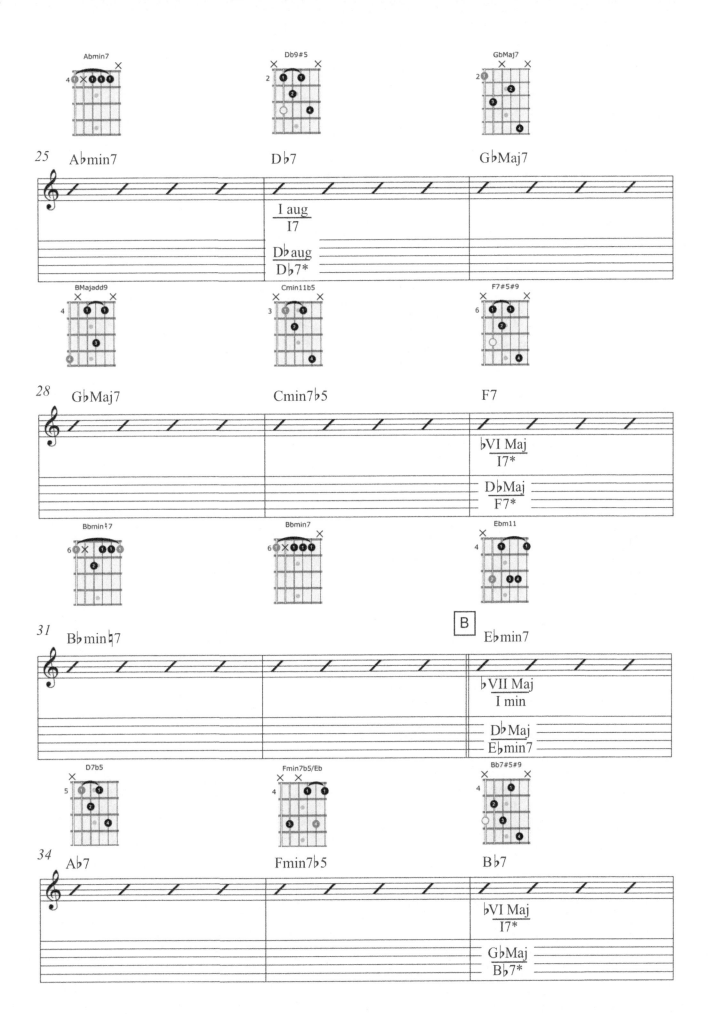

301

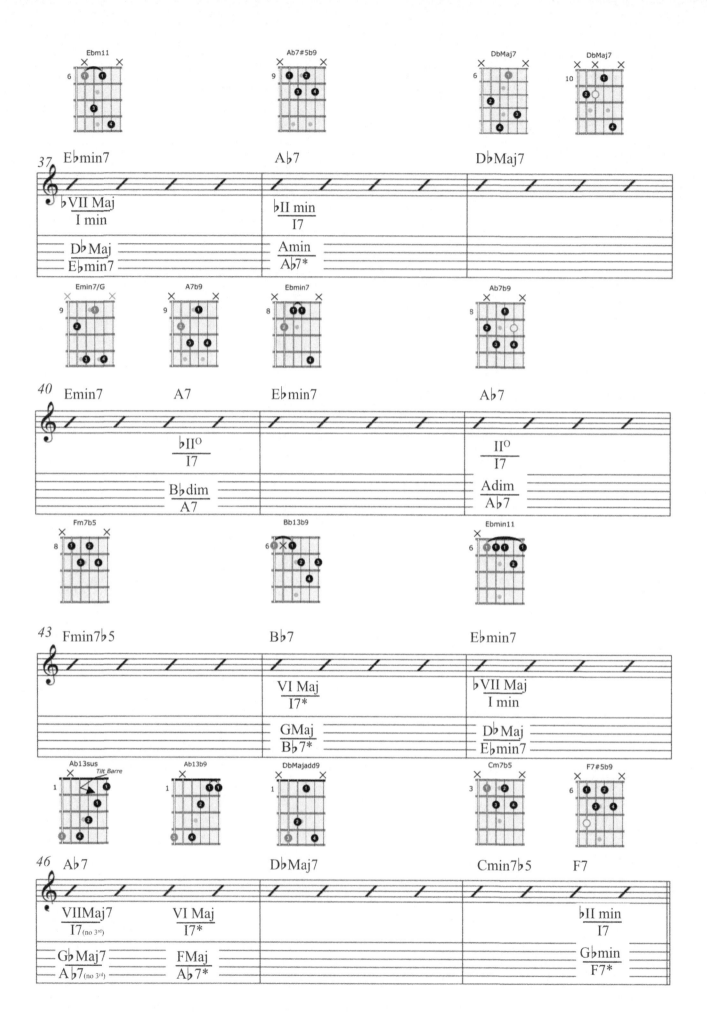

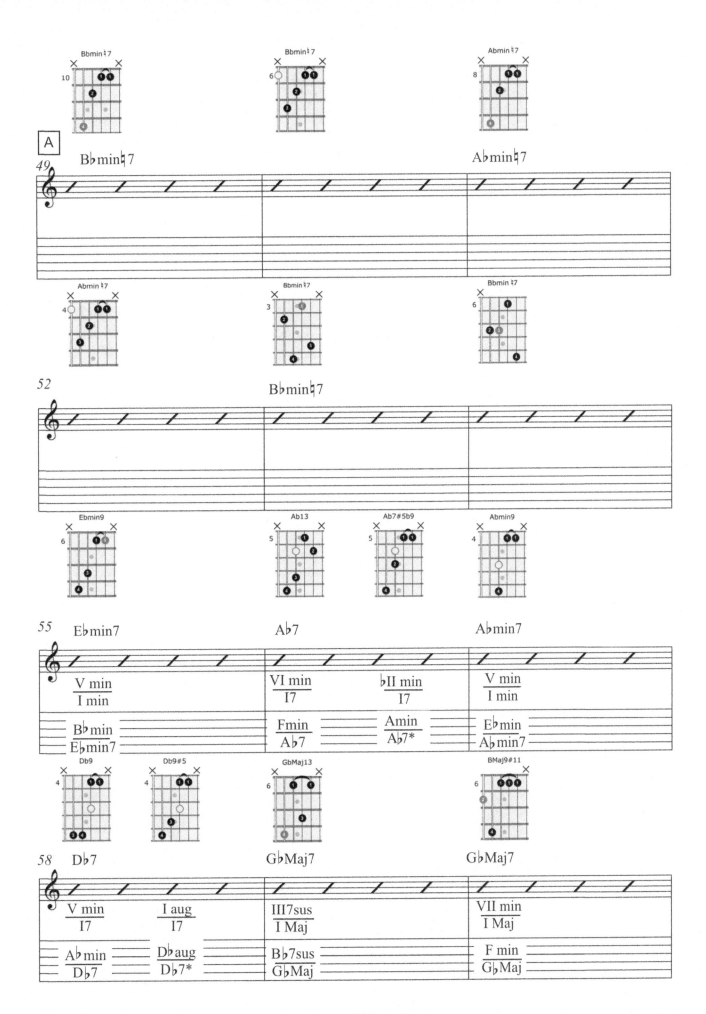

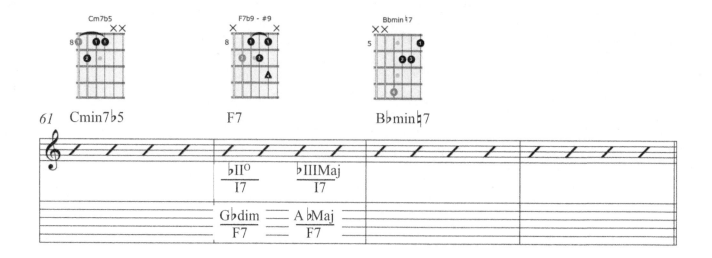

61   Cmin7♭5   F7   B♭min♮7

$$\frac{♭II^O}{I7} \qquad \frac{♭IIIMaj}{I7}$$

$$\frac{G♭dim}{F7} \qquad \frac{A♭Maj}{F7}$$

Song #3

"Whose Dream Is This?"

Notated Solo...

WHOSE DREAM IS THIS?

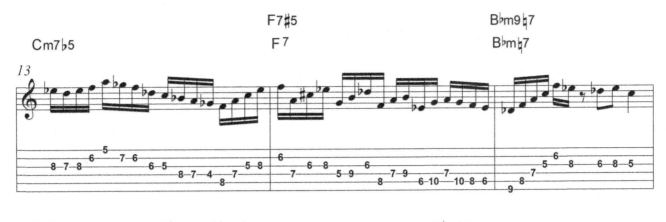

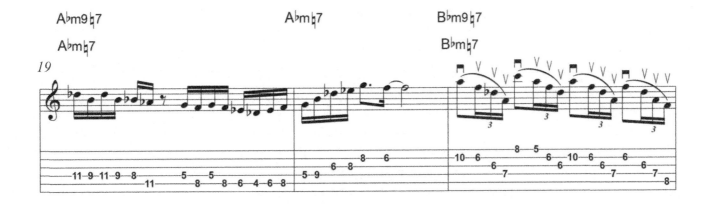

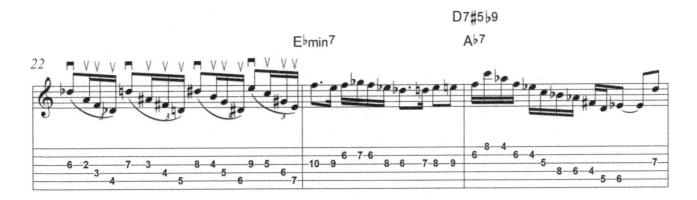

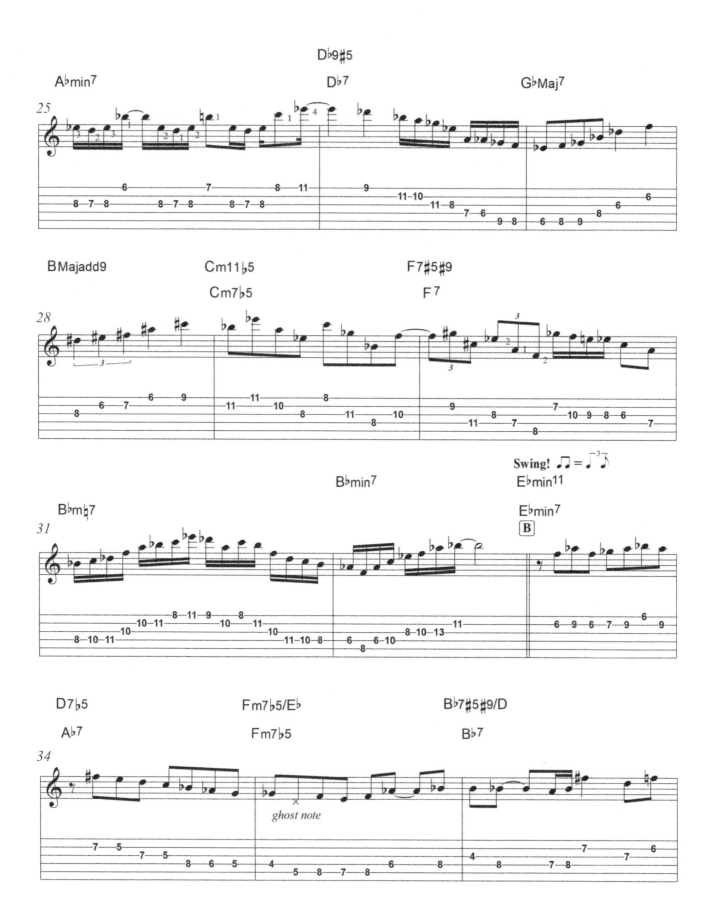

Latin Feel

Song #3

"Whose Dream Is This?"

Melodic Analysis of the solo…

"WHOSE DREAM IS THIS?" MELODIC ANALYSIS...

BARS 1 - 2: In these opening bars I play the same idea an octave apart, or at least I play the same idea twice then develop the initial concept on the repeat.

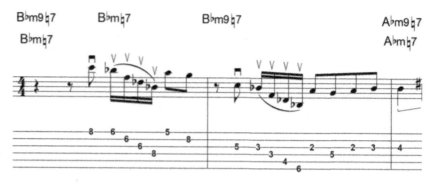

Often, players never repeat themselves and I mean ever! Learning to repeat yourself is a good habit to get into. It helps shape other ideas that may come to mind as well as help create a sense of continuity within a solo.

I have included picking instructions on the opening notes which will be of use to you. Although if you have a strong technique, using alternating down and up strokes on this repeated figure will certainly be an option. Surprisingly I don't actually play the natural seventh until after the main arpeggio figure. However, the ear does pick up that natural seventh in sharp relief with the eighth notes that follow the initial flurry of activity. Note that the initial arpeggio outlined and repeated is a B flat minor nine.

BAR 3: A couple of points about bar three. Firstly, the initial three notes played outline a B augmented triad which has the same notes as E flat augmented. This is outlined in the formulae for upper voicings (chord V augmented over I minor) which can be found in the appendix.

Secondly, take note of the slide from the upper B note to the D sharp which then slides back down to the B again. The use of a slide is of course completely voluntary. If you'd rather play the notes individually then that is fine.

BAR 4: This line idea, or something like it, may have come up before and I seem to use it quite a lot so don't be too surprised if you see this, or something like it appearing all over this solo. It's a good exercise to look at and consider what you play because it's easy to get into melodic habits as I obviously have!

In any case, this idea over a minor chord with a natural seventh is based around yet another augmented triad, G augmented. You may be wondering how many augmented triads actually work over these chords and it's a fair question. The answer is found in section one chapter four which deals with symmetrical harmony. Also take note of what I say about the subject of whole tone scales.

In the case of A flat minor with a natural seventh, E flat, G and B augmented chords will sound great over this chord form. You can experiment with the other augmented chords from the family of chords generated from the harmonised whole tone scale. For me, these are the best and strongest melodic options

This chord sound is another reason for practising augmented chords, augmented arpeggios and whole tone scales. If you are anything like me when I was studying these subjects, it all seemed very discordant and hard to hear and utilise. I hope you can see that there is a lot to be gained from memorising and making use of these musical tools in a variety of different ways.

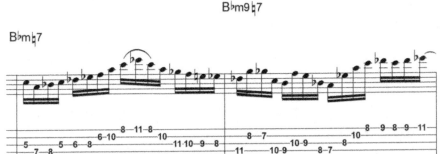

BARS 5 - 6: These are the first two bars of a four bar double time phrase.

If you find this difficult then I would urge you to build up the tempo of the line from an initial slower tempo, trying to ensure that there are no glitches heard.

The second bar of the phrase, which is bar six in the solo, is just an idea that I had to mix up the melodic content. I do this on occasion to create dissonance which can then be resolved. In this case, the dissonance is created by playing chromatically descending tri-tone pairs alternating as they descend, as you can see above. If this kind of melodic improvisation is of interest to you, my advice is don't worry too much about the notes that you play, think more about the dissonance you create. On most occasions when you resolve this dissonance, everything that came before will make sense. It's almost a musical conundrum that only works itself out in the listener's ear when everything is heard, perceived and resolved.

BARS 7 - 8: The second two bars of the line play over a II - V in the expected key of D flat major, however, this is not where the progression finally leads. The A flat thirteen flat nine chord is outlined by playing an F major arpeggio from the VIth degree of the A flat seventh chord.

As mentioned above, this whole line may prove challenging but taking things slowly and building your tempo up over time will make all the difference and increase your technical dexterity.

BAR 10: I have included bar ten to specifically highlight the rhythmic aspect of this section of the solo as opposed to the nature of the notes being played. Coming so close to the double time feel section, this rhythmic change helps to break up the movement of the melody from the frenetic nature of what has come before and is a bridge passage to what follows, which is less "cluttered" and more relaxed from a rhythmic perspective.

I have not explicitly outlined the last altered chord from a playing perspective. However, within this bar the flattened seventh, flattened ninth, sharpened ninth as well as the unaltered ninth early in the bar are all played.

From a technical perspective, there is some string skipping undertaken here which is in contrast to the linear scalar lines that came before so this may feel difficult to get your fingers round at first.

The point to take from this line from a melodic/harmonic perspective is that you do not need to play every single note that is outlined in a chord symbol either from an extension or alteration point of view.

BARS 13 - 14: Another example of a II - V - I phrase (or lick) idea which would be a good candidate for memorisation and development for your own use. The scale used in bar thirteen is B flat harmonic minor.

The fourth beat of this bar is an F minor seven arpeggio which leads into the F altered dominant as played and outlined by a whole tone scale lick. This is a bit of a finger twister.

The first two beats of bar fourteen could be used as the core material in learning this sound and how to technically play it all over the guitar neck.

This idea is a cliché which I am sure I probably first came across in the Jerry Cocker book "Patterns For Jazz". If you have never heard of this book I'd highly recommend it and it is still available for purchase.

BARS 15 - 17: The following circled bars are being used and linked to demonstrate how rhythm is just as important in the development of a solo as the notes you play.

The initial idea of four sixteenth notes which are outlining a B flat minor nine with a natural seventh is stated.

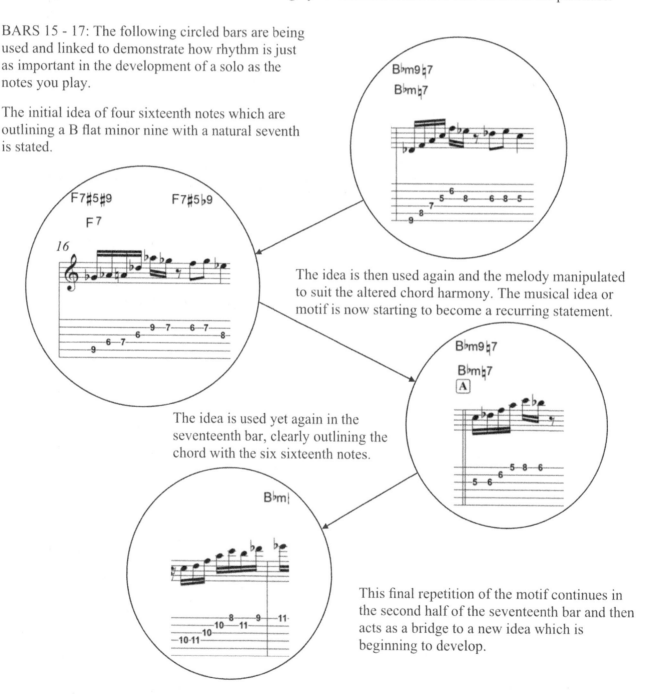

The idea is then used again and the melody manipulated to suit the altered chord harmony. The musical idea or motif is now starting to become a recurring statement.

The idea is used yet again in the seventeenth bar, clearly outlining the chord with the six sixteenth notes.

This final repetition of the motif continues in the second half of the seventeenth bar and then acts as a bridge to a new idea which is beginning to develop.

BARS 18 - 19: This rhythmic repetition is seen again in bars eighteen and nineteen, being used four times in two bars. The musical idea (or motif) used is once again six sixteenth notes and may have been inspired by the previous rhythmic idea shown on the last page. On this occasion, however, the idea has now been flattened out slightly and is less angular in its construction.

Everything that was stated on the last page regarding the use of motifs and rhythmic repetition applies to this example as well.

The initial statement is six sixteenth notes, the first two notes repeated and are a tone apart.

The total distance from the first and last notes in each motif to the next motif is a perfect fifth interval except in the last example where the the interval distance of the first notes changes to a diminished fifth.

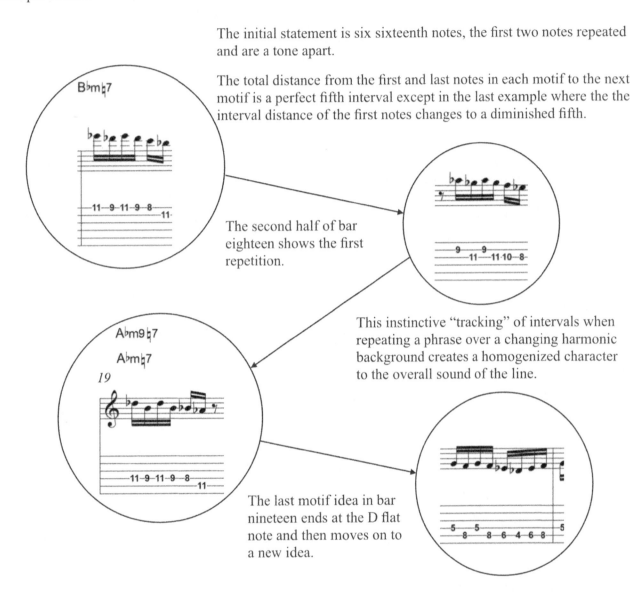

The second half of bar eighteen shows the first repetition.

This instinctive "tracking" of intervals when repeating a phrase over a changing harmonic background creates a homogenized character to the overall sound of the line.

The last motif idea in bar nineteen ends at the D flat note and then moves on to a new idea.

BARS 21 - 22: The final rhythmic idea that I want to discuss can be viewed and heard in bars twenty one and twenty two. This is a rhythmic idea and technique I use quite a lot and is shown below. Note the use of the pick! This will be quite difficult to play for some and it's the moving around the strings that is generally more challenging than the actual notes and rhythms being played. You do need to learn to keep your left hand in a set shape to execute this idea properly.

BAR 24: The chord that was played over the A flat dominant seven was the flat five substitute, D altered dominant. As per the formula that you will find for sharp five/flat nine chords, the arpeggio that is usually played over the tri-tone would be E flat minor.

In this case I played an F minor which is what I heard over the line. This would in most cases be better suited to another altered dominant; D flat five sharp nine.

This part of the solo is a good example of how the reflection of the altered tones as stipulated in the chord symbols is advisory only. It is up to you the performer to decide how you wish to play against the song's harmonic structures.

BARS 29 - 30: Bar twenty nine's commentary is about the oblique nature of what I played at this point. As was discussed in bar fourteen, here is another way of creating dissonant sound, or if not dissonant, then at least sonically uncomfortable. On this occasion, I played an angular line full of wide intervals which creates the discomfort and then paradoxically resolved to a more relaxed sound in the next bar, due to the harmony and melody. I say paradoxically because the chord and the notes played are very dissonant in their own right.

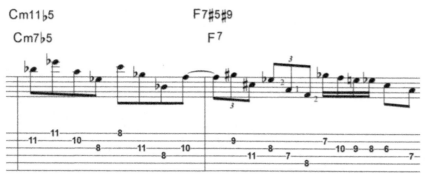

The sharp five/sharp nine chord has the respective tones highlighted in the first triplet of bar thirty within the fundamentals of the chord structure, the flattened seventh and third are played in the second triplet.

By the fourth beat I play a flat nine and you'll see an E natural! It is of course fine to play a natural seventh over a dominant seventh chord as long as it is resolved. This is possibly the best way to use the natural seventh; as a descending line from the tonic moving downwards towards the flattened seventh tone.

BAR 32: In bar thirty two I played on F minor seven arpeggio over the B flat minor seven chord. This would mean that I am playing a minor seven on the fifth of the notated chord which results in a minor eleventh sound being heard.

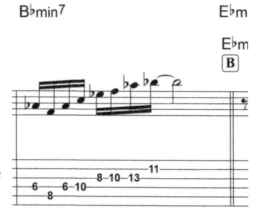

F minor seven consists of F, A flat, C and E flat. The F in relation to B flat minor is the fifth degree. The A flat is the flattened seventh, the C is the ninth and the E flat is the eleventh degree as stated, in relation to B flat minor seven.

From a practical point of view, if you enjoy this sound which, as always, is created through the layering of one arpeggio over another, then practise this relationship of a minor seven based on the fifth of a target minor seven all over the guitar neck. Use as many different shapes and positions as you can and as you practise you will find the playing of these ideas will become instinctive.

D7♭5

A♭7

34

BAR 34: This bar of music does not include any upper voicing related material but I have added it to display the use of a whole tone scale in action.

As you can see, the whole tone scale, due to its construction, would be applicable over A flat seven as well as the performed D dominant seven altered chord which was substituted in its place.

Remember that the whole tone scale can be named after any of the notes that are within it and that there are only two actual whole tone scales available to choose from at any one time.

BAR 38: The altered dominant is predominantly outlined by playing a diminished arpeggio that is one semi-tone higher than the root of the dominant chord. This can be viewed on beat two of the bar providing a flattened seven, flattened ninth, third and fifth of the A flat dominant seven chord.

Other altered tones that are found within the bar are flat five (the D note that the idea begins with) and a flat nine (A natural) found at the end of the phrase although only in passing and as an ornamentation. The A note being part of the played diminished seventh.

A♭7♯5♭9

A♭7

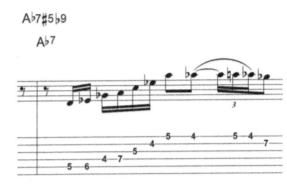

BAR 39: In beat three you can see an A flat major triad. This is the "V" chord of the D flat major chord. As such, playing a major triad based on the fifth of a major chord automatically provides the player with the fifth, natural seventh and ninth tones of the respective "I" chord.

Also, you will see a common substitution idea being used in the first beat and a half of this bar of music where the III chord (F minor) arpeggio is played over the I chord. This is probably not that interesting from a theoretical perspective because it will come naturally for most to play this kind of idea. However, this is worth considering and remembering.

D♭Maj7

BAR 44: The "B" or bridge section of this solo turned out to be more scalar than arpeggio based and here is another example of scale superimposition taking place over an altered chord form.

The underlying scale is an E flat harmonic minor scale and its modal centre is the B flat note which is the fifth. So, the name for an E flat harmonic minor scale starting from the fifth degree is a Phrygian dominant scale.

You can hopefully see that by playing this mode you automatically generate the flattened ninth, the flattened sixth, the flattened seventh and natural third of a B flat dominant seven chord.

B♭13♭9

B♭7

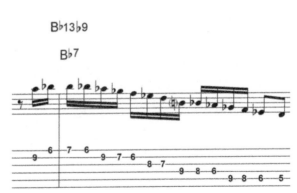

BAR 45: Here is a novel approach; the arpeggio being played actually outlines the initial notated chord, E flat minor seven. The very last note in the bar, however, is the ninth of this chord.

When improvising, play what you hear, not what you think you should play. When we think more about the names, theory and formulae than the music, then we are beginning to walk a sterile musical path.

You can practise perfecting certain techniques, concepts and ideas away from a performance scenario, however, be ready to try and leave this all behind when you are actually on the stand performing or actually playing songs with friends.

D♭Majadd9

D♭Maj7

BAR 47: Back in bar four I discussed using a specific idea over and over and here again is that idea, this time used over D flat major seven.

I think that this is quite an interesting use of the arpeggio as it is a B flat minor nine with a natural seventh played over its relative major. What this means is that the sound of a D flat major seven with a flat five is heard against the chord. Held within the B flat minor nine/natural seven arpeggio is a D flat augmented chord which is where the reference to bar four comes in.

The interchangeability of relative major and minor chords will become increasingly apparent the more you work with extended voicings. In essence, this means that you can utilise a range of known chords and arpeggios in at least two musical scenarios and often in many more.

BARS 49 - 52: The next four bars are not so much about notes as rhythm. You will hear that I am playing against the underlying meter of the piece and it has another unsettling effect on the musical line.

Many of you will be able to play this no trouble at all, but I have a feeling that some may find this line a little harder to play than thought at first glance.

The arpeggios are faithfully outlined as per their chord symbols during the course of this four bar sequence.

A♭13   A♭7♯5♭9

A♭7

BAR 56: Finally an example of upper voicings at work! The A flat dominant seven with a sharp five/flat nine is outlined by playing a minor arpeggio that is a semi-tone higher than the root. This means that A minor is being played and when you play this, you will see that visually it is now obvious.

320

BAR 60: The final bar to be considered in this solo consists of an arpeggio that does not fully describe the chord symbol it is being played over but seems to work nonetheless.

The B major chord symbol is extended and altered but I heard and played a straight major seven arpeggio. There is no sharp eleven present (which would have meant playing an F natural note).

The line does, however, include an interesting technical idea which is often referred to as movable forms.

The shape that is used to play the initial four notes is repeated again and again across the neck. This concept creates a lot of horizontal movement on the guitar neck and is a good way of moving into other areas and not constantly playing in one position all the time.

There are many shapes that make use of this useful technique but this book is long enough and I hope that it provides you with enough ideas to go on and find out your own moveable arpeggio forms.

Song #3

"Whose Dream Is This?"

Harmonic Analysis of the solo…

WHOSE DREAM IS THIS? HARMONIC ANALYSIS...

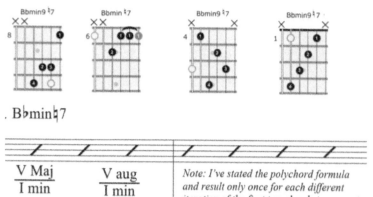

. Bbmin♮7

V Maj	V aug	
I min	I min	

Note: I've stated the polychord formula and result only once for each different iteration of the first two chords to prevent the pages from becoming cluttered by repeating the same information.

FMaj	F aug	
Bb min	Bb min	

BARS 1 - 6: This song sequence starts with two bars of a minor chord with a natural seventh. In most playing scenarios I probably would not play as many chord forms as shown here. For this book, however, I thought that it would be a good way of highlighting a range of potential chords that could be used individually over these bars.

As you can see, if you want to add the ninth to the basic chord add a major triad on the fifth of the minor. If you want a plain minor chord with a natural seventh you can think of the chord as having an augmented chord rising from the fifth of the original I minor.

The last paragraph again demonstrates the strength of thinking about melody/harmony in upper structures forms. Many guitarists would struggle to play a minor ninth with a natural seventh, but you can see that if you have a major triad, put a note based on that major chord's flattened sixth, you create a minor nine with a natural seventh. The flattened sixth as the root note of the new chord. These chord types are used right through until the beginning of bar seven. See the appendix C for written examples.

BAR 7: Again, in this example I use what most people would consider a G flat major nine chord form to represent an E flat minor eleventh chord. As already mentioned, if you are using these forms make sure that either you have a bass player to pin down the harmony or ensure that the chords used make sense in the musical context.

In this example, I play a difficult "A" flat altered dominant chord but it helps justify the previous minor eleventh chord when played together.

Another crucial part of bonding this relationship between chords is the voice leading used which, even from a physical and visual sense, is reasonably obvious in this particular example.

Eb min7   Ab7

bVII Maj	VI Maj
I min	I7

Db Maj	FMaj
Eb min7	Ab7

BAR 9: You will have probably worked out by now that this chord form is one of my favourites. I often play it for the relative minor of its respective major.

In this example, I am playing a B major nine chord but considering it as a G sharp minor form. Due to the prevailing harmony of the piece, I've re-spelt the chord as its enharmonic equivalent, A flat minor 9/11.

Ab min7

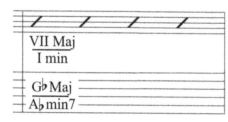

VII Maj	
I min	

Gb Maj	
Ab min7	

BARS 10 - 12: These bars follow on from the previous example detailing the A flat minor chord. What this means is that, with the previous bar included, you have a II - V - I progression in G flat major.

Now, what I heard and substituted in at bar twelve was chord IV in the key of G flat which would be C flat (to keep things simple I have spelt the chord B major). Some people may not wish to do this and feel that what I have done is musically inappropriate and that's fine. I have included chord IV ideas for you to consider.

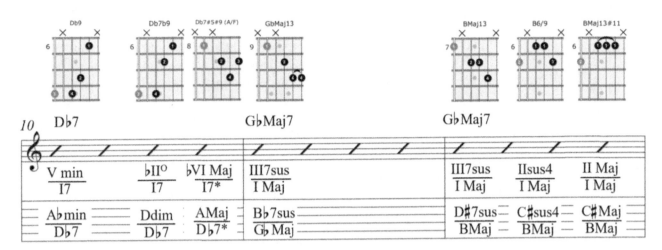

Just to be clear, I included the "B" root note in the backing tracks which helps underpin the harmonic flow.

The D flat seven chord sees both extensions and alterations added as we move to the I chord which is G flat major. Once again, I used both my ear and voice leading considerations when coming to a decision regarding the type of chord voicing to use.

BAR 16: Here is another example of two altered chord types that will more often than not work together really well. As you can see, the chords played move from F dominant seven with a sharp five/sharp nine to F dominant seven with a sharp five flat nine. I often use this chordal pairing as it works in many different musical scenarios such as intros/ending and as a way of creating movement when "comping".

When playing over these chords you can obviously use the arpeggios and ideas presented in this book. Another option open to you is to play a scalar run. If this was the case, F sharp melodic minor would be a great choice as it is a heavily altered dominant acting as a V chord. By starting this scale on the melodic minor's seventh degree (F), you would in effect be playing an F Super Locrian scale.

This way of superimposing scales and then applying them modally is very effective. The notes found in F sharp melodic minor as related to an altered F dominant seventh chord would automatically generate the following tones from F: root, flat nine, sharp nine, third, flat five, sharp five and flattened seventh.

By knowing how chords and scales work together, a lot of the hard work can be taken out of the process (as hopefully shown above) in figuring out what is the best way to play and inject increased dissonance over chord progressions.

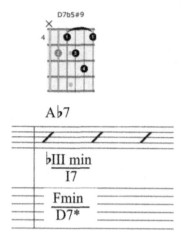

Ab7

bIII min / I7

Fmin / D7*

BAR 24: Here you can see that I have used flat five substitution with chromaticism of the harmonic progression in mind. This chord leads onto a D flat major and was arrived at from E flat minor giving an E flat, D seven and D flat major progression and a descending chromatic bass line.

If you study the actual shape of the flat five/sharp nine chord, you can see other shapes within it. For example, if the A flat *was* played on string six the resulting chord with exactly the same shape would be A flat thirteen flat five.

You can also see a D minor seven chord with the notes of the fifth, third and second strings only. A D seven sharp nine is of course also within the shape. Once you become aware that chords with long and difficult sounding names can be built from other triads and chords, suddenly you'll start physically seeing many other chord shapes within these chords.

BAR 34 - 36: I've highlighted these bars as I wanted to draw attention to the use of the minor seven flat five chord which has the flattened seventh in the bass. This chord in conjunction with the next chord in the progression almost gives a classical feel to the harmony.

The last chord, which is being thought of as a dominant seventh with a sharp five/sharp nine, is one of the chords that you will by now recognise as being used in a multitude of ways. This would include it also being potentially used as a dominant ninth, a minor seven flat five and a minor sixth chord as well. Therefore the minor seven flat five chord shown in bar thirty five above could also be thought of as

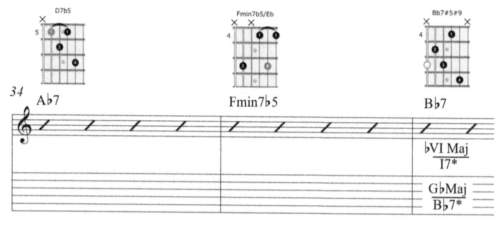

34 Ab7   **Fmin7b5**   **Bb7**

bVI Maj / I7*

GbMaj / Bb7*

potentially three other chord classifications, depending on the harmonic context.

You will find an easy to follow chart regarding these types of chords in the appendix.

BAR 46: This harmonic analysis is shorter than previous solos as I am trying to pick out specifics that have not already been covered and this is one of them.

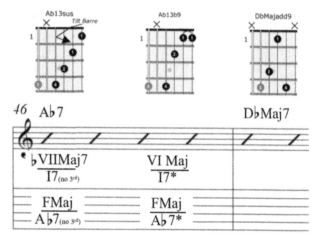

46 Ab7   **DbMaj7**

bVIIMaj7 / I7(no 3rd)

VI Maj / I7*

FMaj / Ab7(no 3rd)

FMaj / Ab7*

The A flat thirteen sus chord could be thought of in many ways, but the easiest would be to think of it as a G flat major seventh chord with an A flat root note in the bass. This chord could have made it into the main part of the book but I don't think it's that common a chord. When I use it, I more often than not use it in conjunction with the altered chord that follows it.

The tilt bar with the first finger is really tricky and will take some time to get used to and execute properly.

BAR 48: This is another good example of the same chord shape being used but for completely different chord types. The more of these physical chord and line ideas you get into your hearing and under your fingers the better.

With this chord shape for example, you will quickly understand the spatial distance that a minor third represents on the fretboard and that this space equals a minor II - V progression.

What will take more time is the memorisation of the upper voicings and how they relate to the underlying chord. To recap and make completely clear, the asterisk beside the F dominant seven means that there is no fifth in the lower chord due to the fact that it is an altered tone with regards the flat II chord above it.

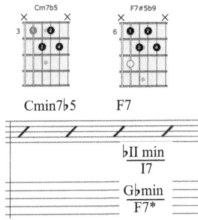

BAR 55 - 56: Here is another example of major chords being utilised as their relative minor cousins and leading to extended then altered chords.

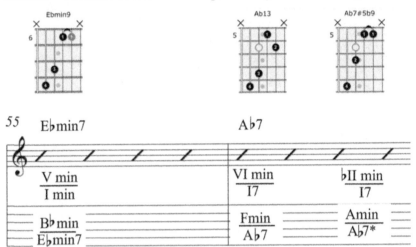

Something that I perhaps need to mention is that a lot, if not most of these types of movements between chord types occur on the inner four strings; string set 2 through 5. The reason for this is that in terms of the timbre of the instrument, I find this string set the warmest. I could and do use string sets 1 through four, however, it sometimes can have an edge to it sonically that I don't want.

If I was to play these ideas on the lower four strings then, although not impossible, a few problems can arise. The first of these is lower bass note limits where the sound becomes very muddy and indistinct. The other problem is often a physical one where it becomes increasingly difficult to play these wide stretch chords.

BARS 57 - 58: Finally, the chords found in bars fifty seven and fifty eight draw from the musical concept of clusters. These chords are not clusters in the truest sense of the word as that would mean that there would be three adjacent notes. In this case there is only two. Other than utilising open strings, which is by the way a distinct possibility, most of the time we create cluster sounds through having a major second or minor second with one other note, usually a major third away, added.

The sound that these close voicings give is quite magical and one that I would urge to you experiment with and introduce to your playing, if you do not already play them.

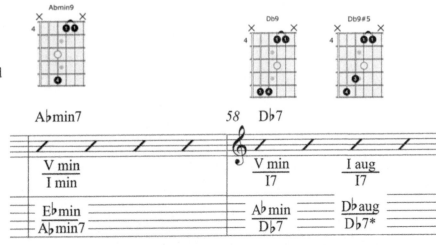

327

Song #3

"Whose Dream Is This?"

The Chords Used In Large Format...

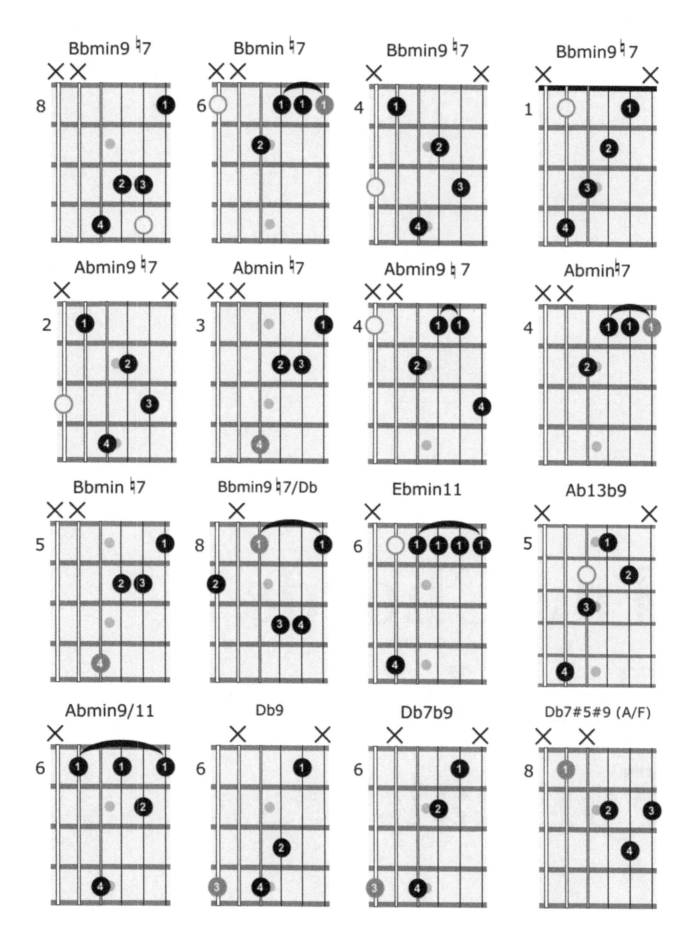

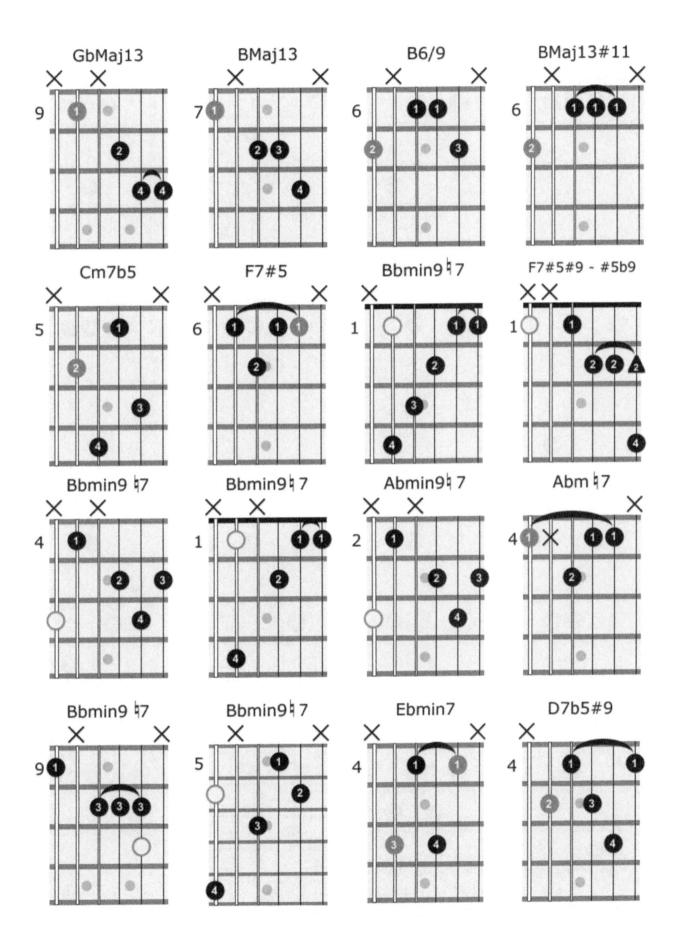

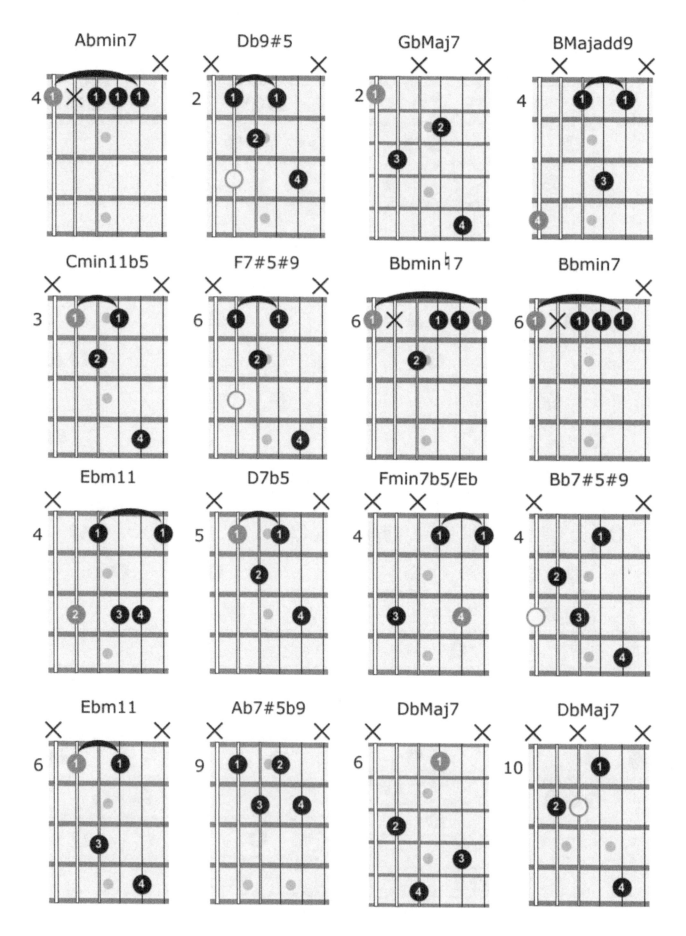

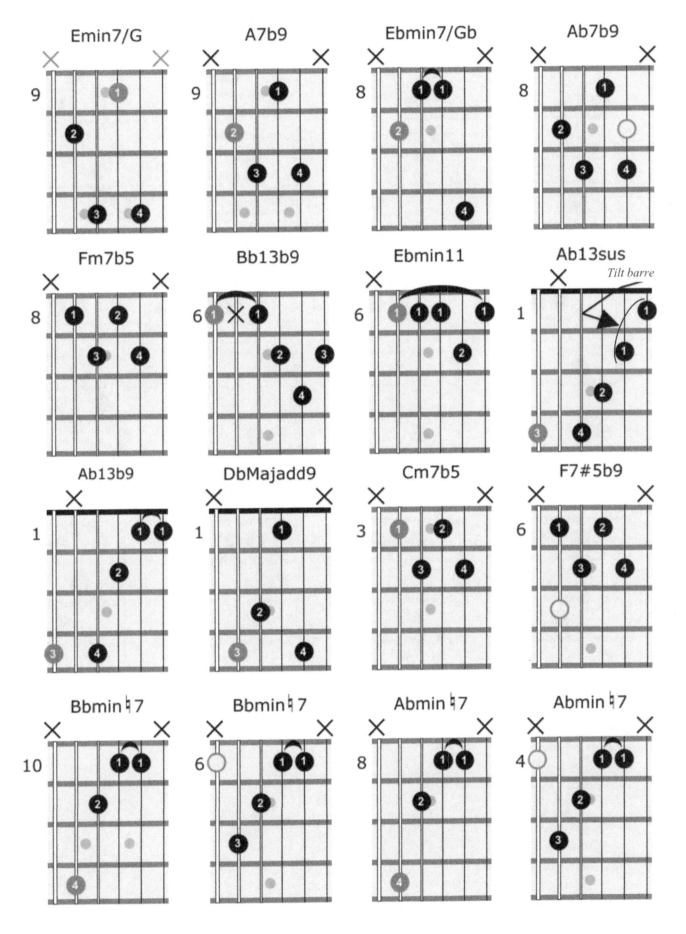

WHOSE DREAM IS THIS? #5

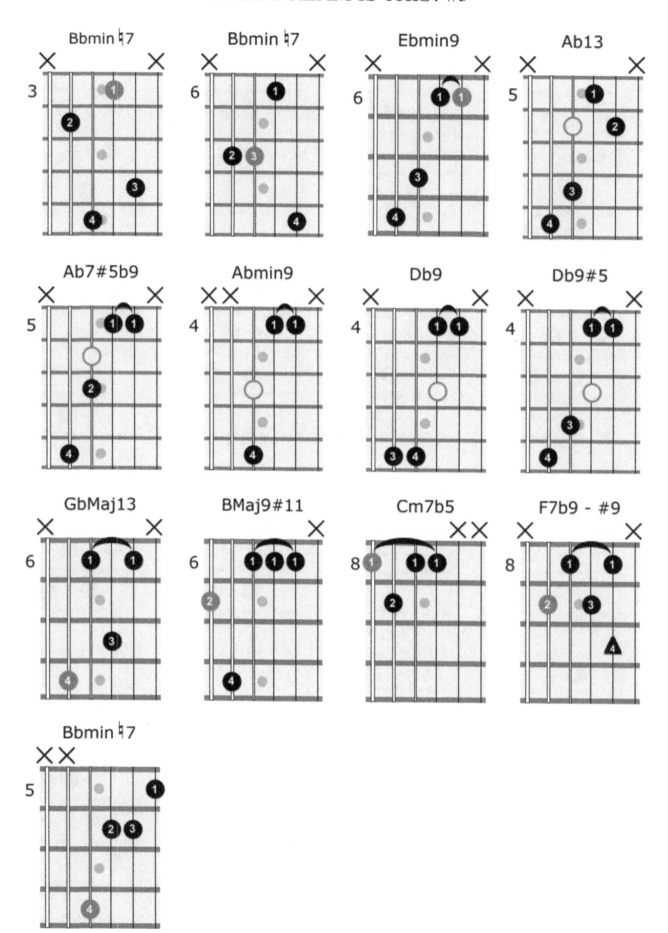

APPENDICES

MAJOR CHORDS

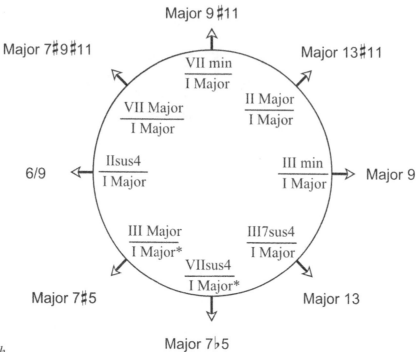

*NOTE: * = no fifth present in the lower chord due to the alteration taking place in the upper structure voicing.*

MINOR CHORDS

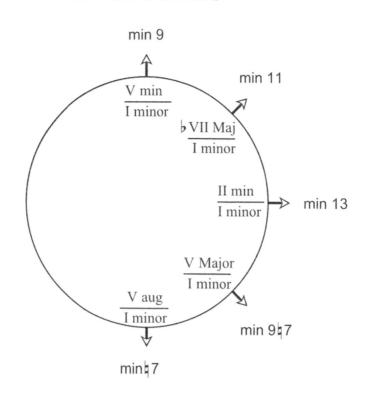

DOMINANT SEVEN CHORDS

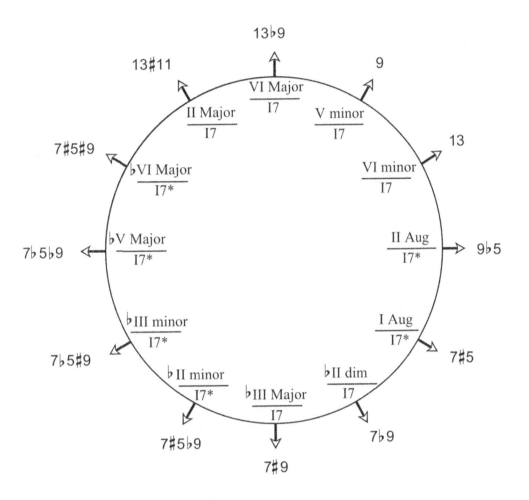

*NOTE: * = no fifth present in the lower chord due to the alteration taking place in the upper structure voicing.*

APPENDIX B - LIST OF POLYCHORDS

Here is a list of chord symbols and the polychords I use to either play the complete sound or infer the sound by utilising slash voicings. This is by no means complete and a quick search will allow you to find others, however, these are the formulae that I have used over the years to get the sounds into my head and playing.

MAJOR SOUNDS   **FORMULA**   **SLASH VOICING*****   **POLYCHORD**

C Major 9$\sharp$11 = B minor over C Major = $\dfrac{\text{VII min}}{\text{I Major}}$ = $\dfrac{Bm}{C}$ = $\dfrac{Bmin}{CMaj}$

C Major 13$\sharp$11 = D Major over C Major = $\dfrac{\text{II Major}}{\text{I Major}}$ = $\dfrac{DMaj}{C}$ = $\dfrac{DMaj}{CMaj}$

C Major 9 = E minor 7 over C Major = $\dfrac{\text{III min}}{\text{I Major}}$ = $\dfrac{Emin7}{C}$ = $\dfrac{Emin}{CMaj}$

C Major 13 = E7sus4 over C Major = $\dfrac{\text{III7sus4}}{\text{I Major}}$ = $\dfrac{E7sus4}{C}$ = $\dfrac{E7sus4}{CMaj}$

C Major 7$\flat$5 = Bsus4 over C Major* = $\dfrac{\text{VIIsus4}}{\text{I Major*}}$ = $\dfrac{Bsus4}{C}$ = $\dfrac{Bsus4}{CMaj\text{*}}$

       * No 5th

C Major 7$\sharp$5 = E Major over C Major* = $\dfrac{\text{III Major}}{\text{I Major*}}$ = $\dfrac{EMaj}{C}$ = $\dfrac{EMaj}{CMaj\text{*}}$

       * No 5th

C6/9 = Dsus4 over C Major = $\dfrac{\text{IIsus4}}{\text{I Major}}$ = $\dfrac{Dsus4}{C}$ = $\dfrac{Dsus4}{CMaj}$

C Major 7$\sharp$9$\sharp$11 = B Major over C Major = $\dfrac{\text{VII Major}}{\text{I Major}}$ = $\dfrac{BMaj}{C}$ = $\dfrac{BMaj}{CMaj}\text{*}$

MINOR SOUNDS   **FORMULA**   **SLASH VOICING*****   **POLYCHORD**

Amin9 = E minor over A minor = $\dfrac{\text{V min}}{\text{I minor}}$ = $\dfrac{CMaj7}{A}$ = $\dfrac{Emin}{Amin}$

Amin11 = G Major over A minor = $\dfrac{\flat\text{VII Maj}}{\text{I minor}}$ = $\dfrac{Gsus4}{A}$ = $\dfrac{GMaj}{Amin}$

Amin13 = B minor over A minor = $\dfrac{\text{II min}}{\text{I minor}}$ = $\times$ = $\dfrac{Bmin}{Amin}$

***   *Often infers the sound of the original chord but with tones missed out*

MINOR SYMBOL	FORMULA	SLASH VOICING	POLYCHORD
A minor 9♮7 = E Major over A minor =	$\dfrac{\text{V Major}}{\text{I minor}}$ =	$\text{Cmaj7\#5} / \text{A}$ =	$\dfrac{\text{EMaj}}{\text{Amin}}$
A minor ♮7 = E augmented over A minor =	$\dfrac{\text{V aug}}{\text{I minor}}$ =	$\text{E+} / \text{A}$ =	$\dfrac{\text{E aug}}{\text{A min}}$

DOMINANT SYMBOLS

	FORMULA	SLASH VOICING	POLYCHORD
C9 = G minor over C7 =	$\dfrac{\text{V minor}}{\text{I7}}$ =	$\text{Em7♭5} / \text{C}$ =	$\dfrac{\text{Gmin}}{\text{C7}}$
C13 = A minor over C7^ =	$\dfrac{\text{VI minor}}{\text{I7}}$ =	$\text{Em11♭5} / \text{C}$ =	$\dfrac{\text{Amin}}{\text{C7}}$
C9♭5 = D aug over C7** *No 5th =	$\dfrac{\text{II Aug}}{\text{I7}}$ =	$\text{D+} / \text{C}$ =	$\dfrac{\text{DAug}}{\text{C7}}$
C7#5 = C aug over C7 *No 5th =	$\dfrac{\text{I Aug}}{\text{I7}}$ =	$\text{C+} / \text{C}$ *** =	$\dfrac{\text{C+}}{\text{C7}}$
C7♭9 = D♭dim over C7 =	$\dfrac{\text{♭II dim}}{\text{I7}}$ =	$\text{D♭dim} / \text{C}$ =	$\dfrac{\text{D♭°}}{\text{C7}}$
C7♯9 = E♭Major over C7 =	$\dfrac{\text{♭III Major}}{\text{I7}}$ =	$\text{E♭Maj*** } / \text{C}$ =	$\dfrac{\text{E♭Maj}}{\text{C7}}$
C7♭5♯9 = E♭minor over C7 *No 5th =	$\dfrac{\text{♭III minor}}{\text{I7}}$ =	$\text{E♭min} / \text{C}$ =	$\dfrac{\text{E♭min}}{\text{C7}}$
C7♯5♭9 = D♭minor over C7 *No 5th =	$\dfrac{\text{♭II minor}}{\text{I7}}$ =	$\text{D♭ min} / \text{C}$ =	$\dfrac{\text{D♭min}}{\text{C7}}$
C7♭5♭9 = G♭Major over C7 *No 5th =	$\dfrac{\text{♭V Major}}{\text{I7}}$ =	$\text{G♭Maj} / \text{C}$ =	$\dfrac{\text{G♭Maj}}{\text{C7}}$
C7♯5♯9 = A♭Major over C7 *No 5th =	$\dfrac{\text{♭VI Major}}{\text{I7}}$ =	$\text{A♭Maj} / \text{C}$ =	$\dfrac{\text{A♭Maj}}{\text{C7}}$
C13♯11 = D Major over C7 =	$\dfrac{\text{II Major}}{\text{I7}}$ =	$\text{D Maj} / \text{C}$ =	$\dfrac{\text{DMaj}}{\text{C7}}$
C13♭9 = A Major over C7 =	$\dfrac{\text{VI Major}}{\text{I7}}$ =	$\text{A Maj} / \text{C}$ =	$\dfrac{\text{AMaj}}{\text{C7}}$

^ I've named this a 13th but it's perhaps stretching the point more than a little. The chord has the 6th added which reminds me of the master guitarist Ted Greene's 6/7 voicing symbol that he would sometimes use when no 9th tone was present.

*** As outlined in chapter four of section one, the actual chord created by playing a D augmented over a C7 chord is C9 with a flattened fifth. As we don't have a direct 7 flat five option this is a good alternative and can be used for 9♭5 chords as is.*

* This slash voicing produces a poor imitation of the original chord and polychord equivalent due to the lack of crucial tones not found in the upper chord and remember **the lower symbol is just a single note**.*

NOTES:

1. *The core identifier of a harmonic structure (chord) is primarily based around the 3rd and 7th tones and this, in most cases, establishes what works within a given musical progression.*

2. *Arrow heads shown in some cases below signify that a major/minor relationship is valid between chords.*

1.   **MAJOR SEVEN ⟨┄┄┄┄⟩ MINOR NINTH**

                                   EXAMPLE: Cmaj7 - Amin9

                              C - E - G - B = (A) - C - E - G - B

2.   **MAJOR SIXTH ⟨┄┄┄┄⟩ MINOR SEVENTH**

                                   EXAMPLE: Cmaj6 - Amin7

                                 C - E - G - A = A - C - E - G

3.   **MAJOR NINTH ┄┄┄┄┄┄ MINOR SEVENTH**

                                   EXAMPLE: Cmaj9 - Emin7

                                 (C) - E - G - B - D = E - G - B - D

4.   **MAJOR SEVEN SHARP FIVE ⟨┄┄┄┄⟩ MINOR NINE NATURAL SEVEN**

                                   EXAMPLE: Cmaj7♯5 - Amin9♮7

                                 C - E - G♯ - B = (A) - C - E - G♯ - B

5.   **DIMINISHED SEVENTH** ┈┈┈┈┈┈┈┈ **DOMINANT SEVENTH FLAT NINE**

EXAMPLE: C^{o7} - $B7\flat9$

$C - E\flat - G\flat - A = B - D\sharp - F\sharp - A - C$

*Dominant seventh flat nine chords can
substitute for diminished seventh chord
one step lower and vice versa.*

6.

MINOR SIXTH   **DOMINANT SEVENTH
SHARP FIVE FLAT NINE**

MINOR SEVEN FLAT FIVE   **DOMINANT NINTH**

EXAMPLE: $C9 = Em7\flat5 = Gmin6 = G\flat7\sharp5\flat9$

*Think of a major triad where X is a variable for the
first three and the altered dominant is the flat five of
the first chord shown. For example:*

X (9th) = X (m7$\flat$5) = X min6th = flat five of first chord

C - E - G and G$\flat$ is the flat V of the C

APPENDIX D - SYNONYM SELECTION OF EXTENDED/ALTERED DOMINANT GUITAR CHORDS & THEIR DOMINANT FLAT FIVE SUBSTITUTE EQUIVALENTS

DOMINANT NINTH ----------- SEVEN SHARP FIVE FLAT NINE

EXAMPLE: D9 = A♭7♯5♭9

D - F♯- C - E - A = A♭- G♭- C - E - A

DOMINANT THIRTEENTH ----------- SEVEN SHARP FIVE SHARP NINE

EXAMPLE: D13 = A♭7♯5♯9

D - F♯- C - E - B = A♭- G♭- C - E - B

DOMINANT NINE SHARP ELEVEN----------- SEVEN FLAT FIVE SHARP FIVE

EXAMPLE: D9♯11 = A♭7♭5♯5

D - F♯- C - E - G♯= A♭- D - G♭ - C - E - A♭

DOMINANT SEVEN FLAT FIVE FLAT NINE ------ DOMINANT SEVEN FLAT FIVE

EXAMPLE: D7♭5♭9 = A♭7♭5

D - F♯ - C - E♭- A♭= A♭- D - G♭ - C - E♭- A♭

DOMINANT THIRTEEN FLAT FIVE ---------- DOMINANT SEVEN FLAT FIVE SHARP NINE

EXAMPLE: D13♭5 = A♭7♭5♯9

D - A♭- C - F♯- B - D = A♭- C - G♭ - B - D

The two diagrams below show all the notes that are needed to play A7 and D7 altered dominant chords. There are many other options and inversions, as this book has shown, available, but this is a good starting point.

In both diagrams, the important initial structure is comprised of the root and tritone interval. Once this initial form is fingered, all other altered tones are then added as desired.

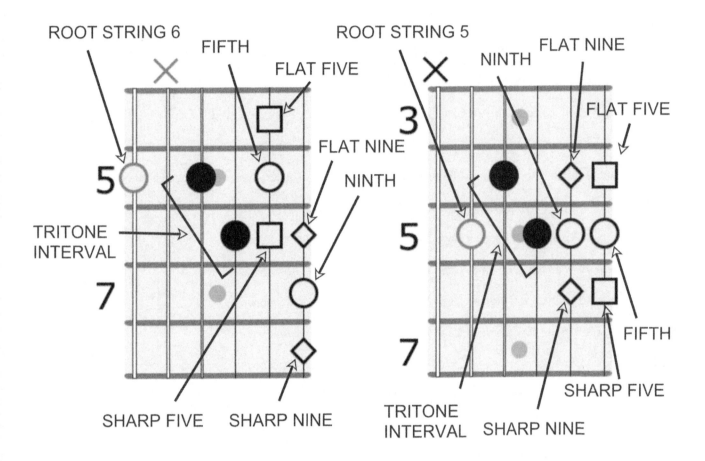

In both diagrams you can see the "fifth" and "ninth" tones clearly labelled. The shapes surrounding these tones (square for the fifth and diamond for the ninth) represent the flattened fifth/ninth and sharpened fifth/ninth.

Any combination of tones can be added to the basic root + tritone interval shape to create an altered dominant. It will not always be possible to play all the the tones you desire together. If you study many of the altered chord forms found in this book, you will see that the templates above are used in many forms.

SECTION ONE

CODE	MP3 FILE NAME	TEMPO	NOTES
S1EX1	Page 14 Chord Progression Example	100	Example of chord being played in progression
S1EX2	Page 34 Both triads up Case 1 Example a	100	C & D major triads combined over major
S1EX3	Page 34 Both triads up Case 1 Example b	100	As above
S1EX4	Page 35 Triads up then down Case 2 Example a	100	As above
S1EX5	Page 35 Triads up then down Case 2 Example b	100	As above
S1EX6	Page 35 Triads down then up Case 3 Example a	100	As above
S1EX7	Page 35 Triads down then up Case 3 Example b	100	As above
S1EX8	Page 36 Triads down Case 4 Example a	100	As above
S1EX9	Page 36 Triads down Case 4 Example b	100	As above
S1EX10	Page 39 Both triads up Case 1 Example a	100	F & G major triads combined over minor
S1EX11	Page 40 Both triads up Case 1 Example b	100	As above
S1EX12	Page 40 Triads up then down Case 2 Example a	100	As above
S1EX13	Page 40 Triads up then down Case 2 Example b	100	As above
S1EX14	Page 40 Triads down then up Case 3 Example a	100	As above
S1EX15	Page 40 Triads down then up Case 3 Example b	100	As above
S1EX16	Page 41 Triads down Case 4 Example a	100	As above
S1EX17	Page 41 Triads down Case 4 Example b	100	As above
S1EX18	Page 43 Triads against dominants	100	D & E flat major triads played over G7 altered
S1EX19	Page 44 Both triads up Case 1 Example a	100	As above
S1EX20	Page 44 Both triads up Case 1 Example b	100	As above
S1EX21	Page 44 Triads up then down Case 2 Example a	100	As above
S1EX22	Page 44 Triads up then down Case 2 Example b	100	As above
S1EX23	Page 45 Triads down then up Case 3 Example a	100	As above
S1EX24	Page 45 Triads down then up Case 3 Example b	100	As above
S1EX25	Page 45 Triads down Case 4 Example a	100	As above
S1EX26	Page 45 Triads down Case 4 Example b	100	As above
S1EX27	Page 46 Combining all lines	100	Triads as demonstrated above over a II - V - I

CODE	MP3 FILE NAME	TEMPO	NOTES
S1EX28	Page 53 Chord Example Without V.L.	100	A Chord progression with voice leading omitted
S1EX29	Page 53 Chord Example With V.L.	100	A chord progression with voice leading included
S1EX30	Page 55 Contrary motion ascending melody	100	Voice leading within chords
S1EX31	Page 56 Contrary motion descending melody	100	As above
S1EX32	Page 57 Parallel motion	100	As above
S1EX33	Page 58 Similar motion	100	As above
S1EX34	Page 59 Pedal tone	100	As above
S1EX35	Page 60 Inverted pedal tone	100	As above
S1EX36	Page 61 Parallel voicing example	100	As above
S1EX37	Page 66 II - V - I example	130	Single line with E flat minor arpeggio upper structure over altered dominant seventh chord
S1EX38	Page 67 E flat minor over C example a	100	Inferring the sound of C dominant seven chord with a flat five/sharp nine with an upper structure
S1EX39	Page 67 E flat minor over C example b	100	As above
S1EX40	Page 67 E flat minor over C example c	100	As above
S1EX41	Page 68 E flat minor over C example a	100	As above
S1EX42	Page 68 E flat minor over C example b	100	As above
S1EX43	Page 68 E flat minor over C example c	100	As above
S1EX44	Page 70 I - VI - II - V - I example	140	Single line with arpeggio upper structures one half step above altered dominant seventh chord
S1EX45	Page 71 D flat minor over C example a	100	Inferring the sound of C dominant seven with a sharp five/flat nine with an upper structure
S1EX46	Page 71 D flat minor over C example b	100	As above
S1EX47	Page 71 D flat minor over C example c	100	As above
S1EX48	Page 72 D flat minor over C example a	100	As above
S1EX49	Page 72 D flat minor over C example b	100	As above
S1EX50	Page 72 D flat minor over C example c	100	As above
S1EX51	Page 86 B flat major over F sharp example a	100	Inferring the sound of D dominant seven chord with a sharp five/nine with an upper structure
S1EX52	Page 86 B flat major over F sharp example b	100	As above
S1EX53	Page 86 B flat major over F sharp example c	100	As above
S1EX54	Page 86 B flat major over F sharp example d	100	As above
S1EX55	Page 87 B flat major over F sharp example e	100	As above
S1EX56	Page 87 B flat major over F sharp example a	100	The same chord as previous example but now functioning within a minor II - V - I progression

CODE	MP3 FILE NAME	TEMPO	NOTES
S1EX57	Page 87 B flat major over F sharp example b	100	The same chord as previous example but now functioning within a minor II - V - I progression
S1EX58	Page 87 B flat major over F sharp example c	100	As above
S1EX59	Page 89 B major over G example a	100	Inferring the sound of E minor nine/natural seventh with an upper structure
S1EX60	Page 89 B major over G example b	100	As above
S1EX61	Page 89 B major over G example c	100	As above
S1EX62	Page 89 B major over G example d	100	As above
S1EX63	Page 90 B major over G example a	100	As above
S1EX64	Page 90 B major over G example b	100	As above
S1EX65	Page 90 B major over G example c	100	As above
S1EX66	Page 90 B major over G example d	100	As above
S1EX67	Page 91 B major over G example a	100	Inferring the sound of G major seven sharp five with an upper structure
S1EX68	Page 91 B major over G example b	100	As above
S1EX69	Page 91 B major over G example c	100	As above
S1EX70	Page 91 B major over G example d	100	As above
S1EX71	Page 92 B major over G example a	100	As above
S1EX72	Page 92 B major over G example b	100	As above
S1EX73	Page 92 B major over G example c	100	As above
S1EX74	Page 92 B major over G example d	100	As above
S1EX75	Page 99 Symmetrical example	100	Example of chords being used in conjunction with symmetrical harmony
S1EX76	Page 102 Symmetrical example a	100	As above
S1EX77	Page 102 Symmetrical example b	100	As above
S1EX78	Page 103 Symmetrical example	100	As above
S1EX79	Page 104 Symmetrical example	88	Single line motif idea used in conjunction with symmetrical harmony
S1EX80	Page 105 Symmetrical example a	88	As above
S1EX81	Page 105 Symmetrical example b	88	As above

SECTION TWO

CODE	MP3 FILE NAME	TEMPO	NOTES
S2EX1	Page 128 Major 9 Example a	90	III minor over I major example
S2EX2	Page 128 Major 9 Example b	110	As above
S2EX3	Page 128 Major 9 Example c	80	As above
S2EX4	Page 132 Major 13 Example a	96	III7 sus4 over I major example
S2EX5	Page 132 Major 13 Example b	80	As above
S2EX6	Page 132 Major 13 Example c	112	As above
S2EX7	Page 136 Major 6-9 Example a	130	II sus4 over I major example
S2EX8	Page 136 Major 6-9 Example b	120	As above
S2EX9	Page 136 Major 6-9 Example c	100	As above
S2EX10	Page 140 Major Flat 5 Example a	112	VII sus4 over I major example
S2EX11	Page 140 Major Flat 5 Example b	103	As above
S2EX12	Page 140 Major Flat 5 Example c	103	As above
S2EX13	Page 144 Major Sharp 5 Example a	132	III major over I major example
S2EX14	Page 144 Major Sharp 5 Example b	136	As above
S2EX15	Page 144 Major Sharp 5 Example c	106	As above
S2EX16	Page 148 Major 9 Sharp 11 Example a	140	VII minor over I major example
S2EX17	Page 148 Major 9 Sharp 11 Example b	110	As above
S2EX18	Page 148 Major 9 Sharp 11 Example c	96	As above
S2EX19	Page 152 Major 13 Sharp 11 Example a	92	II major over I major example
S2EX20	Page 152 Major 13 Sharp 11 Example b	96	As above
S2EX21	Page 152 Major 13 Sharp 11 Example c	80	As above
S2EX22	Page 156 Major 7 Sharp 9 Sharp 11 Example a	110	VII major over I major example
S2EX23	Page 156 Major 7 Sharp 9 Sharp 11 Example b	94	As above
S2EX24	Page 162 Minor 9 Example a	206	V minor over I minor
S2EX25	Page 162 Minor 9 Example b	78	As above
S2EX26	Page 162 Minor 9 Example c	136	As above
S2EX27	Page 166 Minor 11 Example a	104	Flat VII major over I minor

CODE	MP3 FILE NAME	TEMPO	NOTES
S2EX28	Page 166 Minor 11 example b	82	Flat VII major over I minor example
S2EX29	Page 166 Minor 11 example c	110	As above
S2EX30	Page 170 Minor 13 example a	116	II minor over I minor example
S2EX31	Page 170 Minor 13 example b	132	As above
S2EX32	Page 170 Minor 13 example c	120	As above
S2EX33	Page 174 Minor n-7 example a	114	V augmented over I minor example
S2EX34	Page 174 Minor n-7 example b	128	As above
S2EX35	Page 174 Minor n-7 example c	126	As above
S2EX36	Page 178 Minor 9 n-7 example a	112	As above
S2EX37	Page 178 Minor 9 n-7 example b	76	As above
S2EX38	Page 178 Minor 9 n-7 example c	104	As above
S2EX39	Page 184 Dominant 9 example a	110	V minor over I_7 example
S2EX40	Page 184 Dominant 9 example b	114	As above
S2EX41	Page 184 Dominant 9 example c	140	As above
S2EX42	Page 188 Dominant 13 example a	98	VI minor over I_7 example
S2EX43	Page 188 Dominant 13 example b	86	As above
S2EX44	Page 188 Dominant 13 example c	78	As above
S2EX45	Page 193 Dominant Augmented 5 example a	120	II+ over I_7 example
S2EX46	Page 193 Dominant Augmented 5 example b	98	As above
S2EX47	Page 193 Dominant Augmented 5 example c	110	As above
S2EX48	Page 198 Dominant 7 Flat 9 example a	96	Sharp I dim over I_7 example
S2EX49	Page 198 Dominant 7 Flat 9 example b	102	As above
S2EX50	Page 202 Dominant 7 Sharp 9 example a	132	Flat III major over I_7 example
S2EX51	Page 202 Dominant 7 Sharp 9 example b	192	As above
S2EX52	Page 202 Dominant 7 Sharp 9 example c	132	As above
S2EX53	Page 206 Dominant 7 Flat 5 Sharp 9 example a	160	Flat III over I_7 example
S2EX54	Page 206 Dominant 7 Flat 5 Sharp 9 example b	142	As above
S2EX55	Page 206 Dominant 7 Flat 5 Sharp 9 example c	108	As above
S2EX56	Page 210 Dominant 7 Sharp 5 Flat 9 example a	118	Flat II over I_7 example

CODE	MP3 FILE NAME	TEMPO	NOTES
S2EX57	Page 210 Dominant 7 Sharp 5 Flat 9 example b	198	Flat II over I_7 example
S2EX58	Page 210 Dominant 7 Sharp 5 Flat 9 example c	124	As above
S2EX59	Page 214 Dominant 7 Flat 5 Flat 9 example a	116	Flat V major over I_7 example
S2EX60	Page 214 Dominant 7 Flat 5 Flat 9 example b	182	As above
S2EX61	Page 214 Dominant 7 Flat 5 Flat 9 example c	122	As above
S2EX62	Page 218 Dominant 7 Sharp 5 Sharp 9 example a	116	Flat VI major over I_7 example
S2EX63	Page 218 Dominant 7 Sharp 5 Sharp 9 example a	120	As above
S2EX64	Page 218 Dominant 7 Sharp 5 Sharp 9 example a	134	As above
S2EX65	Page 222 Dominant 13 Flat 9 example a	78	VI major over I_7 example
S2EX66	Page 222 Dominant 13 Flat 9 example b	102	As above
S2EX67	Page 222 Dominant 13 Flat 9 example c	110	As above
S2EX68	Page 226 Dominant 13 Sharp 11 example a	120	II major over I_7 example
S2EX69	Page 226 Dominant 13 Sharp 11 example b	120	As above
S2EX70	Page 226 Dominant 13 Sharp 11 example c	160	As above

SECTION THREE - INTRO VIDEO + DEMONSTRATION SOLOS & BACKING TRACKS

CODE	MP3 FILE NAME	TEMPO	NOTES
S3EX1	Page 240 I Can't Hear A Thing - Guitar SOLO + Band	140	Demonstration of guitar solo with full band
S3EX1b	I Can't Hear A Thing - Rhythm Guitar - Piano - Bass - Drums	140	Backing track with full band no solo
S3EX1c	I Can't Hear A Thing - Rhythm Guitar - Bass - Drums	140	Backing track as above with no piano or solo
S3EX1d	I Can't Hear A Thing - Rhythm Guitar - Drums	140	Backing track as above with no piano, solo or bass
S3EX2	Page 272 The Day We Renamed Night - Guitar SOLO + Band	74	Demonstration of guitar solo with full band
S3EX2b	The Day We Renamed Night - Rhythm Guitar - Piano - Bass - Drums	74	Backing track with full band no solo
S3EX2c	The Day We Renamed Night - Rhythm Guitar - Piano - Bass - Drums	74	Backing track as above with no piano or solo
S3EX2d	The Day We Renamed Night - Rhythm Guitar - Drums	74	Backing track as above with no piano, solo or bass
S3EX3	Page 306 Whose Dream Is This - Guitar SOLO + Band	120	Demonstration of guitar solo with full band
S3EX3b	Whose Dream Is This - Rhythm Guitar - Piano - Bass - Drums	120	Backing track with full band no solo
S3EX3c	Whose Dream Is This - Rhythm Guitar - Bass - Drums	120	Backing track as above with no piano or solo
S3EX3d	Whose Dream Is This - Rhythm Guitar - Drums	120	Backing track as above with no piano, solo or bass

FILE STRUCTURE OF MP3 PACKAGE COMPRESSED TO SAVE SPACE WITH WINRAR

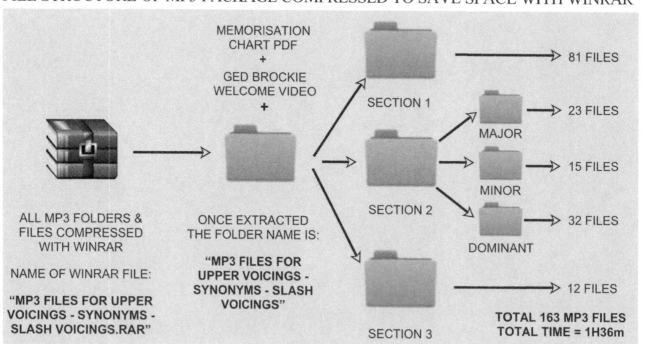

The WINRAR file is 234MB, UNCOMPRESSED THE SIZE OF THE PACKAGE IS 246MB. Full details on how to download WINRAR for PC & MAC owners available on the download page on the GMI website. Full details on where to get your FREE download found on the last page of section one in this book. Most computers, however, now automatically see and open zipped files as a matter of course.

APPENDIX G - UPPER VOICINGS MEMORISATION CUT OUT

Cut following the dotted lines and use to aid memorisation of upper structures & the chord symbols they equal.

✂

Major 7♯9♯11	minor 9	9♭5	Major 9	minor 11
7♭5♭9	7♯9	minor 9♮7	Major 7♯5	13♭9
minor 13	7♭5♯9	6/9	Major 13	7♯5
Major 7♭5	7♯5♯9	7♯5♭9	7♭9	Major 13♯11
minor♮7	9	Major 9♯11	13♯11	13

If you do not wish to cut this page of your book, I have included these two pages as a PDF for you to print out. This PDF is provided as part of your free download that accompanies this book. See the last page of section one for details on where to download. *(Any lower triad with an asterisk means the 5th is not present).*

$\dfrac{\flat\text{VII Maj}}{\text{I minor}}$	$\dfrac{\text{III min}}{\text{I Major}}$	$\dfrac{\text{II Aug}}{\text{I7}}$	$\dfrac{\text{V minor}}{\text{I minor}}$	$\dfrac{\text{VII Major}}{\text{I Major}}$
$\dfrac{\text{VI Major}}{\text{I7}}$	$\dfrac{\text{III Major}}{\text{I Major}}$	$\dfrac{\text{V Major}}{\text{I minor}}$	$\dfrac{\flat\text{III Major}}{\text{I7}}$	$\dfrac{\flat\text{V Major}}{\text{I7}}$
$\dfrac{\text{I Aug}}{\text{I7}}$	$\dfrac{\text{III7sus4}}{\text{I Major}}$	$\dfrac{\text{IIsus4}}{\text{I Major}}$	$\dfrac{\flat\text{III minor}}{\text{I7}}$	$\dfrac{\text{II min}}{\text{I minor}}$
$\dfrac{\text{II Major}}{\text{I Major}}$	$\dfrac{\flat\text{II dim}}{\text{I7}}$	$\dfrac{\flat\text{II minor}}{\text{I7}}$	$\dfrac{\flat\text{VI Major}}{\text{I7}}$	$\dfrac{\text{VIIsus4}}{\text{I Major*}}$
$\dfrac{\text{VI minor}}{\text{I7}}$	$\dfrac{\text{II Major}}{\text{I7}}$	$\dfrac{\text{VII min}}{\text{I Major}}$	$\dfrac{\text{II Major}}{\text{I7}}$	$\dfrac{\text{V aug}}{\text{I minor}}$

Ged Brockie (right) playing with friend and fellow guitarist Dougie Urquhart and Dougie's son Fraser on piano

Ged Brockie has spent a lifetime playing, composing, recording and teaching music. Here is a selection from some of his band and video recordings as well as the other books released through GMI - Guitar & Music Institute. His music and books can be found online at Amazon worldwide and all good online retailers.

CD release 2005 (Circular Records) - The Last View From Mary's Place

CD release 2009 (Circular Records) - The Mirror's Image

DVD release 2011 (Circular Records) - Five Innovations For Guitar & Orchestra

Ged was a member of the critically acclaimed Scottish Guitar Quartet (SGQ). As one of the main writers, Ged contributed and performed on the bands three albums: Near The Circle, Fait Accompli and Landmarks from 2000 - 2007.

"SCALES YOU CAN USE!" IS MORE THAN JUST A BOOK OF SCALE PATTERNS

Learn the scale patterns that are both powerful and meaningful and will really make the difference to your playing, improvisations and performances.

A thought through method of learning including a template system of progressive scale tuition that acts as a force multiplier for your overall understanding of how the guitar and scales are created and used.

This is a full colour publication including large easy to read scale forms, fretboard diagrams and descriptive images.

Covers the widest range of scales that guitarists need to know including: major, natural/harmonic and melodic minor scales over the entire neck in seven positions. Pentatonic, Blues, Diminished, and whole tone scales are also included.

Learn how you can play major and minor pentatonic patterns in 10 different keys in just one position.

This book also includes how to play fourteen different keys in one position using modal scales giving you complete musical control over key changes!

Included are fret maps detail, a simple to understand root based system in two key positions giving you complete understanding over the entire guitar fretboard.

Theoretical explanations of pentatonic, major, melodic and harmonic minor, blues, chromatic, whole tone and diminished scales.

A large suite of "exotic" scales are also included for those that are looking to learn patterns that are on the fringe.

Scales You Can Use!

Learn to truly understand the patterns guitarists need for soloing, sight reading and general musicianship regardless of musical style.

Supercharge your guitar playing with easy read scale boxes, music/TAB ideas, original concepts, exercises and a simple to understand scalar template accompanied by our Youtube videos.

Open String Scales That Matter

Pentatonic & Blues Scales

Major/Relative Minor Scales

Harmonic/Melodic Minor Scales

Diminished, Whole Tone & Exotic Scales

The Truth About Modes & How To Utilise Them

How To Play In Fourteen Keys In One Position

GMI
Guitar & Music Institute

Original music examples and pieces provided in music and TAB throughout Guitar Scales You Can Use! enabling you to learn the patterns whilst you actually play music and not just patterns.

SOME REVIEWS…

"The book is very clear, well explained and you have Youtube links with free lessons with the author, completely value for money. I highly recommend it."

"This book is quite useful, it gives you scales that are easily accessible and to use as well with techniques and some stuff that is also song writing related. I would recommend this to anyone who is trying to expand their horizons, not just on the scales but also on their music theory and techniques."

DROP TWO VOICINGS UNCOVERED

Drop Two Voicings Uncovered is a full colour instructional guide for guitar created by guitarist Ged Brockie. This book focuses on helping the guitarist understand chordal knowledge in all keys, all string sets & across the entire fretboard using a systematic concept to learn the power of drop two chords. This is really a course, not just a book. Read below to find out why.

Guitarists of all ages who are beyond the beginner stage will benefit from this detailed and thought through publication which gently guides the player through the various stages of learning.

Easy to read large chord diagrams are used throughout Drop Two Voicings Uncovered. All music is offered in both music and TAB.

The book is supplemented by almost two hours of Youtube video tuition where guitarist Ged Brockie discusses in detail the theoretical and technical issues covered in each lesson within the book. These videos are accessed via QR codes within the book to view on your mobile while the book is on the music stand.

Book owners have access to an additional download of twenty one backing tracks which accompany the lessons and additional chordal ideas in PDF format for extended study.

You can buy the wire bound version directly from https://gmiguitarshop.com or the perfect bound version from Amazon and all good online bookstores.

SOME REVIEWS...

"This book is a revelation! I am an experienced classical guitarist who wanted to find out about other styles. Drop Two Voicings Uncovered is quite mind blowing. Its like a Pandora's box. Not only does is set out chords, their inversions across 4 adjacent strings, it presents them in the most useful chord progressions. Each lesson has YouTube videos and many supporting downloads. Highly recommended."

"The book is clear, has plenty of information, it's easy to read, well organised, this book is very useful in real-life situations for the musician.

Also it has links to Youtube video lessons with the author of the book for free plus some extra material like backing tracks to play along. I highly recommend it."

"Very well designed book, which covers all of the areas of ii V I progressions and drop two voicing I can highly recommend it to any guitarist who is seeking to learn more in depth about the most common in jazz progressions."

If you have enjoyed this book then we're sure you will find James Akers transcriptions found in his Scottish Classical Guitar Collection Volume 1 an absolute must have.

For the intermediate to advanced player, this volume of work includes Mauro Giuliani's beautiful settings of six favourite Scottish songs; Fernando Sor's masterful 'Variations on Ye Banks and Braes' and Johan Kaspar Mertz's dramatic evocation of the landscape of the Outer Hebrides, 'Fingal's Cave.'

Scottish Classical Guitar Collection Volume 1 is available to purchase from Amazon and all other good online sellers in both printed and electronic format. PDF versions of individual songs found within the book are available to buy direct from the GMI - Guitar & Music Institute online shop at https://gmiguitarshop.com

There is also a wire bound lie flat version of this publication only available at the GMI Guitar Shop at the web address above.

The second GMI publication by James Akers is Theorbo music transcriptions for classical guitar.

The book includes works by Kapsberger, Piccinini and Castaldi but this large publication also includes the following:

- All works offered in both music and guitar tabulature.

- Selected works include an audio commentary that is accessed via QR codes placed alongside specific titles. Use your mobile (cell) phone or tablet to listen to James's commentary from both a technical and musical perspective about the work you will be learning.

- Selected works include a QR code that opens up a performance video of the piece currently being considered. Listen to this stellar guitarist play and interpret the musical composition for your guidance as well as listening pleasure.

- Owners of the book will be able to access further musical works that accompany this publication. Your copy of this book will include a code which enables you to access this PDF download completely free of charge.

Italian Theorbo Music is available to purchase from Amazon and all other good online sellers in both printed and electronic format. A wire bound flat lie version of the book is available only from https://gmiguitarshop.com

An introduction PDF book containing extra works for pre sale of this book or as mentioned free for those who have already purchased the printed version is available to buy direct from the GMI - Guitar & Music Institute online shop at https://gmiguitarshop.com

GMI - Guitar & Music Institute publishes a wide range of books. Check out our books on Amazon and at our web shop at https://gmiguitarshop.com

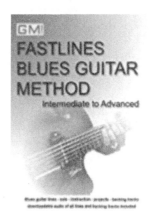

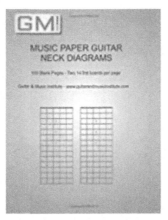
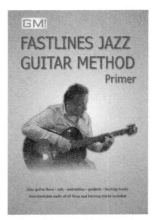

If you enjoyed this publication, then please visit the following websites below for a huge amount of free guitar content including lessons, articles, videos, podcasts and much more…

If you bought this book from Amazon we'd really appreciate a positive review on Amazon if you found this book enjoyable and helpful to your guitar playing education.

www.guitarandmusicinstitute.com

gmiguitarshop.com

gedbrockie.com

A

accidentals, 31, 121

alteration   13–15, 25, 30, 31, 39, 41–43, 46, 51, 53, 54, 56, 57, 66, 69, 70, 73, 77, 83, 85, 88, 91, 97, 102, 103, 105, 111, 115, 117, 121, 140, 144, 148, 152, 162, 166, 184, 202, 204, 210, 214, 222, 226, 234, 244, 246, 247, 249, 252, 253, 276–79, 284–87, 315, 316, 318, 319, 321, 324–27, 341

appoggiatura, 102

arpeggios, 14,26, 30, 39, 61, 65, 69, 82-83, 93, 128, 132, 148, 162, 170, 192-193, 198, 202, 217, 222, 279, 285, 314, 320, 325

B

Blues, 188, 354

bluesy, 170, 188, 279

C

cadence, 14, 41, 156, 248, 252, 285

cadential, 104, 288

chromatic, 31, 56, 61, 77, 81, 82, 93, 109, 111, 117, 132, 140, 156, 162, 166, 178, 184, 193, 198, 202, 210, 214, 218, 245–47, 249, 252, 254, 278, 280, 281, 286, 288, 298, 315, 326, 354

comp, 229

comping, 253, 325

contour, 46, 140, 144, 210, 214, 218, 222, 249, 277

contours, 34, 48, 162, 210, 277

contrary motion, 3, 51, 55, 56, 91, 156, 266, 287, 288, 345

counter clockwise, 80

counter melodies, 54

counter melody, 287

cross-string, 140

D

decrescendo, 103

demisemiquaver, 280

descending bass, 3, 55, 254

descending line, 184, 255, 318

descending melody, 3, 56, 57, 345

diatonic, 14, 101, 128, 166, 246, 278, 281

dissonance, 14, 25, 41, 48, 73, 80, 82-83, 93, 104, 111, 210, 252, 253, 279, 280, 315, 318, 325

dominant 13, 348, 349

dominant 9, 348

dominant altered, 4, 179, 278

dominant augmented, 348

dominant chord, 46, 56, 69, 116, 226, 249, 279, 284, 319, 324

dominant chords, 3, 48, 53, 59, 73, 110, 115, 184, 202, 226, 343

dominant ninth, 4, 58, 285, 326, 341, 342

dominant pedal, 103

download instructions, 118

E

enharmonic, 58, 66, 79, 88, 110, 111, 116, 193, 218, 324

enharmonic equivalent (enharmonic equivalents), 58, 66, 79, 88, 110-111, 116, 218, 324

enharmonic spelling, 193

extension, 14, 23, 25, 38, 42, 56, 252, 253, 315, 325

extension & alteration, 23

extension notes, 38

F

fermata, 188

figured bass, 13

finger, 26, 79, 121, 152, 202, 284, 288, 316, 326

fingered

214, 343

fingering

25, 105, 136, 214, 218, 222, 234

fingerings

121, 174, 229

fingers

61, 79, 132, 136, 178, 247, 281, 315, 327

fingertips

276

G

Guitar and Music Institute, 1, 358

H

harmony, 3, 5, 25, 36, 43, 51, 55, 59, 61, 66, 73, 82, 97, 99, 101–3, 105, 115–17, 136, 152, 156, 178, 192, 197, 229, 233, 244–48, 255, 265–67, 279, 285–87, 297, 314, 316, 318, 324, 326, 346

polytonal, 32, 117, 210, 222, 246

quartal, 136, 184, 248

quintal, 136

hemiola 128, 156, 222

I

improvisation, 11, 25, 34, 36, 54, 174, 315

improvisational, 14

improvisations, 4, 104, 234, 246, 285, 354

improvise, 61, 69, 99, 156, 166

improvised, 110, 121, 210, 240, 286

improviser, 46, 210

improvises, 83

improvising, 25, 65, 66, 184, 277, 320

improvisor, 83, 244

improvisor's, 83

inferred root (inferred roots), 8, 15, 58, 80, 81, 85

interval distance, 13, 55, 58, 317

interval leaps, 140, 226

Intervallic, 226

interval melodic, 132

intervals, 54, 68, 79, 103, 105, 136, 156, 184, 197, 206, 210, 214, 245, 248, 266, 276, 317, 318

interval structure, 105, 148

L

leaps, 140, 226, 276

M

melodic analysis, 5, 243, 244, 275, 276, 281, 313, 314

melodic contour, 46, 140, 144, 210, 214, 218, 222, 249, 277

melodic contours, 34, 48, 162, 277

melodic minor, 178, 198, 325, 354

melody/bass, 3, 55, 57–60

modulations, 286

motif idea, 105, 317, 346

motif shapes, 4, 105

N

neighbour tones, 178, 198

nomenclature, 42, 103

notated arpeggio, 11

notated chord, 82, 246, 318, 320

notated solo, 5, 234, 239, 271, 305

O

octave playing, 174

organically, 48, 61, 103, 148, 284

Ornamentation, 319

P

pseudo scale (pseudo scales), 23, 26, 48, 69

R

rallentando, 103, 162

relative major, 38, 91, 204, 210, 320

relative minor, 38, 226, 324, 327

Resolve (resolves), 104, 166, 178, 193, 276, 286, 288, 315

resolution, 14, 54, 104, 105, 210, 276, 286

resolved, 61, 104, 315, 318

resolving, 102, 248, 276

rhythm guitar, 350

root movement, 54, 255

S

scale extended, 25

scale patterns, 354

scales, 14, 23, 30, 97, 99, 100, 109, 110, 117, 245, 248, 278, 314, 319, 325, 354

dorian, 38, 166, 198, 245, 281

lydian, 25, 26, 136, 156, 202, 206, 218, 247, 255, 278

mixolydian, 79, 188, 245

modal (modes), 25, 109, 166, 206, 248, 255, 319, 354

phrygian, 248, 319

scale superimposition, 319

secondary dominant, 41, 48

semitone, 25, 54, 69, 89, 110, 111, 117, 148, 156, 280, 281, 284, 319, 320

sequence, 11, 105, 128, 140, 174, 229, 244, 266, 276, 284, 288, 320, 324

soloing, 1, 26, 73, 82, 104, 148, 266

solos & backing, 350

string sets, 27, 47, 89, 327, 355

string skipping, 315

superimposed, 23, 46, 48, 73, 82, 83, 105, 144, 170, 184, 210, 226, 244, 319, 325

symmetrical harmony, 59, 97, 99, 101, 102, 117, 192, 197, 245, 314, 346

symmetrical ideas, 4, 104

symmetrical scales, 245

synonyms, 1, 3, 5, 7, 11, 15, 17, 18, 32, 59, 77, 88, 93, 162, 226, 253, 279, 284, 286, 340, 350

synonyms & slash, 1, 350

synonyms & substitutions, 340

T

TAB, 121, 229, 354, 355

tabulature, 356

Technique, 11, 27, 34, 43, 47, 55, 56, 73, 79, 99, 102, 121, 132, 140, 144, 166, 178, 184, 193, 202, 244, 247, 249, 276, 278, 279, 284, 286, 314–17, 320, 321, 354–56

targeting, 48, 166, 184, 280, 318

tension, 14, 43, 61, 104, 128, 198, 252, 284

tertian, 136, 248

theory, 7, 14, 25, 27, 36, 101, 110, 246, 286, 320, 354

triadic diminished, 116, 197, 198

triadic overlays, 188

triadic voicings, 79, 80, 93

Turnaround, 152

U

upper chord, 26, 339

upper structures, 7, 23, 26, 31, 51, 65, 69, 80, 118, 121, 148, 156, 197, 202, 229, 234, 237, 267, 277, 280, 285, 324, 345, 346, 351

polychord, 26, 31, 103, 105, 116, 170, 188, 222, 244, 267, 299, 338, 339

formula, 23, 31, 43, 48, 53, 65, 69, 229, 234, 235, 244, 246, 267, 284, 285, 287, 299, 314, 318, 320, 336, 338, 339 polychordal, 48

polychords, 4, 5, 7, 17, 18, 26, 27, 32, 85, 115, 121, 188, 338

upper triads, 25

upper voice, 5

upper voicing (upper voicings), 3, 5, 11, 17, 25, 26, 61, 66, 70, 82, 83, 118, 144, 156, 166, 170, 246, 284, 287, 314, 319, 320, 327, 336, 350, 351

V

vagrant harmony, 51, 73

voice leading, 3, 14, 41, 51, 53, 54, 61, 66, 73, 79, 91, 156, 253, 324, 325, 345

voicing choice, 255

voicing chord, 13, 15

voicing equivalents, 99

voicing example, 26, 345

voicing formula, 5, 284, 336

voicing polychord, 339